COMMUNICATION IMPACT

COMMUNICATION IMPACT
Designing Research That Matters

Edited by
Susanna Hornig Priest

ROWMAN & LITTLEFIELD PUBLISHERS, INC.
Lanham • Boulder • New York • Toronto • Oxford

ROWMAN & LITTLEFIELD PUBLISHERS, INC.

Published in the United States of America
by Rowman & Littlefield Publishers, Inc.
A wholly owned subsidiary of The Rowman & Littlefield Publishing Group, Inc.
4501 Forbes Boulevard, Suite 200, Lanham, Maryland 20706
www.rowmanlittlefield.com

PO Box 317, Oxford OX2 9RU, UK

Copyright © 2005 by Rowman & Littlefield Publishers, Inc.

All rights reserved. No part of this publication may be reproduced, stored in a retrieval system, or transmitted in any form or by any means, electronic, mechanical, photocopying, recording, or otherwise, without the prior permission of the publisher.

British Library Cataloguing in Publication Information Available

Library of Congress Cataloging-in-Publication Data
Communication impact : designing research that matters / Susanna Hornig Priest [editor].
   p. cm.
Includes bibliographical references and index.
ISBN 0-7425-3097-3 (cloth : alk. paper) — ISBN 0-7425-3098-1 (pbk. : alk. paper)
1. Communication in social action—Research—Case studies. 2. Communication in the social sciences—Research—Case studies. 3. Action research—Case studies. 4. Communication—Research—Case studies. I. Priest, Susanna Hornig.
HN29.C615 2005
302.2'072—dc22
                      2004015474

Printed in the United States of America

∞™ The paper used in this publication meets the minimum requirements of American National Standard for Information Sciences—Permanence of Paper for Printed Library Materials, ANSI/NISO Z39.48-1992.

Contents

Preface: Why Another Book?	ix
Part I: Community-Based Research	1
1 Why Did the Scholar Cross the Road? Community Action Research and the Citizen-Scholar *Lana F. Rakow*	5
2 Creating Informed Deliberation: The Role of Impact Surveys in Community Decision Making *Dietram A. Scheufele*	19
3 Community Action for Drug Prevention: A Behind-the-Scenes Look at a Sixteen-Community Study *Michael D. Slater*	33
4 Designing Communication Research for Empowering Marginalized Populations: A Participatory Methodology *Chike Anyaegbunam, Aaron P. Karnell, Wai Hsien Cheah, and John D. Youngblood*	49
Part II: Organizations and Institutions	67
5 Gender and Professional Identity among Caribbean Journalists *Marjan de Bruin*	69
6 Patient Satisfaction in a Medical Setting: An Emergent Design Approach *Robert L. Krizek and Paaige K. Turner*	85

7 Interpreting Signs: Reflections on Research Design in Context *Robert J. Balfour*	101
Part III: Problem-Focused Research	**111**
8 Peer Influence and Prosocial Behavior: Ten Years of Study *Timothy P. Meyer and Thomas R. Donohue*	113
9 Adolescent Memory for Health Information: Mixing "Micro" and "Macro" Variables *Brian G. Southwell*	129
10 Communication at the End of Life: Volunteer-Patient Relationships in Hospice *Elissa Foster*	143
11 Scientific Knowledge and Personal Experience: Mutually Exclusive? *Loreen N. Olson*	159
Part IV: Research across Cultures	**165**
12 Stories in the Sand: Field Research with Pitjantjatjara Yankunytjatjara Media in Central Australia *David I. Tafler*	167
13 Adventures in a Foreign Field: Complexity, Crisis, and Creativity in Cross-Cultural Research *Karen Ross*	185
14 On Our Way, On the Ground, On Cloud Nine: Research Planning and Adaptation in Belize *Joy L. Hart and Kandi L. Walker*	197
15 Choices and Voices: Assesssing Television Preferences of Teenage African-American Girls *Lynne Edwards*	207
Part V: New Technologies and Research	**223**
16 Health Communication Research on Hard-to-Reach Populations Using Telephone Interviews *Jennifer L. Gregg and Pamela Whitten*	227

17	Using the Internet to Conduct Communication Research: Two Scholars' Experiences *Tara L. Crowell and Traci L. Anderson*	239
18	Finding Out What's on the World Wide Web *James W. Tankard Jr. and Cindy Royal*	253

Afterword: Purpose and Direction 265

Index 269

About the Contributors 273

Preface: Why Another Book?

WHY ANOTHER RESEARCH METHODS BOOK? Dozens of adequate texts are already on the market setting forth both quantitative and qualitative approaches (and, very occasionally, both). Some are designed specifically for communication research scholars and students, as this one is. But none of them seem to fully convey the excitement, the value, and the pitfalls of actual communication research projects focusing on real-world problems. Laying the technical foundations for an in-depth understanding of particular methods seems to take precedence over illustrating how—and why—they might be applied.

Perhaps as a result of this omission, communication students at all levels can have a difficult time getting interested in research. Either the algebra behind the quantitative methods is too formidable, or the philosophical rationale provided for the qualitative ones is too obtuse.

This book was put together to help address this limitation. The chapters included were chosen not so much to illustrate the details of particular methods (for which some instructors might want to refer students to a traditional text), even though most—perhaps all—of the traditional social and behavioral science methods applied in communication research appear here. Rather, the goal has been to include effective narrative pieces from authors who are willing and able to tell the stories of their projects in a form that engages readers.

These projects were all worth carrying out because they all had the potential to make a difference in the real world, a criterion for their being included here. But you would probably never know it from studying their methods out of context, and perhaps not from reading published journal articles on the results—which tend to omit both the passion and the problems. This book tries to tell the story of research as it is actually practiced by people using their research skills in hopes of having an impact on the world.

The case studies in this book discuss research on compelling real-world problems involving questions of health, technology, community, development, media, gender, politics, culture, and ethnicity. So it is not necessarily just for students in research classes, but should also be useful for students in specialized communication classes focused on one or more of these areas.

And for communication scholars across a range of subdisciplines, it is an invitation to look more closely and sympathetically at what colleagues down the hall and around the corner might be up to.

I learned a lot about some interesting and exciting new approaches in putting together this book. I hope you will, too.

Part I
COMMUNITY-BASED RESEARCH

FOUR VERY DIFFERENT STUDIES make up Part I, but all are focused on understanding the dynamics within particular communities. Two of these studies are quantitative (resting primarily on numerical data) and two are qualitative (resting primarily on non-numerical information). Two are directed toward members of the researchers' own local communities and were conducted in large part with student labor (Rakow's discourse analysis project and Scheufele's impact survey project). The two others represent more complex efforts directed primarily toward those who were initially strangers (Slater's quasi-experimental project and the trio of qualitative projects presented by Anyaegbunam and colleagues). These latter contributions are concerned with more than one individual community. Interestingly, however, all illustrate that in community-based projects, the success of the researcher depends on effective interaction with the community being studied—even when he or she is initially an "outsider" to the research context.

Together, these four studies illustrate most of the primary methodological approaches that are especially prominent in social research: polls and surveys, experiments, textual or discourse analysis, and the use of interviews and focus groups. And they suggest some of the important decisions researchers make quite early in the design stage: whether to use qualitative or quantitative methods (and which ones), whether to consider the individual or the community as the unit of analysis, how much and in what ways to involve those being studied in setting the goals of the project, and how much flexibility is available to revise the goals of the study as it moves along—whether the study is intended as a formal hypothesis-testing effort, or whether it is more exploratory in nature.

In the traditional quantitative research model, especially in experimental work, hypotheses to be tested are determined ahead of time and there is relatively little flexibility once the design is in place. While this is not completely practical in community work, field experiment designs such as the one Slater discusses in this section attempt to imitate the laboratory model as closely as possible in a field setting, in order to gain some of the advantages of formal experiments in terms of statistical explanation. Similarly, while polls and surveys do not necessarily test hypotheses, the value of survey work depends on asking each participant the same question in exactly the same way. So the form of each question must be completely specified in advance—it cannot be revised partway through.

Quantitative work usually demands that the researcher remain as independent as possible from those he or she is studying, in order to remain as objective as possible. On the other hand, some researchers—generally those using qualitative methods—believe that to be true to the lived experience of those being studied, it is more important to become immersed in the culture than to remain "objective," and more important to record what people have to say about their lives and experiences than to try to generate accurate measurements of a limited number of previously specified variables.

Qualitative techniques such as depth interviews, discourse analysis, and focus groups are more often used in such projects because they provide valuable insights into community dynamics that may not be available through quantitative methods and that can help shape the emerging project by teaching the researcher a great deal about how things appear from the community's point of view. This is often interpreted as requiring a sacrifice in terms of the extent to which results can be generalized to other situations (as opposed to being unique to the community and to the individuals under study). Qualitative methods do not provide statistical proof of cause and effect. However, it is not necessarily the case that lessons learned through qualitative research cannot be applied in other contexts.

Some researchers also believe that community involvement in setting the goals for a project is necessary to produce meaningful and relevant results, that facilitating community action and change may be a legitimate research goal, and that the research design must therefore be flexible enough to accommodate both of these dimensions. These types of research projects—action research and participatory approaches—can be qualitative or quantitative, but they are more often at least partially qualitative, and they rarely involve formal hypothesis testing because they are designed to accommodate community feedback.

The projects included in this section show that both qualitative and quantitative research projects are valuable, and also that the separation between them is not always as complete as textbooks would have it. The participatory approaches described by Rakow and Anyaegbunam produced knowledge of community dynamics that is very likely to apply to other community settings at future times, not just the specific ones they looked at. Slater's field experiment had to be modified to accommodate real communities and real people, and Scheufele's survey work has community mobilization as an explicit objective. Both of these quantitative designs, as well as the two qualitative ones, had the built-in capacity to bring about important change in the communities being studied.

1
Why Did the Scholar Cross the Road? Community Action Research and the Citizen-Scholar

Lana F. Rakow

Most academic departments divide up the study of communication research into interpersonal, organizational, and mass media communication courses. But many of the authors included in this book take a variety of other approaches to understanding human communication processes, as dictated by the particular problems and circumstances they are studying. In this piece Lana Rakow describes her experience with community-based research and explains the challenges she and her students encountered studying the dynamics of their own local community after its devastation by a natural disaster—the 1997 flooding of Grand Forks, North Dakota, by the waters of the Red River.

Rakow and her graduate students initially found that most communication theory provided little assistance for designing such a study, and she also discovered that her qualitative approach did not generate lists of interview questions that were specific enough to satisfy her university's Institutional Review Board (IRB)[1] for human subjects. In response, instead of using interviews as originally planned, they redesigned their project to rely more heavily on analysis of public discourse—something Rakow now regards as a happy accident.

In order to complete this project, Rakow was forced to step outside of the traditional scholar's role of "objective observer" who is indifferent to the events being studied. Because she herself was a member of the community under study and had an undeniable stake in the outcomes of the community's decision making, she was at once a researcher and someone who cared about and might influence the events being researched. She reflects on this experience at length in this chapter.

ACCORDING TO THE TIMEWORN JOKE, the chicken crossed the road to get to the other side. So why did the scholar cross the road? To do research on the other side, presumably. Why do scholars go elsewhere to do research, like the proverbial wandering chicken, instead of staying right where we are? Is there nothing of significance in our own communities that is worthy of study? Is there no role for our research in the daily struggles of local citizens to create healthy and just communities? Is a scholar also a citizen?

This is a story about one scholar, myself, who didn't cross the road but stayed put to conduct community research. In the title of this chapter, I have used the cliché question to emphasize the need for us to be citizen-scholars in our own communities. I want to share with you why this scholar didn't cross the road and what difference I think it makes—to me and to my community.

To tell you why I chose to stay on my own side of the road, I need to explain that this is a story about a story. The story I am telling here recounts the telling of another story about my own community, the result of a research project I conducted with graduate students at the University of North Dakota. That research resulted in a story I have told to the community in several venues—through the news media and a public lecture—and now have published in *Southern Communication Journal* (2003). With its publication comes another opportunity to share the story with the community to elicit more discussion and possible action, and more occasions to do research that feeds into the life of the community.

Consequently, this chapter is only one piece of a larger life history of the intersection of this community and me as a citizen-scholar. This part of the story will recap why we need scholarly attention to communities, why this research project was undertaken, how the project was conducted, and its results. I'll be telling you about the uncertainties, decisions, and political realities we encountered along the way. Finally, I'll end by advocating for the ongoing, thoughtful engagement of other scholars in their own communities, despite the complexities and ethical dilemmas resulting from our dual role as citizen-scholars.

Research *of* and *for* Communities

The lack of sustained attention to community by communication scholars has been both disappointing and troubling to me for some time. It is disappointing because as a field we have tended to overlook one of the most significant features of human communication. Consequently, our understanding of communication and our theories accounting for it are underdeveloped at best, inaccurate at worst. Our lack of attention is troubling because the consequences for neglecting community go beyond our field. Communities are the worse for our neglect because public understanding of the problems and possibilities of communities is deficient. It is interesting to note that, unlike discussions of community, discussions about interpersonal communication, organizational communication, political communication, and news and entertainment media can readily be found in public discourse and on best-seller lists. Popularized discussions of communication issues, while often troublingly simplistic, at least raise levels of awareness. Why aren't the communication issues of communities and their citizens subject to the same scholarly and popular attention?

Unfortunately, gaining a foothold for community in communication studies has been difficult, despite fine work by individual scholars, because current specialty areas of communication have reified the omission of community studies. The omission has resulted from the field's overemphasis on the individual at the expense of understanding the collective, a feature of the dominant positivistic approach to studying communication in the U.S. This approach has been concerned with preserving the social order (reconciling individuals to existing social processes by improving individual, organizational, or political communication competence), forgetting that what lies between the individual and society is community, not simply a layer of opinion leaders and institutions. Cultural studies scholars, on the other hand, have roots in community studies dating to the early part of the twentieth century and share an interest in understanding social meaning making. Yet their current interests have focused on media and social groups (characterized by gender, race, class, and sexual identities and identification) far more than on communities. Cultural studies scholars have been concerned with a critique of society at the expense of developing solutions. Between the two major approaches to communication, the study of communities has fallen through the cracks of our institutionalized boundaries of study.

I have proposed elsewhere that scholars not only have the opportunity to make a difference by attending to communities, but also have a responsibility to do so (Rakow 2002, 151). Putting communities at the center of new models for understanding human association, models designed around principles of inclusion, participation, and voice for citizens, is the kind of intellectual leadership we should be providing as a field. While we need to reconsider how we have defined and described communities and the histories we have made for them, I urge us to attend to geographic communities, the places where people live, where their physical needs must be attended to, and where their participation in social and political purposes is most likely to occur—in other words, where public and private spheres intersect.

> **Box 1.1: Research Paradigms**
>
> Ethnographic research was developed primarily within cultural anthropology in order to discover and document the "insider" point of view characteristic of members of a particular group or culture. In other words, it tries to answer the question, "How does the world seem to them?" rather than understanding the people being studied only in terms defined by the researcher's own sociocultural perspective. Traditionally, ethnography has relied on qualitative research techniques such as depth interviews and participant observation to support these goals.
>
> Depth interviews generally use interview "guides" or "schedules"—lists of general questions to be covered rather than rigidly prespecified lists of questions to be asked verbatim. The goal is to let the person being interviewed take the lead in determining the themes of the interview conversation, and to leave the researcher free to pursue these themes with follow-up questions (or "probes") as they arise. The interviewee is sometimes referred to as an "informant" because his or her role is often that of a guide to the researcher working in an unfamiliar culture. Participant observation refers to the researcher's direct personal participation in the social life of those being studied in an attempt to grasp the deeper significance of their everyday activities. The result of an ethnographic study is sometimes referred to as "thick" description. It is a descriptive account but one that takes into account the complex cultural nuances of even ordinary social practices.
>
> In this account Rakow reports that she and her student collaborators relied primarily on textual analysis of public discourse, meaning they studied what was said in public communication contexts (such as public meetings, official documents, and media reports) to produce a similar kind of end result.
>
> Ethnographers and other qualitative researchers are generally concerned with how our perceptions of the world around us are built up or "constructed" in our interactions with others, whether current or historical, person-to-person, or mass mediated. Rather than take our ordinary understandings of the world as given, they want to investigate where these perceptions come from.
>
> Researchers using the ethnographic paradigm sometimes argue that quantitative methods such as survey research or formal experiments can "reify" the way people respond to their social surroundings, tending to take it for granted that the social world is something much more solid and immutable than it actually is and that intellectual constructs such as "attitudes" and "beliefs" fully explain this world. (To "reify" something literally means to treat it as though it were real.) They may reject the "positivist" assumption that human societies are best studied by methods that are as "scientific" as possible, rather than through exploratory and interpretive approaches. And they are willing to sacrifice the arguably greater reliability of numerical measurement for what they see as the greater validity of descriptive approaches.

I have believed in the importance of studying community for some time, but I had been a scholar crossing the road for my own research. Most notable in this regard was my ethnographic study of women and the telephone in a small rural community in the Midwest, the subject of my dissertation and a subsequent book (Rakow 1992). In that study, I confronted the dilemma of being an outsider who brings a new interpretation to the construction of gender in a community. What responsibilities did I have to the participants I interviewed? How could I honor their interpretations while offering my own? I have also been an advocate of being a public scholar who puts her expertise at the service of communities. Another research project (Rakow 1995a, 1995b, 1995c) took me to a very small community in North Dakota where I was affiliated with the newspaper for a week, conducting a communication audit of the community and reporting on the results in a series of columns.

I became involved in my own community of Grand Forks, North Dakota, after moving back to my home state in 1994, following seventeen years of living elsewhere. My first project involved working with local groups on an electronic community conversation. That experience convinced me that we needed scholars "at the table" of community decision making, both to bring our expertise into the community and also to make a place for citizen participation in public matters (Rakow 1999). With these projects as a prelude, a major physical disaster in Grand Forks took my work to another level of involvement in the community, opening up for me a new understanding of my rights and responsibilities as a citizen-scholar and of the potential for research at the service of the public.

Our Story of the Flood

Grand Forks, North Dakota, is a community of about 50,000 residents on the border between North Dakota and Minnesota, a border created by the Red River. In April of 1997, Grand Forks succumbed to the worst disaster in its history and among the worst per capita in the United States at the time. After record snowfalls that winter, the melting snow filled the Red River, which spilled over its banks across the flat land on both sides of the river, resulting in the evacuation of 90 percent of the population of Grand Forks and shutting down electrical service, telephones, the water supply and sanitary system, city and county government offices, the police station, the hospital and the local newspaper, and most businesses. As water boiled into the city and over the rooftops in some neighborhoods and to several feet in the rest of the city, a fire broke out in the flooded and deserted downtown, resulting in the loss of much of the downtown before it was contained.

Most residents were allowed to return to their homes a week after the evacuation, but electrical and water service took several weeks to restore, even months in some parts of the city. Many homes in neighborhoods closest to the river sustained damage to the first floors or rooftops. Most of the rest of the homes in the city sustained at least flooded basements in a part of the country where basements are used for bedrooms, family rooms, storage, furnaces, water heaters, and electrical service. Consequently, most people sustained considerable financial loss of possessions and repair and replacement costs. Over 700 homes were earmarked for a federally funded city buyout program because the city determined the homes were too damaged to be repaired. Another 300 homes were marked for buyouts to make way for a proposed—and controversial—permanent dike.

Thus began a long and painful period of community turmoil that seven years later still lies beneath the surface of its "recovery." The city has lasting physical, economic, and social scars, despite a massive infusion of federal and private money, expensive building and relocation projects, and official proclamations about the success of its recovery. And thus began my deep involvement as a citizen-scholar in my own community. No longer was I a scholarly observer who hoped to increase citizen participation in the community. I became a participant observer in the unfolding drama of the flood and its aftermath. I and my family of a husband and two children lived in one of the neighborhoods closest to the river and hardest hit by the flood. My home took in over eight feet of water, to the ceiling of the walkout level of our home—half of our home, altogether. We escaped first-floor damage by a few inches, which put us on one side of the line that divided those who could repair their homes and those who could not, but it also put us in the group close to the river subject to a buyout program of homes to make way for the proposed dike. Like many others, we felt we had been plunged into a nightmare that had only begun the night we were evicted from our house at 2:00 a.m. by the sound of bullhorns from police cars ordering us to leave.

While the University of North Dakota was closed in April that year by the flood and the semester was declared ended, it was open again in the fall. Despite the havoc in our lives caused by damaged homes and altered routines, I was in the classroom with a small group of graduate students in a communication theory class. The students all had been affected by the flood, mostly by having been evacuated from apartments and disrupted from jobs and classes. They, too, were involved in discussions in the community about decisions being made to remove entire neighborhoods, to rebuild the downtown with the federal money that came to the city, and to build a permanent, massive dike, further altering the physical and social landscape of the community. With the city full of evidence of the disaster and with public and bitter disagreements being expressed about city decisions, it was impossible to ignore what was around us and affected us.

Yet the communication theories that I was introducing to students seemed irrelevant in the face of such social upheaval that demanded explanation and resolution. Why was communication theory so beside the point or absent, at least not without digging for it and stretching it to fit what surely is neither an isolated event nor an insignificant one for understanding conditions experienced by so many? I proposed to the students that rather than ignore what we saw around us, we take it on as a project. What communication theories would be helpful for our task? How is communication theory constructed and by whom, to explain what? Could we do our own study that would modify or create theories about communities and disasters?

Conducting community research of the type we wanted proved to be a challenge in both design and execution. We had no simple formula to apply. Our approach can best be described as emergent, as we immersed ourselves in the communication processes of the community, looking for clues to themes that structured the debates over the flood and recovery and struggling with how to study the phenomenon of which we were a part. Over the few months of that fall semester, the students did reviews of relevant literature, and we discussed what we were seeing and hearing. Since none of them were homeowners in Grand Forks, they were on the periphery of the struggles of those most affected by the decisions of the mayor and city council. I introduced them to homeowners from the hardest-hit and working-class neighborhood. Some were resisting the city's efforts to force them from their homes without a declaration of eminent domain, which gives homeowners rights under the Uniform Relocation Assistance and Real Property Acquisition Policy Act of 1970. We noted the discrepancies between the official versions of the city's decision making and recovery with expressions of anger and frustration by citizens. What was happening to this community?

Clearly, communication was at the core of the issues of power and voice we saw playing out in front of us. For me, the issues were even closer to home than they were for the students, as I attended city council meetings and public hearings, navigated the bureaucracy of disaster assistance and paperwork, and faced our own showdown with the city over the seizure of our home for the dike project. Feeling disaffected and voiceless in the face of contradictory official information and decisions without recourse and, it seemed, without accountability, I was a citizen in the community experiencing what others with even less voice, less access to resources, and fewer avenues for redress had available to them. Even the extensive coverage of the flood and its anniversary a year later by outside national news organizations succeeded in silencing dissent in order to tell the story of the plucky little community that overcame adversity. As a citizen, I felt the need to act. As a scholar, I had the means to do so.

Unlike research designed from outside the phenomena, our project, conducted by insiders, had its own special challenges. From the outset, I planned the research to be qualitative, allowing issues and insights to arise from participants in the drama and from the public discourse that framed it. I wanted a systematic "thick description" of what was unfolding. While I knew there were conflicts in the community, I lacked a sophisticated vocabulary and an analysis of how and why the conflict was occurring. There was no platform available for the insights I did have, nor was there a venue for citizens to discuss their concerns. I thought we should do interviews with a variety of city officials and homeowners affected by their decisions as a way to examine the conflict flaring in the community, as well as examine the public discourse found in official documents, meetings, and news media.

As luck would have it, our Institutional Review Board (IRB), inspired by more stringent federal oversight of human subjects research and ill prepared to deal with qualitative research methodologies, asked us to resubmit our application for approval, insisting that we provide the list of questions we planned to ask informants. Since we had intended the interviews to be sufficiently open-ended to allow the emergence of themes, we felt providing the questions in advance was impossible and a subversion of the project. Consequently, we decided to eliminate interviews and focus on a textual analysis of public discourse, tested against our own knowledge as participant observers in the lifeworld of the community. I say "as luck would have it" that we were dissuaded from conducting interviews because I am glad we did not include them in the research. As I look back on the uses to which I have been able to put the research, interviews, while they would have provided more concrete evidence and permitted a sharpened analysis, would have placed me, as a continuing member of the community, in a politically awkward situation. Since the community is small and the major players known to all, we either could not have guaranteed informants confidentiality or we could not have freely used what we were told. The research would have been shaped and tamed in directions that would have constrained the analysis and our political efficacy.

Another confounding problem was the unfolding nature of events. A disaster does not begin and end in a discrete period of time; we found ourselves in the middle of a flowing stream of change with no known outcome or ending point and no final analysis to be neatly drawn. We ultimately decided to draw our own boundaries on our study by focusing on the one-year period after the flood. Despite the usefulness of a cutoff point, even the events of that period shifted and required reinterpretation as context and historical perspective continued to change. For example, even as I was putting the last changes to the manuscript published in *Southern Communication Journal*, new information was coming forward about the events of that first year. The Federal Emergency

Management Agency (FEMA) demanded a refund from the city government over money the city had claimed for sewer damage from the flood, which FEMA now claimed was not flood-related. We have learned to resist the temptation to declare our analysis final and complete, a caveat that all scholars might remember even if they do not stay around to see events unfold after their research is done.

Another complication that interfered with conducting and completing the project was the extraordinary personal toll the disaster and its aftermath took on me and my family, as it did on so many in Grand Forks. It began when we lived in a small travel camper for months while we hauled our ruined furniture and possessions to the curb (like every other homeowner in the city) and stripped and disinfected about 1500 square feet of house. Like others, we waited for weeks and months for contractors to restore our electrical service, install a water heater and a new furnace and ductwork, install drywall and carpet, and replace plumbing and bathroom fixtures. We did paperwork for insurance companies, FEMA, our mortgage company, and the city. We attended meetings to find out what the city planned for our neighborhood and made our own protests about the dike that was proposed for our neighborhood, planned to run through our house that was under repair. In the end, the city did not declare eminent domain until 2000, after we and nearly every homeowner on the city's list already had been forced to sell our homes.

What difference did it make to our research that I shared this experience with other residents? It certainly gave me access to a standpoint and to the knowledge of those residents that I might never have known had existed had I been an outsider. I was aware of alternative definitions and explanations that countered official ones. Perhaps most significantly, it spurred me to want to document and narrate a different story about the community than the official versions that justified and lauded the actions of city leaders.

The Analysis and Its Uses

As we gathered and attended to the public communication from that one-year period, we discussed the patterns that emerged from the public discourse. We began by thinking about the nature of communities as the product of communication, created by the ongoing routines of people and institutions embedded into the landscape of a social and geographic location. We considered the nature of disasters, called into being by those with authority to declare them to be so outside the realm of the expected and so disruptive of the normal order of things as to require a bracketing and a special handling. With that theoretical understanding, we were left to find a point of view and a voice to speak about what had transpired in our community, which was difficult given the personal nature of our own experiences. Of all the stories that could have been told about what happened, we decided to tell the story that stood out the most to us, the one that brought the conflicts into the sharpest relief. That choice meant we were not ourselves at the center of the story but put ourselves in the position of speaking for and about others, a role not without its theoretical and ethical problems. It was a story about the conflict between two groups that we dubbed "Movers" and "Shakers." The Movers were city officials and self-appointed business and professional leaders. The Shakers were a group of homeowners from the hardest-hit and lowest-income neighborhood who fought back by (among other avenues) filing a class action lawsuit against the city to force it to declare eminent domain. After considering other names, we were pleased to find a pair that we thought gave the "underdog" group equal status with the elite group. We liked that our names subverted the usual use of the label given to an elite group in a community whose members supposedly get things done. While I had traveled between the two groups, as a member of organizations to which Movers belonged and as a friend of people from the resistance group, I did not count myself as a member of either. Therefore we found a point of view that looked at both but clearly was sympathetic to the Shakers, a position we felt was justified from our evidence of how they had been treated.

Briefly, from our analysis we concluded that the conflict between the two had a class origin that positioned members of each group in different social *and* physical locations in the community. They differed on the basis of defining the events (Movers defined the flood as a natural disaster, Shakers defined the "recovery" as a disaster); political ideology (Movers advocated progress by "moving on," while Shakers argued for justice); and control over material and symbolic resources (Movers had access to the primary means for voice in the community, enabling them to make their vision of the community material reality, while Shakers were frustrated in their attempts to be heard and to keep control over the small amount of material resources they owned). We concluded that by Movers "winning" in the short term, the community continued to suffer from unresolved class conflicts and unresolved issues of justice produced by decisions after the flood. Conflicts continue to simmer in the community, surfacing when major community decisions are to be made. Until these differences are acknowledged and steps taken to include citizens in decision making in a meaningful way, we concluded, the city could not "move on" in the way some imagined it already had.

Conducting the research and the analysis and writing a manuscript for submission to a journal is one thing; figuring out how to put results to good use are another. As for other scholarly work, various venues for presenting the work were available. I discussed the research at a talk given at the University of Illinois. The paper was accepted for presentation at the annual convention of the

Association for Education in Journalism and Mass Communication. The manuscript was accepted for publication in the *Southern Communication Journal* special issue on community. In other words, the research took its place in standard ways in our fields. But what of the community? What responsibility did we have to the Shakers, whom we felt deserved a hearing? What were the political risks of "going public" with the research results? What was our responsibility as scholars to a community we felt needed to address serious communication issues? How could we address these issues and more in the community?

I got the opportunity to raise them in a very public manner in the fall of 2003. I was asked to give the first lecture in the annual University of North Dakota Faculty Lecture Series, an honor to be invited, a privilege to have the floor for whatever research I wanted to present. While other research projects would have been easier to present and less risky to make public, I chose to base my presentation on this community research project. Coincidentally, the community was in the middle of a major controversy over spending tax money on a large water park to replace neighborhood swimming pools. Callers to a local talk radio program articulated the same feelings of disenfranchisement that we had found characterized conflicts in the community after the flood. I was invited to be on the show twice, the second time with a city council member in the studio with me and another on the telephone line, talking about conflicts in the city and the need for citizen voice and participation. My lecture brought members of the community to the audience, including members of the city council, generating public discussion about the flood and communication problems. Since then, I have been approached by the mayor's office (a new mayor since the flood) about working together on improving communication in the community.

Clearly, the work has just begun. We succeeded in getting some attention to the situation of the group called Shakers and some attention to the communication issues that threaten the community. With the published research now in our hands, we are in a position to extend the reach of our analysis. I am aware, however, that we will be in for criticism and contradiction when the full research record is made available. Public scholarship is not for sissies or for those who aspire to be a member of the club of Movers in whatever city or institution they reside. Yet few others in a community are in the position to raise issues as scholars are. We can be dismissed, but not as easily as others with less material and symbolic capital to leverage.

Which Side of the Road Are We On?

This story about one researcher's road to acquiring the identity of citizen-scholar raises questions and concerns, I understand. Were we too close to the subject matter to be "objective"? Did my own experience in the community mean I had an "axe to grind" that led to the research project and its analysis? Did we let our political affinity for the group called Shakers influence what we studied and what we found? Have we misrepresented or mischaracterized communication issues in the community to justify our interpretation?

It certainly is possible to accuse us of any of these. However, I remain convinced that engaging with our communities and even *taking sides* on the issues citizens confront there is part of our right as citizens and our responsibility as scholars. Had we aligned ourselves with city leaders and their official courses of action, helping citizens "understand" and accept decisions, we would have fulfilled a traditional role for applied communication scholars. We need to be clear that standing with the centers of power in a community is no less a political activity than community action research that seeks social change and the empowerment of citizens.

Although our research did not fit the usual definition of community action research, in which community members are active participants in the design and implementation of the project, our study was an important step toward their inclusion in future projects. Our communicative vision for geographic communities is one described by Lewis A. Friedland as the "communicatively integrated community" (Friedland 2001), whereby deliberative democracy is carried out in the lifeworld of communities. To create such communities requires that researchers link their expertise to communities. Transformative change requires our participation, according to one university group committed to such collaborative work: "One of the clear needs in community change efforts is to bring together expert knowledge with local knowledge about neighborhood life and people" (Maher et al. 2003, 62). Integration of the knowledge of the academy with the knowledge of the community is best carried out by the integration of our identities as citizens and as scholars. While not all of our research needs to be carried out in and with our own communities and not all of the research carried out in a community needs to be conducted by its scholarly citizens, we should continue to remind ourselves why we thought we should cross the road in the first place.

Questions for Reflection

What is meant by the distinction between "insider" and "outsider" points of view in this article?

What is gained, and what might some argue could be lost, when communication researchers step out of their stance as "objective observers" and become advocates within their communities? Do you believe the gains outweighed the losses in this case?

What were the advantages and disadvantages of the decision made by Rakow and her students to substitute discourse analysis for an interview methodology in this study?

Rakow criticizes communication theory for not providing enough guidance for a study like this, yet in the end her analysis makes extensive use of theory. How did theory help her, after all?

Do you agree or disagree with Rakow's argument that applied communication research typically serves to maintain social order by fixing small problems (improving communication competency and effectiveness) within an existing system?

Note

1. Further discussion of IRB issues takes place in Part V.

References

Friedland, L. A. 2001. "Communication, Community, and Democracy: Toward a Theory of the Communicatively Integrated Community." *Communication Research* 28 (4): 358–91.
Maher, T., J. Pennell, and L. Osterman. 2003. "Sociology in the Neighborhood: A University-Community Collaborative Model for Transformative Change." *Humanity & Society* 27 (1): 50–66.
Rakow, L. 1992. *Gender on the Line: Women, the Telephone, and Community Life.* Champaign: University of Illinois Press.
Rakow, L. 1995a. "Noon Siren and Rhubarb Pie Make Crosby a Familiar Place." *Divide County* [North Dakota] *Journal*, July 26, 2.
Rakow, L. 1995b. "Crosby Has Many Strengths but Needs a Common Vision." *Divide County* [North Dakota] *Journal*, August 2, 2.
Rakow, L. 1995c. "In Crosby, Everybody Knows What Everybody Knows." *Divide County* [North Dakota] *Journal*, August 9, 2.
Rakow, L. 1999. "The Public at the Table: From Public Access to Public Participation." *New Media and Society* 1 (1): 74–82.
Rakow, L. F. 2002. "The Return to Community in Cultural Studies." Pp. 150–164 in *American Cultural Studies,* eds. Catherine A. Warren and Mary Douglas Vavrus. Champaign: University of Illlinois Press.
Rakow, L. F., J. L. Hallsten, B. L. Belter, H. Dyrstad, J. Johnson, and K. Indvik. 2003. "The Talk of Movers and Shakers: Class Conflict in the Making of a Community Disaster." *Southern Communication Journal* 69 (1): 37–50.

2

Creating Informed Deliberation: The Role of Impact Surveys in Community Decision Making

Dietram A. Scheufele

Not all research focused on community engagement uses a qualitative paradigm, however. Here, public opinion researcher Dietram Scheufele describes his survey work on local community issues in Ithaca, New York. This work is very different in methodology from that presented in the previous chapter by Rakow, but shares some of the same goals. Scheufele and his students use the results of survey research to stimulate public discussion and dispel misinformation about what most citizens think about local issues. What people think that other people think is often an important determinant of their willingness to express their views and get involved.

Since media accounts often focus on the views of vocal minorities who are more likely to show up at meetings, protest, and write letters to the editor, Scheufele believes that his survey data play a crucial role in the local community by putting those minority views into perspective, providing citizens with a more accurate view of the "climate of public opinion" than would be available just by reading the newspapers.

But his goal is not just providing accurate information. As he relates in this chapter, he also wants to encourage public debate and discussion. He believes that the "impact surveys" conducted by his students can serve this role as well. Drawing from the idea of "differential gains," a theoretical model that stresses the way interpersonal discussion interacts with media information to produce an engaged community, Scheufele and his students design surveys intended to stimulate involvement, not just take an opinion "snapshot."

However, because survey research is so often manipulated to meet political objectives, he stresses the importance of evaluating poll data by considering sampling procedures, question wording, and knowledge of survey sponsorship. In fact, he has written columns in a local newspaper, the Ithaca Journal, *to educate people outside the university on these points.*

MANY COMMUNITIES TRY TO make decisions about issues, such as fluoridation of drinking water or new housing developments, at least in part based on citizen input. This input takes different forms, including deliberative forums, hearings, or letters to the editor of the local newspaper. Most of these different forms of citizen participation, of course, are based on the assumption that the citizenry is informed and capable of making decisions about issues that do not just affect them as individual citizens but also have social, economic, and environmental implications for the larger community. This approach is especially surprising, given that most citizens tend to be largely uninformed about political affairs or other issues relevant to their communities (Delli Carpini and Keeter 1996).

But, of course, there are differences between various groups. More educated members of the community and those who read local newspapers frequently also tend to be more aware of issues that affect their communities. So do people with more firmly held ideological belief systems and those who are already more knowledgeable about community affairs in general (Scheufele et al. 2002).

This, of course, creates an interesting dilemma. As newspapers are engaged in civic journalism efforts trying to bridge these gaps, they might in fact just do the opposite and widen them. This has often been referred to as "knowledge gaps" (Tichenor et al. 1970). In other words, more educated and knowledgeable citizens are also more likely to read local newspapers. More importantly, however, they also tend to pick up more quickly on information presented about various issues in newspapers than do those with less education. As a result, their knowledge gain is higher and the gaps between them and the less educated groups widen.

So what can research do to address this issue? Can it inform and stimulate community discourse? The answer is "yes." In this chapter I will give an overview of a survey project designed to tap into cognitions, opinions, and beliefs of citizens in the local community, but also to stimulate discussions among citizens and ultimately inform community decision making. The research design is based on a theoretical framework called the differential gains model of media effects (Scheufele 2001, 2002). In other words, the informational and mobilizing effects of community media depend to a large degree on how much citizens discuss what they have seen in the newspaper, for example, with other people. Only these discussions will allow them to make sense of what they have heard, integrate the facts into a coherent picture, and make informed and rational decisions.

The Differential Gains Model: A Theoretical Idea Driving Applied Research

As outlined earlier, the potential of newspapers for bridging the gaps between highly informed and active citizens and those people in a community who are less concerned with and less informed about local issues is often limited. Instead, more in-depth coverage of controversial issues, such as fluoridation of drinking water or urban sprawl, often widens existing gaps because the already informed tend to extract factual and mobilizing information at a much faster rate. Researchers have tried to explain these knowledge gaps as a function of differences in motivation, preexisting knowledge structures, and other explanatory variables (for an overview, see Eveland and Scheufele 2000), but few have offered concrete solutions for the problem. How can these gaps be bridged? How can we effectively use newspapers and other informational channels to inform all members of a community instead of just a small subgroup about issues that are directly relevant to their lives and the well-being of the community overall?

A first solution focuses on television as a potential knowledge leveler. Television tends to inform the less educated at a higher rate than the more educated. Unfortunately, this is largely a function of the minimal informational content even in television news. In other words, television will inform the less educated or less aware viewers. But the more educated will find little new content beyond what they already know (Eveland and Scheufele 2000). In addition, the role of television during community conflicts tends to be limited.

A second solution focuses on the two variables that tend to shape community conflicts most directly: coverage in the local newspaper—including articles, editorials, and letters to the editor—and interpersonal discussions among citizens. Interpersonal discussion of politics, of course, is at the core of much scholarly debate about democratic citizenship (for an overview, see Schudson 1998). More recent research, however, suggests that the influence of interpersonal discussion of politics on democratic processes is far more complex than previously assumed (Eliasoph 1998; Scheufele 2001). These researchers have suggested that the impact of media content on citizens' understanding of politics and ultimately on participatory behavior might be strengthened or weakened by a number of other variables, including political discussions with others. Interpersonal discussion of politics, in other words, *moderates* the influence of mass media on its audiences.

While there is an overall positive impact of various types of public affairs media use on understanding of politics and political behavior, this influence differs depending on the degree to which individuals talk about politics with other people. Talking about issues with other citizens seems to be a necessary condition for fully understanding these issues, for tying them to other, preexisting knowledge, and consequently for meaningfully participating in political life.

This idea of interactive influence of interpersonal discussion and media use on political participation, the "differential gains" model mentioned earlier, assumes that mass-mediated information alone is not what allows citizens to participate meaningfully in their communities. Only if citizens talk with others about what they have read in newspapers will they be able to extract mobilizing information and meaningfully participate in local community affairs (Scheufele 2001, 2002). In other words, it is the combination of talk *and* mass-mediated information that allows citizens to make informed decisions and participate meaningfully (see figure 2.1).

The following is a case study of a collaboration between the local newspaper in Ithaca, New York, the *Ithaca Journal*, and my undergraduate course in Industry Research Methods at Cornell University (also in Ithaca). The project is unique since it brings together three groups: academics, local media, and the community. The project has tapped levels of support for various issues that are relevant to our community among a great many citizens. It has assessed what the public knows and how it feels about these issues. In doing so, not only has it stirred up and informed public discussion about the issues, but it has also helped policy makers tailor their decisions toward the larger public rather than a very vocal and therefore highly visible minority. By doing so, this project has demonstrated the usefulness of "impact surveys" as catalysts for community deliberation, as well as sources of information about where the community stands and what its concerns might be.

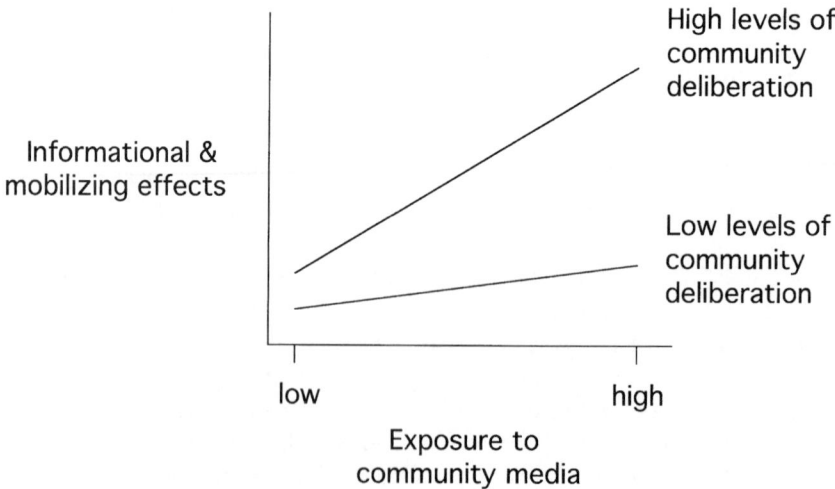

FIGURE 2.1
The "differential gains" model of media communication and political participation.

Doing Research for and about the Community: A Case Study

The idea for this unique survey project originated from the perception that public discourse in the Ithaca area and the county that surrounds it (Tompkins County) tends to be relatively uninformed and dominated by a small, vocal minority. Other views are often crowded out in public discourse. And when it comes to scientific controversies, such as a recent vote on fluoridation of drinking water, credible scientific information is not widely distributed and citizens rely mostly on "heuristic cues" (shortcut strategies for processing information).

This is somewhat surprising in a county with the demographic makeup of Tompkins County. People in this area are highly educated—about 48 percent of all residents twenty-five years and older have at least a bachelor's degree, which is almost twice as high as the national average. And, at least in Ithaca, citizens also tend to be more liberal than in the rest of the country. Registered Democrats outnumber Republicans three to one. That explains some of the more extreme issue stances in the area. Opposition to new cell phone towers is as automatic and certain as anti-Wal-Mart bumper stickers on rusty Volvos. The above-average levels of educational attainment, however, are strangely at odds with the absence of factual information or seemingly rational arguments from much of the discussion about these issues among citizens. On the issue of fluoridated drinking water, for example, much of the electorate was uninformed about the history and background of the proposed change to the city charter they were voting on.

In response to this largely uninformed community discourse, my students and I created the annual *Tompkins County Community Survey*. It brings together students, news organizations, and the community in order to stimulate and inform public deliberation. The survey is designed as a semester-long research project in which the students design and conduct a survey with a probability sample of about 700–800 citizens on important issues in the larger Tompkins County community. Issues studied in the past have included civil liberties, fluoridation of drinking water, and the environmental risks of mall expansions in the community.

The survey is conducted almost entirely by the students. They design the sampling frame, design the questionnaire, and conduct the survey itself. The interviewing is done by students in collaboration with the Survey Research Institute at Cornell. Students go through multiple rounds of training in class and at the survey center and are constantly supervised by professionals while they are conducting the interviews in order to ensure the integrity of the data. At the end of the semester, students write up results for the local paper, other media outlets, and interested citizens in the community.

> **Box 2.1: Survey Terminology**
>
> Surveys are a well-established approach to measuring public opinion in a population. While students new to survey methodology are often skeptical that a relatively small sample of people can accurately reflect the opinions of a much larger group, this is not the main problem with survey research. The main problem is very often how the questions are worded, because subtle differences in wording can produce very different results. Pollsters willing to manipulate wording to arrive at a predetermined conclusion are (unfortunately) not rare in our society. And even with the best of intentions, writing a question that is a valid measure of the factor that we have in mind is quite difficult.
>
> Using survey techniques rather than qualitative methods raises the question of the validity of the results. The results are likely to be reliable in the sense that if we repeated the survey we would probably get the same results. But some might argue that because of the issue of question wording and the artificiality of asking people prespecified questions from a list, the validity of survey research is more often in question.
>
> Just how likely is it that the results of a survey are accurate? The usefulness of survey results rests on the concept of a "probability sample" taken from the larger group. (That larger group need not be the population as a whole; it most often consists of all voters, or all people over eighteen, in a given geographic region, but it could also consist of any other specific group—all kindergarten students, all sailboat owners, all readers of a certain newspaper, and so on.) A probability sample is one in which every member of the population has an equal chance of being included in the sample. Knowing the size of this kind of sample allows the researcher to calculate the "sampling error" (an estimate of the accuracy of the results, usually expressed as plus or minus so many percent) for a given confidence level (the probability that the results from the survey are actually accurate within this range). Of course, the larger the sample (all other things being equal), the lower the sampling error and the higher the confidence level.
>
> Surveys in areas such as North America or much of Western Europe, where telephone service is nearly universal, most often rely on telephone contact, although with the proliferation of cell phones and unlisted numbers this is becoming more complex. Mail surveys are a common alternative, of course. Other kinds of survey samples—such as those based on recruiting shoppers in a mall or advertising in a magazine or on the Internet for volunteers—introduce distortions because not everyone in the population being studied has an equal chance of being selected.
>
> The term "sampling frame" refers to a list or set from which the survey respondents are going to be chosen. It might be a telephone book or a voter registration or membership list. The sampling frame is usually imperfect; no list of any large population is likely to include up-to-date information on everyone involved. These days, in phone surveys of the general population, the numbers to be called are most likely generated by a computer program rather than actually selected from a list. This sidesteps the unlisted number problem but may still miss those with only cell phones—or, of course, those with no phones at all.

> Another significant problem with surveys is that response rates (the proportion of people willing to participate in a survey) are getting lower as the number of telemarketers, political campaigners, and legitimate researchers trying to contact each of us rises. This increases the probability of bias, or inaccuracy that is not random but systematic, in a survey because those who agree to answer our questions do not necessarily give answers characteristic of the larger group. For example, our respondents in such circumstances may be less busy, more lonely, more helpful, or less suspicious than others in the same population, or they may be more interested in the survey topic. This may be true even if the distribution by demographics such as gender, age, education, income, and so on closely resembles that of the population.
>
> When response rates are low, even with a large sample, the generalizability of the results (that is, the extent to which what members of the sample think really reflects what members of the population think) is low because there may be systematic bias. This is true no matter what the sampling error and confidence level might be; these statistics only take random error into account, not systematic bias.

The intriguing part about this survey is that the community is informed about all the steps along the way. The *Ithaca Journal* covers the research process in a series of articles leading up to the reporting of the final results. This includes articles on interviewing, on the issue itself, and also on the pros and cons of polling. The goal of this continuing coverage is to get the community informed and involved in the process and to familiarize it with polling as a method of accurately assessing public opinion. These student-run surveys can mobilize citizen interest and have an effect on local policy deliberations. For this reason we refer to them as "impact" surveys."[1]

Quality assurance and informing both students and citizens about the nature of survey work are extremely important, as exemplified by the recent controversy surrounding the Peterson Survey, conducted by criminology professor Stephen Schoenthaler and students in his class at California State University, Stanislaus. The survey tapped public opinion about the murder trial and presumed guilt of Scott Peterson, who is accused of murdering his pregnant wife. After the trial had been moved, in part based on the survey's results, seven students from Stephen Schoenthaler's class came forward and alleged that they had falsified the results. The problems with Schoenthaler's pseudosurvey are obvious. Students were asked to conduct surveys from their homes and on their own dime. And to make matters worse, they went into the field with little training and no supervision or other forms of quality checks. In other words, Schoenthaler violated every rule in the book when it comes to conducting sample surveys. Nonetheless, the publicity that came with this survey exacerbates already existing problems with low levels of public trust in survey researchers and a general lack of confidence in their findings.

Our Tompkins County community survey is no exception. The articles and editorials based on our findings in the *Ithaca Journal* are usually hotly debated, as is the methodology itself. Letters to the editor talk about specific survey questions, about potential biases in the sampling design, and about the validity and, more importantly, the interpretation of our findings more generally. These discussions do not just take place on the opinion pages of the local daily, however. Other media organizations usually pick up on the story or on specific controversies surrounding it. The local radio stations tend to focus on the initial release of the poll. But the *Ithaca Times*, a left-leaning weekly in our community, often runs in-depth follow-up stories that address specific measurement issues or interpret the findings on a concrete issue, for example, a specific development project, in the context of the larger community problem, such as urban sprawl. Our findings have also been used repeatedly as evidence by one side or another in common council meetings of various townships in the Ithaca area.

Learning from Ithaca: Three Goals of Impact Surveys

Our survey project has been designed for and about the local community. By collaborating with the local newspaper we try to get the community involved from the outset in order to achieve three major objectives.

Informing Community Decision Making

Our survey is explicitly designed to inform community decision making and deliberations among citizens. This means, when designing the survey, we take great care to not dichotomize complex issues into simplistic agree-disagree questions. Rather, we measure various dimensions of support for or opposition to policy proposals using stable, multi-item measures for each dimension. A good illustration is a survey we conducted on a proposed development project called "Southwest Park Development." We polled the Tompkins County population in early 2000 in order to get its opinions on a plan that proposed a development close to a state park in order to expand an existing strip mall.

In our survey we tapped people's concerns about environmental impacts, such as pollution of ground water and traffic increase. We measured people's willingness to drive to bigger cities to shop there and their levels of satisfaction with the commercial sector in the Ithaca area. And, of course, we assessed the degree of support for different proposals related to the new development. All of these variables were important factors in the decision-making process in the community, especially since various vocal minorities had used perceived public opinion as a key argument in favor of their own issue stance. Our survey found broad support for the new development among different constituencies in the community and showed that the perceived benefits among the public outweighed risks that people associated with the proposed development.

Measuring Opinion Climates; Countering Spirals of Silence

The issue of vocal minorities, however, highlights the importance of measuring real and perceived public opinion as a second key goal for any type of community impact survey. This is especially important during community conflicts where different interest groups dominate public discussion. A good example is a recent discussion about fluoridation of drinking water in the City of Ithaca. In November 2000, the City of Ithaca, a part of the larger Ithaca area, voted on two referenda that would have allowed a countywide vote on fluoridation of drinking water, which was not in place at the time. Since water cannot be provided individually to separate municipalities, the vote in the City of Ithaca had implications for neighboring cities and townships as well and therefore triggered a heated debate in the larger Tompkins County community.

The referendum was ultimately rejected in a very close vote. The turnout was lower than expected, in part because it was paired with a Senate vote (Clinton vs. Lazio) and a presidential vote (Gore vs. Bush) that were all but decided in advance. (New York State tends to vote Democratic in national races.) Interestingly enough, however, the discussions leading up to the vote suggested a very different picture. In fact, opponents of fluoridation, who were in the minority overall (though they had a slight majority among likely voters in our survey), dominated the discussion on the editorial pages of the *Ithaca Journal* and in town hall meetings. A key contribution of our survey, therefore, was to accurately measure and portray "climates of opinion." Who was really in favor and against fluoridation of drinking water? And where did the people stand who were most affected by the vote, that is, families with small children who relied and continue to rely on fluoride tablets?

Information like this is critical, of course, when it comes to countering "spirals of silence" during community conflicts (Noelle-Neumann 1993). The idea behind the spiral of silence is that people who perceive themselves to be in the minority or see their viewpoint as losing ground will tend to speak out less in public. The spiral of silence idea is not new. But seldom is it more apparent than for an issue, such as Ithaca's fluoridation of local drinking water, where opinion dynamics play out over a relatively short period of time and culminate in a vote. The tendency to silence minority views reinforces or exacerbates public perceptions of minority and majority distributions of opinions, and as a result, one group will ultimately fall silent and the other one will win the debate (for a discussion of the theoretical model, see Scheufele and Moy 2000).

This dynamic is very functional in democratic societies that rely on social cohesion and reaching consensus through discussion. It is very dysfunctional, however, if the initial perception of public opinion among citizens is incorrect, either because of biased news coverage or because of vocal minorities that dominate public discussion and silence other viewpoints. Opinion (mis)perceptions stifle deliberation among citizens and ultimately prevent an open exchange of ideas and viewpoints. This is certainly what happened with the fluoridation vote in Ithaca, and our survey provided key information about the true distribution of opinion in the area, especially among new parents and low-income families who did not get heard adequately in this debate.

Triggering Discussion: The Differential Gains Model in Practice

The most important outcome of our impact surveys, however, has been their effect as catalysts for discussion. News coverage of an issue certainly has positive effects in terms of learning and promoting citizen participation. As outlined in the differential gains model, however, this impact is much stronger among people who discuss what they have read or heard with others. Talking an issue through with others and potentially being confronted with opposing viewpoints, people are forced to develop a more integrated understanding of the issue. And as some of my own recent research shows, discussions with others play a key role in helping people make sense of what they have read in the local newspaper and also in promoting a more active citizenry by deepening people's understanding of the issues and of the different ways of getting involved (Scheufele 2001).

Community impact surveys are therefore not just an important gauge of public opinion in a community. They can also play a key part in informing *and* triggering discussions among various constituencies in a community and ultimately contribute to better decision making and a more participatory citizenry.

Community Impact Surveys: Lessons from the Field

In order to make impact surveys a useful tool in creating informed citizen deliberation and in promoting a more in-depth understanding of complex issues, such as fluoridation of drinking water, it is crucial to report findings that citizens can trust and that they understand. Especially with important decisions at stake, vocal minorities will often try to shoot the messenger and to discredit polling as a manipulative tool. Poll results, they argue, are arbitrary and can be tweaked and manipulated to support any point of view. While this criticism is not unjustified, it misses the point. Of course, any type of information can be manipulated and used for partisan causes, but that does not mean that there is not reliable and valid information out there that people can and should trust. There are good polls and there are bad polls, and usually it is very easy to tell if a poll is carefully done and if the results are valid. There are three things that I usually emphasize in my columns in the *Ithaca Journal* as key guidelines that everyone should be aware of when interpreting public opinion polls: sampling, question wording, and sponsorship.

Every survey is based on the assumption that we can't talk to all voters, all citizens, or—in technical terms—the complete target population. As a result, we need to draw a sample, that is, a smaller group of, say, 500 people. But how representative are these 500 people of the whole population? Unfortunately, it is impossible to answer this question without some degree of uncertainty, called sampling error. Sampling error—which should be reported with any legitimate survey—tells us how accurate our results are likely to be, and just *how* likely that is. For example, let's assume that 56 percent of all respondents in a survey express support for fluoridation of drinking water in Tompkins County. In this case, a sampling error of ±4 percent would indicate the overall support for fluoridation in Tompkins County is somewhere between 52 and 60 percent.

Another problem is that some groups in society are more likely to respond to surveys than others. Females, for example, are far less reluctant to talk to a pollster than males, making the results less representative and therefore less generalizable. This, of course, creates problems for survey researchers. Pollsters have also had to come up with new techniques for sampling hard-to-reach populations such as people with cell phones, answering machines, and unlisted phone numbers.

The second problem inherent in many public opinion polls is the way they ask questions. Even seemingly similar questions can produce startlingly different results. Two different polls on affirmative action, for example, asked respondents if they supported certain policies. The only difference between the two polls was the label they used: "affirmative action" in one poll and "preferential treatment for minorities" in the other. Needless to say, levels of support in the second poll were significantly lower. The exact wording of each question should be presented along with the poll results themselves.

Finally, the media and the public should be wary of any poll that does not identify the sponsor. The American Association for Public Opinion Research (AAPOR) has very clear guidelines as far as this issue is concerned. Pollsters who do not identify the sponsor, either to the respondent, during the interview, or to the public, if the poll is publicized, violate AAPOR's Code of Professional Ethics and Practices (see www.aapor.org).

Questions for Reflection

Imagine a controversial issue that interests you personally. Do you think that knowing more about what other people think would change your own opinion? Would it change your willingness to express that opinion in public, or to become involved?

The term "climate of opinion" is commonly used by public opinion scholars. Do you think public opinion is actually like the weather? In what ways?

Public opinion polls do a poor job of representing strength of conviction. Some people, or "stakeholders," have more to gain or lose in a given situation than others, and may have stronger opinions. Given this, should most public issues be decided by majority vote? Why or why not?

What problems will arise in trying to do surveys in countries where most people do not have telephones, or those where levels of literacy are low?

Note

1. Note that this term *is not* synonymous with "push polls," a kind of partisan survey intended to influence policy in a particular way. "Push polls" are considered unethical (see www.aapor.org for details).

References

Delli Carpini, M. X., and Keeter, S. 1996. *What Americans Know about Politics and Why It Matters.* New Haven: Yale University Press.
Eliasoph, N. 1998. *Avoiding Politics: How Americans Produce Apathy in Everyday Life.* New York: Cambridge University Press.
Eveland, W. P., and Scheufele, D. A. 2000. "Connecting News Media Use with Gaps in Knowledge and Participation." *Political Communication* 17 (3): 215–37.
Noelle-Neumann, E. 1993. *The Spiral of Silence. Public Opinion—Our Social Skin.* 2nd edition. Chicago: University of Chicago Press.
Scheufele, D. A. 2001. "Democracy for Some? How Political Talk Both Informs and Polarizes the Electorate." Pp. 19–32 in *Communication and U.S. Elections: New Agendas,* eds. R. P. Hart and D. Shaw. Lanham, MD: Rowman and Littlefield Publishers.

Scheufele, D. A. 2002. "Differential Gains from Mass Media and Their Implications for Participatory Behavior." *Communication Research* 29 (1): 45–64.

Scheufele, D. A., and Moy, P. 2000. "Twenty-Five Years of the Spiral of Silence: A Conceptual Review and Empirical Outlook." *International Journal of Public Opinion Research* 12 (1): 3–28.

Scheufele, D. A., Shanahan, J., and Kim, S. 2002. "Who Cares about the Issues? Media Influences on Issue Awareness, Issue Stance, and Issue Involvement." *Journalism and Mass Communication Quarterly* 79 (2): 427–44.

Schudson, M. 1998. *The Good Citizen: A History of American Civic Life*. New York: The Free Press.

Tichenor, P. J., Donohue, G. A., and Olien, C. N. 1970. "Mass Media Flow and Differential Growth in Knowledge." *Public Opinion Quarterly* 34: 159–70.

3
Community Action for Drug Prevention: A Behind-the-Scenes Look at a Sixteen-Community Study

Michael D. Slater

The third chapter in this section presents yet another example of community-oriented research, but of a quite different sort. Thanks to a major governmental grant, this complicated and ambitious project involved a total of sixteen different communities, rather than just one. The scale of the effort is truly daunting—involving the management of personal relations with school district personnel, students, and parents, and local community leaders in each area, as well as the actual conduct of a research project based on a formidably complex design.

Like the projects described in the two previous chapters, the intent of this research is not just to generate data to answer scholarly questions but to intervene in the lives of real people at the community level. Yet the design of this project is fundamentally different because it has been conceptualized as an experiment by a researcher familiar with experimental designs of the type commonly used in controlled laboratory tests. Moving this research idea into actual community settings where the conditions are never completely under the control of the research team is difficult, presenting a kaleidoscope of ever-shifting challenges to a research plan.

While both Rakow and Scheufele report on projects that were implemented within their own local areas, in which they are simultaneously acting as citizens and as scholars, Slater's role as described in this chapter is more the traditional researcher's role—that of objective outsider. The goals of this research were influenced by federal government policy and the availability of research funds rather than defined primarily by local events and controversies arising within the communities under study, so the cooperation of the affected communities had to be secured for the project to be successful. However, for this project Slater joined forces with a preexisting group of researchers who had a track record in community mobilization efforts.

This kind of research also presents special ethical challenges because the information collected from the study is highly sensitive, concerned with assessing drug and alcohol use among school-age subjects.

Nevertheless, all things considered, Slater clearly believes the results were well worth the effort!

A FIVE-YEAR, SIXTEEN-COMMUNITY, almost $2.5 million field experiment represents a large slice of someone's professional life. The relationships built, the problems tackled, the nail-biting crises shared, and finally the knowledge that is generated can all shape a person as well as a career. More importantly, such a project has the potential to influence policy and practice, and ultimately to touch human lives for the better.

Colleagues sometimes ask how a project of this scope came about, and what it takes to run a national field study. What does it offer? Is it worth it? How do you make it work? Major field studies such as this one still are a rarity in the field of communication, though they are reasonably commonplace in the public health field. So these are good questions. This chapter is an effort to answer these questions, at least anecdotally and from my own particular experiences. In so doing, I hope to highlight opportunities and warn of potential pitfalls, as well as to give colleagues and students considering future involvement in such ventures an opportunity to vicariously taste the sweet and the bitter of such an enterprise.

Community Action for Drug Prevention in a Nutshell

Since this is a retrospective view, let me begin with an orientation to the project as it actually took shape. Community Action for Drug Prevention (CADP) was a field experiment. We were testing a multilevel intervention strategy, seeking to combine school-level social marketing interventions with community-level, participatory media efforts in the hopes of reducing alcohol, marijuana, and cigarette use among younger adolescents. Our premise was that to be successful, social marketing strategies focusing on individual behavior change needed to operate in a community context (Slater et al. 2000), consistent with social-ecological models of public health (Coreil et al. 2001). We approached this in two ways. First, we focused social marketing in a school setting, in which it might impact the social climate within an institutional community. Second, we also worked with community prevention activists to launch community media efforts designed and managed locally but based

Box 3.1: Field Experiments

Most people are familiar with the general concept of a laboratory experiment in which some variables are held constant and others are manipulated by the researcher. The term "field experiment" refers to a study based on experimental methodology, of the same general type designed for use under controlled laboratory conditions, but under natural or "field" conditions instead—that is, in real-world settings where many things cannot be held constant by the researcher. This particular type of "field experiment" is testing "social marketing" strategies, or strategies designed to "sell" a particular form of social behavior. Experimental laboratory studies, like surveys, are higher in reliability, but (some argue) they can be lower in validity. Field experiments address this by studying real communities, yet retain the ability to show cause-and-effect relationships.

The goal of all experiments is to identify those factors responsible for a particular effect or result. In order to do so, it is necessary to isolate the factors being tested and "control" or account for as many other potential influences as possible. So, for example, if we are trying to test which teaching method results in the greatest student learning, we might compare the experiences of two similar classes, but first we would want to be sure the two were comparable in terms of intelligence, attitude, preparation, skill of teacher, prior knowledge, and so on. This would be one form of "experimental control." Such considerations are a big challenge in fieldwork.

Just as surveys attempt to "generalize" to a larger population on the basis of a smaller probability sample, or the teaching experiment would be intended to "generalize" results to predict effects in other, future classes, a field experiment of the type described here tries to determine if an intervention strategy that is successful in one community would have a similar effect in another. This is also a form of "generalizability." But it is never perfect because no two communities are ever exactly alike, and conditions that might change the result may never be completely accounted for or fully understood.

The term "treatment" suggests origins in medical research, where it would refer to a medication or another treatment for a disease. In social and behavioral research, of course, the term means any intervention (such as exposure to a message) that we think might be responsible for an effect we are studying (such as a change in attitudes or behavior). Because conditions may change whether a treatment is applied or not (in other words, the patient might get better even if the doctor did nothing), a second group may not receive a treatment at all. This is called a "control" group because this is another way we can isolate effects to a single known cause.

Just as the names imply, "pre" and "post" tests assess the conditions before and after a "treatment" is applied. A "factorial design" looks at the effects of more than one such treatment, or "factor."

Sometimes causative factors may interact with one another or with other variables. For example, a teaching method such as group discussion may be more effective than

(*continued*)

Box 3.1: Field Experiments (*continued*)

standard approaches with highly motivated students, yet fail with less motivated students. This is called an "interaction effect" (distinguished from a "main effect"). In experimental design, finding interaction effects can be tricky but important. In this example, it might appear that group discussion has no effect on learning if we look just at the total results for the two classes taught with and without discussion. In reality, the discussion method might be having a large positive effect on a small number of students and a small negative effect on a larger number of others.

Note that the "unit of analysis" of the project in this chapter was the community, not the individual. In survey work and most experiments involving people, the individual human being is almost always the "unit of analysis." All of the statistical tests treat the individual as the object of study. But communities are not just the sum of everything that goes on at the individual level added up. (To continue with the classroom example, every class seems to have a sort of "group personality" that can be quite distinctive and is difficult to reduce to explanations based on characteristics of the individual students, even though in this relatively simple type of case it is customary to consider the student and not the class as the unit of analysis.) Where effects on entire communities are being assessed, Slater and others argue that the community should be treated as the "unit of analysis."

As Slater notes in this chapter, this "nested design," studying individuals within communities, greatly complicates the statistical analysis, in part because far fewer "units" are included at the community level. Only sixteen communities were involved, even though thousands of individual subjects were included, and sixteen is a very small number from which to generalize about all communities.

---

largely on a media "toolkit" that we provided. Our hope was that these community-based media efforts would reinforce the in-school messages in the larger community, hopefully creating both greater exposure to the message (Hornik 2002) and a sense that the anti-use norms advocated were endorsed throughout the major social contexts in which these middle and junior high school students lived.

We were also quite interested in how such media efforts would function to reinforce in-school prevention curricula, the most common approach to youth drug prevention efforts in school settings (Flay 2000; Worden and Flynn 2002). Therefore, we created what is called a factorial design. Eight communities would receive the treatment, and eight others would serve as controls. Within each of these sixteen treatment and control communities, one school would receive a research-based prevention curriculum and one would not. This permitted us to test the main effects of the media treatment and those of the school curriculum, and to find out how the effects of the media treatment and those of the school prevention curriculum interacted.

Emergence of a National Field Study

Most projects start at some point with a simple idea that gains its own momentum. That was certainly the case with CADP. Over several years, I had been involved in some modest collaborative projects with the Tri-Ethnic Center for Prevention Research, a group of prevention researchers with several decades of funding from the National Institute on Drug Abuse (NIDA). The Tri-Ethnic Center, which is deeply committed to community-based efforts, had developed what it called the Community Readiness Model (Oetting et al. 1995; Edwards et al. 2000), a stage model for how communities move forward in the mobilization process. They had also developed a one-day workshop intended to help community leaders and activists move a community forward more quickly in this process. It had struck me, when I heard about this model, that community-based media efforts might have particular potential for helping facilitate community mobilization (Olien et al. 1984; Van Leuven and Slater 1991).

NIDA had announced a request for communication- and media-focused proposals regarding adolescent substance use prevention. Tri-Ethnic Center researchers (notably Gene Oetting and Ruth Edwards) and I got together to chat about the NIDA request and my idea. They agreed that community media hadn't gotten close attention before and that it had potential in the context of the community readiness model. We also discussed how this kind of community-based effort might create a climate that would validate and reinforce school-based prevention efforts. That led, logically, to including school-based media efforts as well, given the media focus of the proposal. Tri-Ethnic Center researchers and I had also worked with a faculty member in the marketing department, Kathleen Kelly, who specialized in substance-use prevention social marketing efforts. Kathleen immediately expressed her enthusiasm regarding the potential for focusing social marketing efforts in the school setting, and for using special events and media relations/media advocacy (Wallack et al. 1993) in the community as a means of supporting such efforts.

A quick review of the literature led us to findings that prior community prevention media efforts had apparently been most successful with youth who had been exposed to in-school prevention curricula (Flynn et al. 1992). Therefore, inclusion of a high quality in-school prevention curriculum in the experimental design seemed an obvious necessity. I had become familiar with the work of William Hansen of Tanglewood Research on the All Stars prevention curriculum (Hansen 1996) from my service on a National Institutes of Health (NIH) grant review study section. Gene and Ruth concurred that Bill would be an excellent collaborator; fortunately, Bill agreed to join us as a subcontractor responsible for the prevention curriculum.

When I raised the idea with Gene and Ruth, I presumed that Tri-Ethnic Center would take the lead on such a proposal. Funded projects that I had led had been tight experimental designs, with controlled exposure to messages either in lab settings or in schools. Moreover, research centers have the staff and resources to more easily develop a large-scale grant proposal of this type on the tight time line required, which is a tremendous challenge for a single faculty member supported primarily by a desktop computer. Their response, however, was that it was my idea, my area of expertise, and I should take the lead.

Those who are unfamiliar with large NIH grants may not understand my hesitation at leaping in. These grant applications involve a twenty-five-page single-spaced project description plus extensive appendixes elaborating the rationale, concept, and the intervention and research methods in exhaustive detail, from design to measurement to power analyses. All of this material must be based on state-of-the-art research methods, as it will be dissected by leading experts in the field from around the country. Dozens of additional pages present detailed budgets, biographical information on the investigators, plans for human research protections, and so on. The time commitment involved can amount to hundreds of hours, to be squeezed in around other responsibilities. This isn't too bad in programs with rolling deadlines and many opportunities to revise and resubmit. But the type of NIH program we targetted was a one-shot opportunity.

The good news is that in such cases there isn't the usual two- to three-year cycle of review and revision before funding, and the competitive pool is likely to be smaller than for an ongoing program. The bad news is that if one isn't funded—and for this type of program the ratio of grants to submissions may range from one in four to one in twenty or more—a great deal of time has been spent with little to show for it, except perhaps the opportunity to rework and resubmit the proposal for some other purpose later on. Fortunately, the Tri-Ethnic Center group, Kathleen Kelly, and Bill Hansen were all extremely supportive and professional, writing parts of the proposal text based on their prior work and forming the core of the research team for this proposal.

Studies like the one we planned are very expensive. There was a time when community intervention research like this relied on comparing results in matched communities (see, e.g., Farquhar et al. 1990). In this kind of "quasi-experiment," impacts are assessed based on data from individuals, often thousands of individuals, even though (as individuals) they are not randomly assigned to a treatment condition (Cook and Campbell 1979). This is rarely acceptable any more. Recent statistical and methodological thinking has led to an expectation that effects be analyzed at the unit at which the treatment is applied (Murray 1995). In other words, an intervention (such as community media involvement) that takes place at the community level means that the treatment needs to be randomized by community and the primary unit of analysis is the community.

Limitations of time and money (even given significant grant funding) dictate that the primary N (or number of individual units being studied) may be quite small. Our project had thousands of individual participants from whom we collected data, but the statistical tests were based primarily on the number of communities, which was just sixteen. The statistics appropriate to these "nested" designs are complex (Raudenbush and Bryk 2002). This requirement for group randomized designs is especially challenging for communication interventions, which typically have small effect sizes (Snyder and Hamilton 2002) that nonetheless may have important impact because mediated communication can reach so many people (Hornik 1988). Having as many communities as possible raises the chances of showing meaningful effects; our design with eight treatment and eight control communities was at the bottom end of acceptable sample sizes. It is hard to think of a study taking place in sixteen communities and thirty-two schools from around the United States, with two years' work in each community and involving over 4,000 youth who participated in longitudinal surveys, as a "small" study from a statistical point of view. But that is the challenging reality of current thinking.

Implementing a National Field Study

I'm afraid I was a source of continuing amusement to my Tri-Ethnic Center colleagues, seasoned as they were in the vagaries of community-based research. My prior background in grant-funded research, as I mentioned, was primarily in carefully controlled experiments with individuals randomly assigned to conditions, testing effects of persuasive messages such as alcohol advertisements and warnings. In field research, control is a brass ring for which we may reach but which we can never grasp.

We think we have recruited enough communities to conduct the research in a given year, but one drops out at almost the last moment due to some internal political issues. Can we recruit another in time? Another school district has an unanticipated 20 percent budget cut due to some fiscal disaster and key personnel working with us are laid off or cut back; can we find ways to help them manage to keep the program going for the coming year? We find out that the two leaders in one community, a senior law enforcement person and a newspaper editor, who have agreed to spearhead activities with the project, are leaving town and have alienated most of the rest of the community leadership over other issues. Can we find new leaders to take over? A key school contact becomes so difficult that project staff members are unable to work with him. Can I step in and smooth his feathers so the project can continue there?

Box 3.2: Levels of Measurement and Statistical Tests

The results of controlled experiments are analyzed using a wide range of statistical tests, depending on the experimental design and the type of data (whether categorical or based on measurement) involved.

Categorical data consists of frequency counts of such things as source type, gender, ethnicity, story theme, eye color, conversational turn, event occurrence, and so on that can be observed, recognized and counted, and possibly classified into categories. No actual measurement is involved. The so-called "chi-square" (χ^2) test for determining whether two frequency distributions should be considered the same or different is a very common test used with this kind of categorical data. Is the distribution of planned college majors the same at two universities, or different, based on a sample from each student body? The chi-square test will give the answer.

Higher levels of measurement involve assessing the degree to which a quality is present on a continuous scale. Age in years, scores on a test, ratings on an "agree-disagree" scale (though some argue these are really categorical), story length in words, and so on are examples of variables that can be measured on a continuous scale. Such data can be used to calculate a mean value, and a statistical test called a "t-test" can then be used to compare the means from two groups. For instance, we could use a t-test to measure whether one group of people recalls advertising or other media content better than a second group, possibly by using their score on a test of recalled knowledge. The t-test is a common example of a statistical test appropriate to continuously measured variables.

The purpose of chi-square tests, t-tests, and other (often far more complex) statistical comparisons is to determine the probability of whether differences based on sample data actually reflect differences between the populations from which the samples were drawn, or if the differences just occurred by chance (sampling error). The distinction between categorizing and measuring on a continuous scale is often the crucial one for determining which statistical tests are appropriate.[1]

Of course, these are only the "barest bones" of elementary statistical analysis. Fortunately, most of the more tedious calculations needed are now commonly done via computer software, and dozens of reference books provide exhaustive detail on how to carry out these kinds of tests—as well as how to perform more complex multivariate analysis, construct scales and indexes, draw different types of random samples, and so on.

Even if you are not planning to learn more about statistical tests, try to remember that they never actually disprove anything. Rather, they are designed to answer the question of whether the statistical evidence is strong enough that we can assume that the two things we are comparing (whether frequency distributions, means from different groups, or something entirely different) are actually different in the populations from which our samples have been drawn. If the evidence is not strong enough, we don't know that the populations are the same—we only know that we cannot rule out a chance difference.[2]

Generally speaking, as for survey data, the larger the number of observations or measurements, the less the probability that the observed results in the sample have occurred by random chance (sampling error). The extreme case is when we have measurements or observations for every unit in two populations we are comparing (census data rather than samples), in which case we can be completely certain about the characteristics of the populations. Any differences between them are actual population differences, not the result of sampling error.

Statistical significance refers to the achievement of a predetermined probability (by arbitrary convention, usually 95 percent or 99 percent) that the results we see have occurred because of something other than chance—that is, the odds that an observed difference or association really exists in the population being studied, not just in the sample being analyzed.

Notes

1. Categorical classifications can often be further subdivided into strictly nominal categories and ordinal, or ordered, categories. Measured variables are often subdivided into those based on scales that actually begin with zero, called ratio scales, and those that do not, called interval scales.

2. Statistical tests are also available to determine the likelihood that a correlation or measure of association occurred by chance (see chapter by Edwards in Part 4 for an example).

I have also had to loosen my definition of experimental control. A treatment school is on a semester system and the comparison school, in the same district, is on hexters? Well, we'll match the data collection times as closely as we can. I learned to say, "We'll just have to do what's possible. This is field research, after all." My Tri-Ethnic Center colleagues smile. I'm finally learning what they know so well.

We asked a lot from school staff in conducting this research. We do provide annual payments to the schools (a minimal ethical responsibility, to my mind) to help compensate for the extra effort. This money is very welcome to cash-strapped schools, but doesn't do much for the overworked teachers and counselors who pass out the surveys and put up the posters. I learned the fine points from the experienced staff at Tri-Ethnic Center. It doesn't cost a lot to create pads and pens and thermos bottles with the project logo and send them along at holidays or after major project efforts as gifts. We truly appreciate what these hardworking people are doing to support the project but only once in a while have direct contact with them. These tokens wind up meaning a lot to people who rarely receive other thanks for their efforts. We also provided recognition plaques for key people and for schools.

In the midst of the project, I spent far less time worrying about whether we would get our hypothesized effects than whether we could simply deliver the project as planned. When the intervention and data collection phases finally ended, after five years of project efforts, I was sorry to wind up efforts with what is a delightful and highly professional research and intervention team. But I was so relieved that this extremely ambitious and complex project had been concluded successfully!

Human Research Protections and Ethics

Community-based research touches lots of lives. Our interventions took place in eight communities. Intensive efforts in treatment schools reached many thousands of young people with what we believed would be an effective substance-use prevention message. Over 4,000 youth participated in four waves of data collection in the assessment of the community and school interventions. Over 15,000 have participated in cross-sectional surveys designed to help schools and communities assess the extent of the substance use problem in their schools. If the intervention is successful, it has the potential (if disseminated) to reach many, many more people than this. There is a moral and ethical responsibility that comes with such research, to minimize the risks of unintended harm as well as to maximize the opportunities for benefits.

Protecting Research Participants

Of course, this research project was carefully scrutinized by the university Institutional Review Board (IRB), in accordance with federal regulations, before this research could be conducted. Our surveys asked detailed questions of twelve- to fifteen-year-olds concerning illegal substance use, a highly sensitive topic that if mismanaged could put them at considerable personal and legal risk. The longitudinal version of the survey included identifying information regarding the respondent, so that we'd be able to link each wave of the surveys. We had to work carefully with our survey form supplier to develop a cover page with the respondent's name that would be removed before the survey was filled out, but that was linked back to the actual survey via a machine-readable bar code. Many hours were spent clarifying procedures, circulating versions of consent forms, recruitment materials, instructions for survey administration, and questionnaire items with our IRB. We applied for and received a Certificate of Confidentiality from the NIH, which provides protection against a worst-case scenario in which a local law enforcement agency would attempt to subpoena research data in order to identify and prosecute young drug users.

Creating a human protections system that passed IRB scrutiny was only the first step, however. Thousands of surveys were being conducted by teachers in remote locations. How could we be sure that only students whose parents had signed a consent form were in fact filling out the surveys? We instituted our own auditing system, having someone check each survey against our list of consent forms. Lo and behold, we found that there were isolated cases in which students with no recorded consent form had been surveyed. They were well under 1 percent of the total. But they did put us, technically, in violation of human research policies, and we had to report them to the IRB and find a solution. Our solution, which they endorsed, was to hire more staff to fill out the cover page for each of the hundreds of longitudinal surveys at each school, prebubbling the name of the student and writing it in longhand. Teachers were instructed to give the surveys only to the students whose names were on the cover page.

We were well satisfied with this solution. We continued our auditing procedure, nonetheless. To our dismay, the next fall we found a school with nine students surveyed for whom we had no consent forms. We checked the forms. Evidently, the teacher gave the surveys for absent students to some classmates eager to participate in the survey (but who hadn't brought in consent forms). They erased the names already bubbled onto the cover sheet and filled in their own names. It was back to the IRB with another report, and time for another solution. We checked back with our forms supplier and identified a special indelible ink that could be read by the scanner. Our staff used this ink to fill in and prebubble the cover pages, so they could not be erased and given to another student. Finally, our audits showed no slips in the consent process. We had evolved a truly effective system.

There are three lessons here that I would recommend to the reader. First, human subjects protection, like any other aspect of a research project, may need continuing refinement. Budget the necessary time and dollars for such efforts. Second, taking a proactive stance, creating one's own auditing systems, and reporting problems before they come in the form of angry letters from community members or parents, is wise as well as responsible. Often, antagonistic relationships develop between researchers and IRBs. Being proactive in this way builds a relationship of confidence and trust between the IRB and the researcher. Third, the well-known "Murphy's Law" (which says that what can go wrong, will go wrong) holds in the realm of human research protections as it does in most other realms of human endeavor. Be prepared.

Finally, be patient with the process. Many hundreds of hours and thousands of dollars were expended on our human protections efforts and on correcting problems we identified. With the approximately 20,000 surveys completed over the five years, I had a grand total of one telephone call from a distressed parent (even though my phone number was included on all the consent forms). This family was upset because the child wasn't sure whether sacramental use of wine counted as alcohol use. We clarified survey instructions accordingly. It may seem as though one is hitting a mosquito with a baseball bat—that such a process is bureaucratic overkill. Sometimes that may be the case. But a legal problem arising from violations of process or a slipup resulting in some negative consequences for a research participant would be a much worse nightmare.

We accept a tremendous responsibility when we engage in community-based intervention research, and this goes beyond the usual obligations of human subjects protection in data collection. We are communicating to young people. Are our messages sound? Are we sure they aren't causing any unexpected negative effects? We are intervening by supporting the development of community coalitions. Are we in fact strengthening the prevention network in communities, building social capital to address substance use problems, or are we somehow interfering in negative ways, despite our best intentions?

We use our best understanding of prior research, our experience, and our formative (early-stage) research to maximize the likelihood that what we are doing is constructive from the outset. We look at the preliminary data from the first few communities and are reassured to find evidence that our efforts are moving youth attitudes and behavior in the right direction (Slater and Kelly 2002). Sometimes, though, the most encouraging evidence is not data-based, but heart-to-heart. Our key contact from our first intervention community called and played an excerpt from a recording of "If Not for You," telling us that our coalition-building effort was just the catalyst they needed to move to the next level of effective and coordinated action in their community. It's not a data point one can enter into the computer, but it's the kind of thing that keeps us going for months, despite the rough spots.

Data and Collaborative Talent: An Embarrassment of Riches

Little sympathy can be expected when I bemoan the fact that I have four waves of extensive longitudinal data on over 4,000 youth, and not enough time or staff with the requisite statistical skills to capture more than a fraction of the knowledge and publications that lurk in such a data set. The intellectual opportunities afforded by research of this scope are extraordinary.

Some communication scholars may belittle funded research of this type as applied work that contributes little to fundamental theoretical knowledge and theory building. I would argue, in opposition, that our field has been slowed by the inability to test our theories with extended data sets reflecting real-world social and developmental processes. It is easy enough to include items important for testing and developing theory in a research instrument that is evaluating an intervention, for example. Such items may provide increased insight regarding the intervention, as well as added value for the field.

For example, the Columbine killings took place just about an hour's drive south of here as this project was being launched, killings that had been linked in the media to the assailants' use of video games and Internet sites. It was an obvious (and in my view, ethically vital) step, especially since media effects are fundamental to my research interests, to include at the last minute a set of items about use of violent video games, Internet sites, and movies; we already had items concerning aggressive thoughts, values, and behaviors. This provided a straightforward opportunity to identify cross-sectional links between use of such media and aggressiveness (Slater 2003a). More important, having such items in our longitudinal data set made it possible to explore some ideas I'd been developing about how a variety of forces described by media theory (selective exposure or uses and gratifications phenomena, for example) might work to reinforce media effects (such as the effects of violent media content) over time. This opportunity was leveraged substantially by the collaborative relationships that a large grant like this makes possible. Tri-Ethnic Center had hired a postdoctoral researcher, Kimberly Henry, who had trained with leading experts at Penn State's Methodology Center. I was able to pick up some of her time to work on our data set and to utilize sophisticated multilevel modeling techniques to assess and find intriguing support for these theoretical notions (Slater et al. 2003). Plenty of other worthwhile analyses can be developed from such data sets, sometimes on a shoestring budget after the main project funding has been spent (see Slater et al. 2000; Slater and Kelly 2002; Slater 2003b; Kelly et al., in press). Clearly, then, such research not only has the potential to impact lives positively, but it can also build knowledge and boost the careers of graduate students and other upcoming scholars who have the opportunity to work with such data sets.

Research Outcomes and Exploring Next Steps

While anxieties about research outcomes may need to be put out of mind when focusing on day-to-day problems, our interim assessments suggested that, at the individual level of analysis at least, we were having statistically significant effects on targeted attitudes, intentions, and substance use behavior. Such results, of course, were very encouraging, and spurred renewed commitment to quality research and intervention efforts. Nonetheless, our goal was to show effects at the community level. In other words, we wanted to show that the community in aggregate, as a single unit of analysis, showed experimental treatment differences, not just be able to demonstrate effects on individuals within each community.

We have now largely completed these rather complex analyses. Our results (currently under peer review) suggest that the media interventions, independent of the in-school curriculum, produced significant reductions in marijuana and alcohol uptake as reported by youth in the study, although reductions for cigarettes were not statistically significant. The increase in alcohol and marijuana use among youth in the treatment communities was almost 50 percent less than among youth in the control communities. Effects on intentions (which are much more variable) were even more robust. Pre-post analyses of changes in community readiness to tackle prevention efforts, as assessed by coded in-depth interviews with community key informants, also provided evidence for treatment impact.

These are exceptional results, even better than we had hoped. Such results, however, pose new challenges. If we have developed an effective model for intervention, we need to take the next steps to encourage dissemination. One step, of course, is to communicate our results as widely as possible, through conferences among prevention practitioners as well as among academics. The second is to continue our research on this effort, with an eye to examining factors that may support dissemination. Intelligent program adoption decisions should be based on cost-effectiveness and fit of various program elements. For example, the in-school media effort is very easy and inexpensive to disseminate, but the community coalition building requires expert labor to execute, and many communities might not be ready for such an initiative. The next step we have proposed involves testing the independent versus the combined effects of the in-school and community-based efforts, and assessing the cost-effectiveness of each element. We'll also be better able to measure and model processes by which community-based communication efforts may influence youth perceptions of norms, and their attitudes and behavior, in the new design.

Based on such findings, we hope to provide the hard evidence needed to support widespread dissemination of these innovative communication interventions. The past five years have taught us how to conduct and evaluate this type of effort. The task before us is to do the necessary work to get the interventions into additional communities.

Questions for Reflection

What are the advantages of this kind of "field experiment" design? Disadvantages?

What factors other than education and media messages (sometimes called "confounding variables" in experimental design) might account for rates of drug and alcohol use by young people in a particular community?

Young people in an experiment such as this may not give honest answers to questions about their drug and alcohol use. Do you think this is likely to be a serious problem? Do you have suggestions for minimizing it?

If you had a choice of using naturalistic inquiry, impact surveys, or a field experiment to study a problem in your own community, which method would you choose? Why?

Note

This research was supported by grant DA12360 from the National Institute on Drug Abuse to the author. Thanks are due to key collaborators: Kathleen Kelly of the Department of Marketing; Ruth Edwards, Barbara Plested, Pamela Jumper Thurman, and Kimberly Henry of the Tri-Ethnic Center for Prevention Research; and Thomas Keefe of the Department of Environmental Health; as well as our research staffs, notably Julie Chen, Beverly Marquart, Dean Helzer, Stacy Biggerstaff, Linda Stapel, Eleanora Comello, Jennifer Anderson, and Rebecca Gumtow, all at Colorado State University, and William Hansen and Kathleen Nelson-Simley of Tanglewood Research, Greensboro, North Carolina. We also express our gratitude for the dedication and efforts of community leaders, school district staff, teachers, and students in our sixteen study communities, without whom this research would not have been possible.

References

Cook, T. D., and D. T. Campbell. 1979. *Quasi-experimentation: Design and Analysis Issues for Field Settings.* Chicago, IL: Rand-McNally.
Coreil, J., C. A. Bryant and J. N. Henderson. 2001. *Social and Behavioral Foundations of Public Health.* Thousand Oaks, CA: Sage.
Edwards, R. W., P. J. Thurman, B. Plested, E. R. Oetting, and L. Swanson. 2000. "Community Readiness: Research to Practice." *Journal of Community Psychology* 28: 291–307.
Farquhar, J. W., S. P. Fortmann, J. A. Flora, C. B. Taylor, W. L. Haskell, P. T. Williams, N. Maccoby, and P. D. Wood. 1990. "Effects of Community-Wide Education on Cardiovascular Disease Risk Factors: The Stanford Five-City Project." *Journal of the American Medical Association* 264: 350–65.
Flay, B. R. 2000. "Approaches to Substance Use Prevention Utilizing School Curriculum Plus Social Environment Change." *Addictive Behaviors* 25 (6): 861–85.
Flynn, B. S., J. K. Worden, R. H. Seeker-Walker, G. J. Badger, B. M. Geller, and M. C. Costanza. 1992. "Prevention of Cigarette Smoking through Mass Media Interventions and School Programs." *American Journal of Public Health* 82: 827–35.
Hansen, W. B. 1996. "Pilot Test Results Comparing the All Stars Program with Seventh Grade D.A.R.E.: Program Integrity and Mediating Variable Analysis." *Substance Use & Misuse* 31 (10): 1359–77.

Hornik, R. 1988. *Development Communication.* New York: Longman.
Hornik, R. C. 2002. "Public Health Communication: Making Sense of Contradictory Evidence." Pp. 1–22 in *Public Health Communication: Evidence for Behavior Change,* ed. R. C. Hornik. Mahwah, New Jersey: Lawrence Erlbaum Associates.
Kelly, K. J., R. W. Edwards, M. L. G. Comello, B. A. Plested, P. J. Thurman, and M. D. Slater. In press. "The Community Readiness Model: A Complementary Approach to Social Marketing." *Marketing Theory.*
Murray, David M. 1995. "Design and Analysis of Community Trials: Lessons from the Minnesota Heart Health Program." *American Journal of Epidemiology* 142: 569–74.
Oetting, E. R., J. F. Donnermeyer, B. A. Plested, R. W. Edwards, K. Kelly, and F. Beauvais. 1995. "Assessing Community Readiness for Prevention. *The International Journal of the Addictions* 30 (6): 659–83.
Olien, C. N., G. A. Donohue and P. J. Tichenor. 1984. "Media and Stages of Social Conflicts." *Journalism Monographs* 90.
Raudenbush, S. W., and A. S. Bryk. 2002. *Hierarchical Linear Models: Applications and Data Analysis Methods.* 2nd ed. Thousand Oaks, CA: Sage.
Slater, Michael D. 2003a. "Alienation, Aggression, and Sensation-Seeking as Predictors of Adolescent Use of Violent Film, Computer and Website Content." *Journal of Communication* 53: 105–21.
Slater, M. D. 2003b. "Sensation-Seeking as a Moderator of the Effects of Peer Influences, Consistency with Personal Aspirations, and Perceived Harm on Marijuana and Cigarette Use among Younger Adolescents." *Substance Use and Misuse* 38: 865–80.
Slater, M. D., K. L. Henry, R. Swaim, and L. Anderson. 2003. "Violent Media Content and Aggression in Adolescents: A Downward-Spiral Model." *Communication Research* 30: 713–36.
Slater, M. D., and K. J. Kelly. 2002. "Testing Alternative Explanations for Exposure Effects in Media Campaigns: The Case of a Community-Based, In-School Media Drug Prevention Project." *Communication Research* 29: 367–89.
Slater, M. D., K. Kelly, and R. Edwards. 2000. "Integrating Social Marketing, Community Readiness, and Media Advocacy in Community-Based Prevention Efforts." *Social Marketing Quarterly* 6: 125–37.
Snyder, L. B., and M. A. Hamilton. 2002. "A Meta-Analysis of U.S. Health Campaign Effects on Behavior: Emphasize Enforcement, Exposure, and New Information, and Beware the Secular Trend." Pp. 1–22 in *Public Health Communication: Evidence for Behavior Change,* ed. R. C. Hornik. Mahwah, NJ: Lawrence Erlbaum Associates.
Van Leuven, J., and M. D. Slater. 1991. "Publics, Organizations, and the Media: How Changing Relationships Shape the Public Opinion Process." *Public Relations Research Annual* 3: 165–78.
Wallack, L., L. Dorfman, D. Jernigan, and M. Themba. 1993. *Media Advocacy and Public Health.* Newbury Park, CA: Sage.
Worden, J. K., and B. S. Flynn. 2002. "Using Mass Media to Prevent Cigarette Smoking." Pp. 23–34 in *Public Health Communication: Evidence for Behavior Change,* ed. R. C. Hornik. Mahwah, NJ: Lawrence Erlbaum Associates.

4

Designing Communication Research for Empowering Marginalized Populations: A Participatory Methodology

Chike Anyaegbunam, Aaron P. Karnell, Wai Hsien Cheah, and John D. Youngblood

In a way each chapter in this section has described an experiment in participatory research, in that every one of them has engaged the community—in some sense—as partners in a research project. This chapter describes yet another approach to community research, one that is more consciously participatory, was created for use in developing countries, and relies on a variety of specific strategies for engaging the community being studied. The difference is not so much in the methods—this is an approach that can make use of a variety of fairly standard qualitative and quantitative tools. But there is a distinct emphasis here on an approach geared to assessing community needs and resources from the community's perspective before deciding on a communication strategy to address the community's problems.

In order to do this, the researcher must sometimes participate in the community, as well as ask the community to participate in the research! Three investigator stories embedded in this chapter illustrate exactly what this means. In so doing, they also help us think about the many meanings of "community"—not only are there geographical communities, but also many intersecting communities defined by factors such as culture, ethnicity, gender, sexual orientation, disease status, age, and experience.

In the first of these, coauthor Aaron Karnell must divorce himself from his initial contacts in the Rwandan Tutsi community in order to "connect" with the Hutu groups he wants to reach, and then allow himself to be absorbed into the lives of those groups in order to develop what qualitative researchers sometimes call "rapport," a mutual sense of understanding, with his interview subjects. Only then are they comfortable and familiar enough with him to give him the information and perspective he needs about the role of radio messages during the Rwandan genocide.

In the second, coauthor John Youngblood—who describes himself as a biracial gay male—gains the trust of members of an African-American male-to-female transgender group by revealing his own sexual orientation and by sharing his personal experience living with a stigmatized identity. Working with the transgender group and with HIV/AIDS patients in other contexts has taught Youngblood how difficult it is for members of these marginalized groups to open up to an "outsider," so he has learned to talk about his "insider" status and experiences in order to help bridge this gap.

In the third, coauthor Wai Hsien Cheah finds he must step out of his "neutral facilitator" role when conducting a focus group made up of college students. His young adult subjects want information on the subject he is investigating, male and female condom use. More information on focus group research is given in box 4.1.

The approach illustrated in this chapter is not really a set of research tools so much as a conceptual framework for approaching research projects aimed at community development and empowerment. The approach uses a variety of actual methods, both qualitative and quantitative. Combining different methodological approaches in the same study is sometimes called "triangulation." Just as a mapper or a navigator establishes new positions relative to multiple fixed points, sometimes a good researcher confirms insights and observations by going at them from different methodological directions.

Action-oriented projects and programs, sometimes funded by national or international agencies, often incorporate a concern with evaluating the impact of those projects and programs. However, conditions and resources in the developing world and within small and marginalized groups elsewhere are rarely conducive to the more formal and elaborate experimental designs of the type Slater was able to use in the previous chapter to determine the effects of his project's interventions, nor are the resources to do this commonly available.

The participatory philosophy described here, along with the practical demands of fieldwork among special populations, makes the concept of "formative evaluation" especially relevant. This means getting feedback about relevance and effectiveness early on in a project's history, before everything has been decided, in an attempt to "form" or shape the effort in response to that feedback. Formative evaluation may be used in the design of educational television, for example, to assess whether its messages are meaningful and informative to a target audience. The program can then be fine-tuned in response to the results. In the type of research described in this chapter, formative feedback is absolutely essential because the community's own needs, priorities, and knowledge are expected to drive the program. The results of formative evaluation efforts also provide the "baseline" or starting point against which future conditions can be judged.

WHICH RESEARCH METHODS would be most effective for involving rural, poor, and illiterate communities in the southern region of Africa in studies that explore their problems, strengths, and communicative behavior? Can such studies empower community members to participate more actively in decision making that affects their development and livelihood? How does a White American communication scholar working in Africa recruit and hold candid discussions with Tutsi and Hutu peasants on the role of radio in the Rwandan genocide? How does a communication researcher successfully identify and penetrate a highly furtive and marginalized subculture, such as an African-American male-to-female transgender (AAMTF) community, and fruitfully explore the influence of stigma on the subpopulation's perceptions of, access to, and utilization of HIV/AIDS prevention messages and facilities? How does a scholar conduct formative research for the design of a theory-based communication campaign on such a sensitive topic as sexually transmitted diseases among self-effacing, taciturn international students in a U.S. university?

These are some of the difficult questions scholars grapple with when they engage in the conceptualization and implementation of communication research on sensitive topics or in the design of communication interventions with marginalized communities. While there are many different ways of answering the questions above, the researchers who collaborated in writing this chapter all found answers in an investigative perspective informed by a novel communication research approach called Participatory Rural Communication Appraisal (PRCA). PRCA aims at empowering the marginalized by involving them as coequal partners in communication research that helps them to define and shape their own livelihoods and realities.

As an international development communication advisor to the Food and Agriculture Organization (FAO) of the United Nations, the lead author of this chapter was commissioned in 1994 to develop a communication research methodology suitable for various rural development projects in about a dozen countries of the southern Africa region. Review of literature about this region revealed that its colonial heritage, especially the policies of the apartheid era and the liberation wars engaged in to topple oppressive regimes, has left the people with an especially distrustful view of outsiders. This view is magnified when the people of this region encounter outsiders who visit them for research purposes. When approached by researchers, these people often size them up and then tell them whatever the researchers want to hear, whether truthful or not.

The literature also revealed that rural people in this region feel that researchers are not interested in their lives, problems, and achievements. Researchers are seen as exploitative data miners who collect information from rural communities and disappear without telling the people what was discovered. At best, researchers have been viewed as treating the people they study as ignorant recipients of innovations developed elsewhere—ostensibly to help them solve their problems—without having paid attention to the community's existing problem-solving capabilities. In this frame of mind it is not surprising that people in the region have become reluctant to divulge to outsiders the results of their own informal experimentation in problem solving. In several instances in which rural people were approached during participatory communication research studies and requested to teach the visiting team their indigenous agricultural methods, the people exhibited disbelief that anybody would be interested in their knowledge. They attributed the request to some ulterior exploitative motive on the part of the team.

This state of affairs has made it difficult to conduct fruitful communication research with the rural poor in this region of Africa. This group has become difficult to reach. To be useful in this peculiar political, sociocultural, and communization environment, any new research method must be able to enhance dialogue among people, researchers, development workers, and policy makers. It must also identify and adapt appropriate methods of collecting data that the people are comfortable with and that do not require literacy as a precondition for participating in the research. In addition, the method should promote respect for rural people (regardless of their economic circumstances), their knowledge, and their traditional means of communication.

As a result of the FAO-United Nations contract, a new participatory research methodology for conducting communication studies with the rural people of southern Africa was developed. This PRCA methodology enables scholars to conduct multidisciplinary and participatory communication research as the first step toward the design of communication programs. The methodology is used to involve marginalized people in the identification of the essential elements for the design of effective communication strategies and programs for community development.

PRCA uses field-based visualization techniques, interviews, and group work to generate information for the design of communication strategies, materials, media, and messages to ensure relevance and a sense of ownership by the people involved. In the rural development context, field-based visualization techniques are used to enhance community-researcher communication about issues related to people's understanding of their current environment, problems, and resources—what they were in the past and, often, what they are anticipated to be in the future. These participatory techniques do not require literacy and range from sophisticated interactive computer animation, simulations, and graphics to video and photography (often shot by the people themselves) and more readily accessible tools such as mapping, wealth ranking, walking transects, or simply touring the community. These techniques are tools for generating discussion or dialogue on the visualized issues, problems, or processes, and for triangulating the results obtained with those from other research processes.

PRCA also adapts other techniques and tools from both the qualitative and the quantitative research traditions. The participatory and qualitative portions of PRCA provide essential formative information rooted in the explanatory models of the people themselves about the issues or problems to be addressed. This information is then used to sharpen the focus of baseline surveys used to triangulate the qualitative results and quantify the prevalence of the identified problems and the ways they are perceived in the communities of concern. PRCA results help set the basis for participatory monitoring and adjusting of communication programs or campaigns as they unfold, and for measuring their immediate outcomes as well as their longer-term impact.

PRCA is premised on a conception of communication as an interactive process characterized by the exchange of ideas, information, points of view, and experiences between people and groups. In PRCA, communication is a multidirectional process in which the receiver is also a source with information and ideas to transmit. Passiveness has no place in this process because PRCA calls for an individual or a group to enter into dialogue and mental cooperation with another individual or group until they come to a common awareness and understanding. It is a process in which the researcher and the community decide on a course of action together. In the context of community development work, this kind of communication presupposes that all actors are equal.

PRCA belongs to the same family as other participatory methods. However, it is unique because of its focus on both traditional and modern communication systems and in the development of strategies and materials to improve information and knowledge sharing among the various stakeholders. PRCA was developed to ensure that communication programs are firmly rooted in the realities of the community. It emerged as an answer to the challenge to develop a communication research approach that involves people as equal partners in studies about their lives, aspirations, and ways of communication, as opposed to treating them as mere objects of research. As Dervin and Huesca (1999) stress, rural people are the most solid vessels of wisdom and knowledge concerning their own living conditions and must become empowered to participate in the decision-making processes leading to policies and activities aimed at improving their lives. Empowerment through PRCA provides a means to enable the marginalized to unleash the power of their innate creativity, cultural values, and knowledge and to harness their potential to forge their own identity, have a say in how they are represented and governed, break the yoke of their oppression, and improve their livelihood (Anyaegbunam et al. 1999).

Each society, whether defined as developed or developing, has its own marginalized groups characterized by their disenfranchisement and alienation from the public sphere. Within such groups a large variety of social experiences can be expressed and exchanged. Communication research, informed by the emerging discourse on empowerment and participation, has become one road whereby the consciousness of these groups can be raised and their liberation attained. Enabling such groups to participate more meaningfully in the public sphere has become an additional agenda item for many scholars.

PRCA enables communication researchers to understand how people perceive and define their world. In addition to any data obtained from secondary sources, PRCA provides the opportunity for a firsthand interaction between the people and the researcher. PRCA enables the researcher and the people to arrive at a mutually acceptable interpretation of the community's problems, needs, and solutions, as well as its socioeconomic and physical characteristics. This is necessary because quite often the way outsiders see the marginalized community or the descriptions given about them in books—their norms, values, actions, and aspirations—might not correspond to the way the people see themselves. PRCA can overcome this because the tools and techniques of the process can break through the suspicion and conspiracies of silence, diplomacy, and courtesy often associated with rural communities.

With PRCA, tools such as communication resource maps, linkage diagrams, focus group discussions, and other methods can help define the communication and information networks, systems, and channels of key interaction groups within the community. Using these tools can help reveal the groups' preferred information sources both within and from outside the community, both modern and traditional. Such sources can range from cultural or religious events, rituals, art, drawings, storytelling, talking circles, dances, songs, role-playing, and drama, to audiovisual and print media. PRCA methods can also help identify influential people and institutions that the groups see as credible (role models, leaders, trendsetters) and help to identify the idioms, vocabulary, cultural norms and associations, symbols, and stories these groups use in discussing development issues.

But PRCA research also raises unique challenges. In the remainder of this chapter, three very different examples of the application of PRCA concepts and methods are described from the points of view of the three researchers. These three accounts illustrate field problems in finding people to interview in an unfamiliar culture, in winning the trust of members of a highly stigmatized community, and in defining a researcher's role as a focus group leader.

Lessons from the Field

A PRCA Study of the Rwandan Genocide

Ascroft (1978) used the term "conspiracy of courtesy" to describe the ability of marginalized populations who are the subject of research to treat outsiders courteously without revealing their true feelings and biases. In the summer of 2002, Aaron Karnell began field research in Kigali, Rwanda, for his dissertation on the role of extremist radio in the Rwandan genocide. The "conspiracy of courtesy" came in many forms. His initial contacts in the country, for example, were especially eager to help him find interviewees, yet precious weeks in the field passed before he realized that these courteous helpers were consistently leading him toward interviews with representatives of only one of Rwanda's two major ethnic groups. Once he finally reached the right subjects, his comparative American wealth, white skin, and status as an outsider introduced bias and influenced what the interviewees chose to reveal and not reveal. Ultimately, according to Karnell, "I would discover that I was not only the researcher, but as often the subject—the one to be sized up, manipulated, talked about, used for political and social purposes, and mined for information."

Aaron Karnell's Story

Genocide in Rwanda claimed the lives of almost a million people between May and June 1994. Most of the victims of this colossal human tragedy were members of the Tutsi ethnic group. The Tutsi are a minority of the Rwandan population. Their killers were Hutu, who comprise the majority and, at that time, represented the political leadership of Rwanda.

Most Tutsi were killed by ordinary people—neighbors, coworkers, fellow villagers. Those who carried out this "work," as the authorities called it, had been organized and encouraged by a racist and despotic central government that commanded them to engage in an act of collective "self-defense." Those who heeded the authorities' call received considerable rewards: the homes of the slaughtered, their cattle and money. Those who resisted faced intense public shame and were sometimes themselves killed as putative collaborators and traitors.

During the genocide, a certain extremist radio station—RTLM radio—exhorted ordinary Hutu to "rise up" in self-defense against their Tutsi neighbors. The station broadcast a constant stream of racist rhetoric justifying violence against Tutsi. It also provided organizational support for those in charge of the killing. As I began my research into this disturbing phenomenon, my goal was to understand the impact of this station by analyzing a sample of its broadcasts and by conducting in-depth interviews with ordinary Hutu citizens of Rwanda who had listened to RTLM in 1994.

Rwanda is 85 percent Hutu. It should have been easy to find Hutu interviewees. A few days into interviewing, however, I began to notice that everyone to whom my initial contacts in the country were referring me for interviews was Tutsi. My translator, a Tutsi, said he "didn't know of anybody" who was Hutu for me to interview. My other contacts—mostly friends and associates of my translator—offered no additional help. I knew that Rwanda was an ethnically divided society, but the wall was even higher than I had imagined. My research stalled. I also had a limited need for certain classes of Tutsi interviews and busied myself with those, but as the days passed, I became concerned that I would not find enough "ordinary" Hutu interviewees to meaningfully answer my research questions.

Reflecting one evening on how I got myself into this situation, I began to better understand the immense barriers I faced to controlling the selection of my own interviewees. The first barrier was the fact that my initial contacts in the country happened to be Tutsi and felt most comfortable introducing me to fellow Tutsi. The second was my own ignorance—of French, of how to get around Rwanda on my own (there are no street signs), and of the differences in appearance or surnames that might have helped me distinguish between Hutu and Tutsi without assistance. Polite society set up yet another barrier. It is considered rude to inquire about someone's ethnic group in a social setting or to make it the first or second question posed to a stranger. Rwandan social norms presented a final barrier. I could not march independently into a Hutu village—assuming I could even identify one—and start interviewing. Permission from local elders and authorities is needed to conduct research. In short, I was lost. This only increased my dependence on my initial contacts.

I do not mean to discredit those who helped me when I first arrived. They translated for me, offered valuable introductions, and made arrangements for transportation. The problem was that they could not—or would not—introduce me to Hutu interviewees. I would have to find a way to leave the comfortable social circle they helped create for me in order to advance toward answering my research questions.

The first lesson for PRCA researchers is this: *Search for subjects far from the tarmac.* Rural development experts have long recognized that when one attempts to carry out social research among the people living closest to the roadside—a cynic might say, those within walking distance of the researcher's Land Rover—the results are skewed toward the wealthy and powerful. The reason is that those living next to a commercial artery such as a road are likely to have more economic and social power than those living in distant villages.

They own the shops that every traveler passes through to buy a cool drink or a beer. They have the houses built from the best material. The enhanced social standing of the people by the road makes them more interested in and less intimidated by a conversation with a rich Westerner than their counterparts in the boondocks. Such people are also more likely to have a vested interest in the outcome of the study, especially if the research is being conducted to determine how best to spend money in the area. The people by the roadside can offer some data, but the researcher must be aware of their bias, and of how their bias interacts with the researcher's own biases.

My initial contacts in Rwanda were the people by the roadside, Tutsi elites. It was no coincidence that Tutsi, not Hutu, were the easiest for me to find and interview. First, I was doing research about a phenomenon in which Tutsi had been victimized; Tutsi, therefore, had the moral upper hand. Hutu, by contrast, were ashamed and afraid to talk about the events of 1994. Second, since 1994 a Tutsi government has been in power. People whose representatives control the government always feel freer to speak than those who are unrepresented. Third, many Tutsi spoke English. Finally, as a foreigner and comparatively wealthy Westerner, I was less intimidating to someone already at the top of the social structure. For all these reasons, it was not difficult for my initial contacts to approach and strike up a conversation with me and for me to talk with them. But this comfortable situation was not getting many research questions answered.

My breakthrough in locating Hutu interviewees did not occur until the third week of fieldwork, when I met the Hutu director of a Christian activist group in Kigali. I had not met him through any of my initial contacts, but through a friend who had given me his telephone number before I entered the field. In order to move forward with my research, I had been forced to pull back entirely from my initial contacts in Rwanda. I had to start afresh, far from the tarmac.

The Christian activist group happened to be implementing a program to promote Hutu-Tutsi reconciliation. It provided a forum for representatives of each ethnic group to meet and, in an atmosphere of confidentiality and trust, talk about the genocide. The director introduced me to the reconciliation groups and permitted me to observe meetings for a few days.

My success with this group led me to my second lesson for PRCA researchers: *Once you find potential subjects, hang around for a while.* Observing the reconciliation groups enhanced my trustworthiness and allowed me to observe Rwandan social dynamics. I felt as if I were watching a society healing itself. Most importantly for my research, however, observing the groups also helped me avoid the necessity of asking individual interviewees whether or not they participated in the genocide—a difficult admission to make and preserve face in an interview.

Instead, it was obvious to me through the stories told who had participated in the killing and who had not. Thus, before even sitting down to interview a subject, I had already compiled important information on the interviewee, and he or she was already familiar with my face and the purpose of my research.

Many of the barriers I faced in my field research can be traced to the unequal power relationship between my subjects and myself, as an American researcher. Rwandans are among the poorest and most marginalized people in the world. Interviewees' judgments about whether and to what extent I could be trusted determined which layer of truth they would make accessible. Rwandan Tutsi elites found it easier to engage with me, and therefore they revealed more. Yet they were not able to help me answer my research questions. When I finally did find Hutu interviewees, the circumstances of Rwandan history and the socioeconomic gap between the participants and myself made it critically important for me to do everything possible to build trust and rapport with the interviewees. Ultimately, I discovered that if one searches far from the road where the elites are and takes the time to become a part of the scene, the feelings and perspectives of the community would be revealed.

Collecting PRCA Data from an African-American Gay Community

Conducting research within ethnic gay communities can be an especially arduous process, considering the stigma of homosexuality, particularly within African-American communities (Fullilove and Fullilove 1999; VanderWaal et al. 2001). John Youngblood conducted communication research with various categories of African-American gay men, including male-to-female transgender persons and gay men living with HIV/AIDS. Youngblood believes that "PRCA requires the researcher to become one with the 'native' or 'real' people, or at least walk in their shoes to understand their world."

John Youngblood's Story

As a researcher interested in marginalized groups, experience has taught me that when you want something from someone (especially if they know it), you must be first and foremost willing to give something of yourself. With this in mind, I typically begin the interview process, after ascertaining that the people understand and agree to the study, by opening myself up to them and revealing my own sexual orientation—a trait that I consider a connection between them (the participants) and myself (the researcher). I also talk about my personal experiences as a biracial (Black and White) gay male and point out that I see my research as a means of helping others like me who have suffered due to some real or perceived marginalized or stigmatized trait or status.

Generally these marginalized communities are quick to accept me, albeit as an educated brother. They often express their happiness about having an African-American scholar approach them for studies concerning African-American issues and concerns. However, despite my racial and sexual affinity with these marginalized communities, I still encounter some difficulties in my interactions with them. For instance, because of differences between their typically underprivileged economic urban background and my middle-class rural background, differences in language and culture emerge, which I strive to handle sensitively and respectfully so as not to come across as "better than them."

During one particular study, to improve my chances of collecting "good" data from a specific African-American gay group, I moved my residence from the college community near campus to the east (mostly Black) side of town, down the road from what are usually called "housing projects." The experience was enjoyable, educational, and reaffirming, both for me and for the community. That community then saw me as one of them, despite the subtle language and cultural differences that remained, and therefore opened up to me for the research study.

In nearly all of my studies I have enlisted a community contact to aid in recruitment of participants and to explain culturally significant occurrences, utterances, and events to me. The contact person also teaches me the proper procedures for establishing and maintaining trust and goodwill among study participants.

I have found that entrance into and establishment of rapport with African-American gay communities is easy compared with gaining entrance and acceptance in HIV-positive populations. Conducting research with African-American gay men who are HIV positive is complex, considering that people with AIDS are typically viewed more negatively than persons with other terminal diseases (Schulte 2002). Further complicating my studies with HIV-positive gay persons is the notion of their inevitable death, which dominates their thoughts. Once, when I was conducting a focus group with HIV-positive persons on the topic of prevention messages and care services, one individual insisted, "Why would I care about housing, health education, medication, or eating, when I can't even stop wanting to kill myself at all times?" This indicates the serious and extremely "real" nature of living with HIV/AIDS and suggests the need for researchers who are sensitive and can convey that sensitivity as well.

I have also had the opportunity to investigate the lives, behaviors, communicative styles, and other cultural aspects of African-American male-to-female transgender (AAMTF) persons living in a nearby city. I first met a group of AAMTF individuals in my first year in the University of Kentucky doctoral program while conducting interviews and focus groups with persons living with HIV/AIDS: homosexual men, male-to-female transgender persons, African-American persons, intravenous drug users, and members of other vulnerable populations.

My research of AAMTF persons has revealed them as a unique, vulnerable, and proud community, one in which too little scholarly attention or empirical research has been invested. For acceptance into the AAMTF community, I incorporated the same strategies I used in my encounters with gay African-American and HIV-positive populations, with the same successful results. Not only am I viewed as an advocate, an ally, and a member of the "queer" community, but I am also viewed as "the researcher" who wants to tell each person's individual story and—more importantly—the story of the AAMTF community as a collective, a story that has never been properly told. Reflecting on the perceived importance of my study to the AAMTF community, one participant remarked, after a particularly revealing interview:

> I'm Black and I'm transgender and I'm a male. That's a lot of strikes. . . . If you really care, you've gotta *become* these people and feel what they feel and see what they see. I think this was a good interview. I think the reason why it was a good interview is I was able to give knowledge to you. . . . There's so much more knowledge that I can give you. . . . Maybe, this knowledge, we can use it to help.

Breaking Researcher Neutrality in a Focus Group

Because "the transmission of information or mere data does not equal effective communication" (Ratzan 1999, 255), it is crucial to understand the audience for which a message is intended. This is often accomplished through formative evaluation research. Common methodological techniques used in such an effort include focus groups, surveys, central location intercept interviews, and theatre testing (Clift and Freimuth 1997). According to one source, the goal of formative evaluation is to "learn as much as possible about the intended audience(s) before specifying campaign objectives or devising message strategies" (Nowak and Siska 1995, 171). Wai Hsien Cheah conducted a formative research study in which focus group participants insisted the facilitators change from collectors of data to information disseminators as a way of empowering the participants.

Wai Hsien Cheah's Story

My communication research project required me to first develop numerous test instruments (pamphlets for gonorrhea prevention) before they were used in the main experiment. Thus, to develop my instruments, I conducted numerous focus groups at the University of Kentucky to elicit college students' knowledge about sexually transmitted diseases (STDs) other than HIV/AIDS and to ascertain their attitudes, practices, and behaviors toward male and female condom use. Ideas on how to target college students and what kinds of messages to use were generated and discussed. American and Malaysian students were recruited for this purpose. I facilitated the male-only focus groups, and my good friend and colleague Dr. Ajlina Karamehic moderated the female-only groups. We used single-sex focus groups because we believed that young adults are less likely to perceive that it is inappropriate to discuss sexually related matters if they are in same-gender groups. Separating males from females also has been discovered to be advantageous to the females because the males "will not be there to dominate the discussion," according to Anyaegbunam (1998, 53). Moreover, students would be able to discuss sexually related matters freely without the fear of intimidation or embarassment in a same-sex group.

Focus groups are a technique "that capitalizes on communication between research participants in order to generate data" (Kitzinger 1995, 299). According to Krueger and Casey (2000), a focus group study is a series of systematically planned discussions designed to ascertain perceptions (along with attitudes, values, and beliefs) about a topic of interest in a supportive environment, generally run by a skilled interviewer or facilitator. Ideally, participants in focus groups are encouraged to share their ideas and respond to comments made by others, but many still consider the focus group methodology to be a one-way process in which it is primarily the participants who do the talking. The facilitator's role is usually limited to asking the necessary questions, ascertaining that the discussion flows smoothly, and ensuring that any single participant does not dominate the discussion. Although this is the "heart and soul" of the focus group approach, I was not comfortable adopting this rigid framework due to the sensitive nature of the topic that I was exploring in the early phase of my research project.

When we conducted these groups, Dr. Karamehic and I both adopted the participatory research approach and used participatory communication as the main tool in our facilitation. White and Nair (1999) define the participatory research process as a process in which knowledge is collectively produced, critical analyses are collectively carried out, and problem solving and decision making are done collectively by both the researcher and all the participants involved. Instead of running these focus groups in the traditional manner, we both adopted the role of the "catalyst" communicator, acknowledging the fact that every participant will have some generalized knowledge, understanding, and opinions about an issue or topic that could be shared for the benefit of the group. Yet at the same time a catalyst communicator does not disregard his or her own contribution and expertise.

> **Box 4.1: Depth Interviews and Focus Groups**
>
> The three specific project activities used to illustrate this participatory approach involve depth interviews and focus groups. Depth interviews have been introduced in an earlier chapter by Rakow. Focus groups are different. One of the authors here refers to focus groups as a kind of group interview, which is accurate, but it is important to recognize that a focus group is not intended as a convenient way to interview several people at once. Rather, the key characteristic of focus groups is that they are affected by the interaction of group members, who stimulate and influence one another's thinking. For this reason the answers gleaned from focus group transcripts may be quite different from those that would have been gleaned from the results of depth interviews with each person.
>
> Focus groups may be especially useful for topics where the participants cannot be expected to be completely familiar with the issues. The group experience gives them a chance to think through and articulate their views on a subject to which they may not have given a lot of prior thought. They are sometimes used in market research as part of the formative evaluation of a product or a message. Very often, people with shared demographic characteristics (gender, race and ethnicity, age, socioeconomic or professional status, education) are put together in their own group. Since some people have more power in society than others, this is a way of helping assure every focus group member a voice. If teenage girls were in a group with middle-aged male doctors, for example, to discuss a medical issue, the doctors would undoubtedly dominate. And the researcher would not gain as much insight into the girls' perspectives, which in many cases would be very different from those of the doctors.
>
> Finally, whereas in a depth interview the interviewer is directing the flow of conversation with his or her questions and follow-up "probes" to explore answers in more depth, the focus group leader or facilitator (a member of the research team) tries to remain neutral and outside the general conversation. With luck and skill, a situation is produced in which the discussion within the group is largely self-directed and the facilitator can limit his or her contribution to introducing a topic, asking a few prespecified questions, and offering more neutral probes if conversation lags or more clarification is needed; while the interviewer and interviewee in a depth interview are engaged in a form of conversation, the focus group leader generally wants the group dynamics to take over. However, this is not always how it might turn out, as the experience of Wai Hsien Cheah attests.

When we asked our research participants whether they had seen, heard of, or used a female condom before, we were surprised that not a single one of them had. The participants did not even have an idea of what a female condom would look like. When the participants asked us where a female condom could be purchased, how much it would cost, how to put one on, and whether it is as effective as the male condoms, we felt obligated to impart our knowledge and understanding to the participants. We did not feel that these questions should be deflected back to the participants or that attempting to provide the answers should be postponed. As catalyst communicators, we felt that it was also our job to empower our research participants by providing the information they wanted.

In addition, when we ran the focus groups, we also disclosed our own condom use behaviors to get the participants talking about their own individual behaviors. Self-disclosure is defined as "any message about the self that a person communicates to another" (Wheeless and Grotz 1976, 338). This strategy was particularly useful because it gave the participants the opportunity to connect with us even when they knew we were researchers and in that sense outside their community. St. Anne argues that "to be able to participate and communicate with each other, people need to connect" (1999, 69). These connections help enhance participation, and it is these connections that help "forge a shared reality."

Conclusion

Ultimately, the success of any PRCA project hinges on the capability of the researchers to use empowering tools and their possession of such requisite attributes as respect for the culture of the people, the ability to listen and learn from the community, alertness, inquisitiveness, and humility. Without them, the PRCA researcher would not be able to create an atmosphere conducive to dialogue. The experiences of the three projects described above all reflect these dynamics.

Questions for Reflection

Compare this participatory approach to the experimental approach of Slater and his colleagues in the last chapter. What are the strengths and weaknesses of each approach?

In all three cases in this chapter, for somewhat different reasons, the researcher needed to step out of a pure research role and act as a member of the community or group being studied in order to proceed. Do you think this is justified? What is gained, and what is lost, by taking this path?

Can you think of additional examples within your own community where a participatory strategy might yield results that are unlikely to be obtained by another approach?

All four chapters in this section illustrate approaches to community-based research, albeit of very different sorts. Yet university programs in communication studies rarely offer courses or programs in this specific area. What might be some of the reasons?

References

Anyaegbunam, C. 1998. *Participatory Communication Appraisal. Starting with the People: An Action Programme Resource.* Harare, Zimbabwe: SADC Centre of Communication for Development.
Anyaegbunam, C., P. Mefalopulos, and T. Moetsabi. 1999. "Facilitating Grassroots Participation in Development: New Training Models and Techniques." Pp. 207–28 in *The Art of Facilitating Participation: Releasing the Power of Grassroots Communication,* ed. S. A. White. Thousand Oaks, CA: Sage.
Ascroft, J. "A Conspiracy of Silence." 1978. *International Development and Reconstruction/Focus* 3: 8–11.
Clift, E., and V. Freimuth. 1997. "Changing Women's Lives: A Communication Perspective on Participatory Qualitative Research Techniques for Gender Equity." *Journal of Gender Studies* 6 (3): 289–96.
Dervin, B., and R. Huesca. 1999. "The Participatory Communication for Development Narrative: An Examination of Meta-theoretic Assumptions and Their Impacts." Pp. 169–210 in *Theoretical Approaches to Participatory Communication,* ed. T. Jacobson and J. Servaes. Cresskill, NJ: Hampton Press.
Fullilove, M. T., and R. E. Fullilove, III. 1999. "Stigma as an Obstacle in AIDS Action: The Case of the African-American Community." *American Behavioral Scientist* 42 (7): 1113–25.
Kitzinger, J. 1995. "Introducing Focus Groups." *British Medical Journal* 311 (7000): 299–303.
Krueger, R. A., and M. A. Casey. 2000. *Focus Groups: A Practical Guide for Applied Research.* 3rd ed. Thousand Oaks, CA: Sage.
Nowak, G. J., and M. J. Siska. 1995. "Using Research to Inform Campaign Development and Message Design: Examples from the 'America Responds to AIDS' Campaign." Pp. 169–85 in *Designing Health Messages: Approaches from Communication Theory and Public Health Practice,* eds. E. Maibach and R. L. Parrott. Thousand Oaks, CA: Sage.
Ratzan, S. C. 1999. "Revolutionizing Health: Communication Can Make a Difference." *Journal of Health Communication* 4 (4): 255–57.
Schulte, A. 2002. "Consensus Versus Disagreement in Disease-related Stigma: A Comparison of Reactions to AIDS and Cancer Patients." *Sociological Perspectives* 45 (1): 81–107.
St. Anne, S. 1999. "Synergizing Participation: Are You Able to Enable?" Pp. 68–79 in *The Art of Facilitating Participation: Releasing the Power of Grassroots Communication,* ed. S. A. White. Thousand Oaks, CA: Sage.

VanderWaal, C., F. L. Washington, R. D. Drumm, Y. M. Terry, D. C. McBride, and R. D. Finley-Gordon. 2001. "African-American Injection Drug Users: Tensions and Barriers in HIV/AIDS Prevention." *Substance Use & Misuse* 36 (6–7): 735–55.

Wheeless, L. R., and J. Grotz. 1976. "Conceptualization and Measurement of Reported Self-disclosure." *Human Communication Research* 2 (4): 338–46.

White, S. A., and K. S. Nair. 1999. "The Catalyst Communicator: Facilitation without Fear." Pp. 35–51 in *The Art of Facilitating Participation: Releasing the Power of Grassroots Communication,* ed. S. A. White. Thousand Oaks, CA: Sage.

Part II
ORGANIZATIONS AND INSTITUTIONS

THIS SECTION DESCRIBES STUDIES concerned with specific organizational and institutional settings—in particular, what goes on in a Caribbean newsroom, in a United States medical clinic, and in a secondary school in South Africa. In each case, despite the very different contexts, the need to understand the communication dynamics within a particular type of specialized human organization was what inspired the project. Once again, the studies presented here provide examples of a broad range of methodological approaches that are possible in such a situation.

Two of the studies (those using newsroom and educational settings, respectively) involve non-U.S., non-European cultures; the third is set in the United States. Two (the newsroom study and the study of patient satisfaction in a U.S. healthcare setting) use primarily the same sorts of ethnographic methods introduced in Part I—depth interviews and observation. The third, although carried out in quite difficult conditions in rural South Africa, uses a quasi-experimental design to assess the impact of educational interventions. This is somewhat parallel to Slater's community-based substance abuse prevention study in Part I, although in the school-based project described here the researcher also had to confront the very different and unique challenges of cross-cultural research in a rural setting at the same time as he tried to implement a formal quasi-experimental design.

In addition to introducing examples of research on organizations and institutions, these three studies introduce another aspect of research design and development: What is the purpose of the research? Academics may talk about research being done to get tenure, to get promoted or get a raise, or to bring in contract or grant funding, but in reality most research involves an enormous investment of time, energy, and resources (very often supported by tax dollars or, in some cases, by client fees). Different motivations and purposes drive research projects. The researcher has to be interested in the question to be answered, but beyond this lie many other questions of purpose and motivation.

Research can be designed to answer theoretical questions or practical ones. Of the studies in this section, one (de Bruin's study of Caribbean journalists) is driven primarily by well-developed theoretical interests in gender and identity within the context of a professional organization. At the other end of the spectrum, another (Krizek and Turner's study of a medical organization) was initiated in response to the organization itself, whose leadership needed a better practical understanding of the reasons for diminishing levels of patient satisfaction. Both are included in this book on "research that matters," but the question of *why* the research matters is somewhat different in these two cases.

Somewhere in the middle of this spectrum falls Balfour's study of South African secondary schools, which was designed as a dissertation project that would evaluate educational materials and teaching strategies. Incorporating both theoretical and practical objectives, this project had the additional goal of advancing the author's knowledge of how to carry out research in a cross-cultural educational context.

# 5

Gender and Professional Identity among Caribbean Journalists

Marjan de Bruin

This part begins with a contribution about a qualitative project concerned with three intersecting concepts: gender identity, professional identity, and organizational identity—what de Bruin calls "sensitizing concepts." Such concepts represent a general theoretical interest rather than a fully developed explanatory theory or a specific list of categories into which her transcript material was to be forced. They are a set of ideas she felt would be useful in helping her to understand the setting she chose for study. Such "sensitizing concepts" are a very useful tool.

As de Bruin points out here, many dimensions of identity other than the three she chose might form the focus of a project about Caribbean newsrooms. There is no one "right answer" as to how to understand a given social setting, but a theoretical focus based on a particular set of concepts (theoretical ideas or abstract constructs) helps make a project more coherent than it otherwise might be and is more likely to lead to clear conclusions. Unlike experimental hypotheses, "sensitizing concepts" tell the researcher something about where to look and what to notice— but without rigidly restricting the kinds of observations that might be made.

Even though driven by theoretical ideas, qualitative inquiry is designed to minimize the number of assumptions the researcher makes about the setting, in order to produce a description that is as free of the researcher's own cultural bias as possible. Instead, the goal is to reflect the lived reality of those being studied. This means that categories for the analysis of interview, observational, focus group, content, or other qualitative data may not be specified in advance. Instead, they are likely to be developed—inductively—from an examination of the material itself.

Such an approach is sometimes called a "grounded theory" approach because the theory, or explanation, is grounded in the material rather than specified in advance. The term "grounded theory" appropriately emphasizes that the work is still connected to theory, but the term itself often misleads students because it actually refers to a research strategy in which theory is derived inductively, not a specific "theory" at all.

Grounded theory analysis of interview or focus group data would be almost impossible without using complete transcripts of the material. It is a fluid and flexible process in which the categories may be revised or refined partway through the project as needed to reflect the material as fully as possible. Some researchers do qualitative analysis with the help of computer software, but in this project de Bruin abandoned her keyboard and tackled the task with paper and pencil instead.

MY RESEARCH, BASED ON IN-DEPTH INTERVIEWS, focused on the intersection of professional identity, gender identity, and organizational identity among newsroom workers in two Caribbean nations: the country of Jamaica and the country of Trinidad and Tobago. The choice of this focus was the result of an interest that developed over many years, starting with the production of a descriptive baseline study on "women and media" in the early 1990s (de Bruin 1994). This initial study addressed simple questions: how many women (and men) were working in the media, what were the positions they occupied, what were their responsibilities, and so on—questions that dealt with quantities and structures, job descriptions and positions. The underlying assumption at that time, inspired by concerns about the stereotyped portrayal of women in media output, was that an increased presence of women in newsrooms might lead to qualitative changes in media output.

Feminist media studies in the 1970s and 1980s was preoccupied with content analyses focusing on portrayal. The leading question was this: If portrayal of women was so biased, would changing the balance in normally male-dominated newsrooms affect the content and quality of media output? Opening up the media to women workers should counterbalance the gender-biased selection of news items and information sources. It seemed widely accepted that if the number of women would only reach this "critical mass," then media content would improve and be less male-oriented.

It turned out not to be that simple; quantity alone was not sufficient. Insight into employment patterns and sexual division of labor were important for getting a better picture of media organizations, but at the same time this information did not go beyond a descriptive level. This quantitative knowledge did not offer any deeper understanding of women and men in media work. In addition, research findings trying to establish a relationship between the presence of women and gender-related characteristics of media output were inconclusive and sometimes contradictory (Mills 1997; Weaver 1998; Weaver and Wilhoit 1996). After doing my baseline study and follow-up surveys, I felt the same kind of ambivalence. It was important to be able to map out newsroom realities, but it also seemed like merely scratching the surface.

My own perspective, and consequently my research focus, began to change. I was not so interested anymore in statistics and percentages but began to search for ways of understanding the processes beyond the numbers. What was actually happening on the work floor? What were the specific functions assumed by women and men? Did the interaction between the sexes show any gender patterns or differences? And if so, how would these differences influence the production processes? How did gender exist—beyond the "body count"?

Media studies over the last two decades had shown a gradual shift from the taken-for-granted idea that the mere presence of women in news organizations would lead to a changed balance in decision-making power, which in turn would influence the quality of news selection and production, to the realization that processes more complex than the presence or absence of women alone were influencing the qualities of media output. But what were the nuances and dynamics of these processes? I started to mark out the territories with which I would have to make myself familiar. I realized that, if my focus was women and men, working journalists who were expected to be guided by professional values while simultaneously fulfilling the demands of the organization that employed them, I would have to consider at least three different areas of study and research: gender, journalism as a profession, and media as organizations.

I read whatever I could find, searching for clues that would spark new ideas. It was Weaver and Wilhoit's (1996) traditional research involving national surveys among U.S. journalists and Weaver's collection of worldwide research (Weaver 1998) that brought me to wonder about the changes in journalists' perceptions of their profession and the shifting balance between organizational interests and professional interests. I read with a rather wide and vague notion of what I was looking for. All I knew was that I was trying to find one or more key words, core concepts that could help me look at the changes in the area of my interest—which by now had become gender, professionalism, and organizations—to be used as anchor points in new research. Each of these topics has been the subject of discussion and study, but the intersection of these areas remained implicit or was described only partially.

Media studies in general had shown a shift in the 1980s and 1990s, attempting to reconcile political economy and cultural studies approaches. There had been a wave of reflection, expressed in the now almost classic titles by leading authors in the field who spoke of "rethinking," "revisiting," "reappraising," and "refining" (Berkowitz 1990; Curran 1990a, 1990b; Schlesinger 1990; Schudson 1991; Shoemaker 1997). As far as the topic of "gender and media" was concerned, after the appearance of Van Zoonen's *Feminist Media Studies* (1994), new perspectives developed in the 1990s had begun to explore the "gendered substructures in media organizations" (Allan 1998; Carter et al. 1998; Skidmore 1998; Steiner 1998; Van Zoonen 1998).

The focus in academic work on media and gender began to be more on cultural interpretations of everyday work in which relations were structured according to often implicit notions of what was "feminine" or "masculine," but how these cultural interpretations of everyday reality in the newsroom were working out in practice was still not very clear. What was clear, however, from the literature on journalism was that professional identities in journalism were undergoing changes, finding multiple expressions. The organizational literature I was reading showed increased attention to subjectivity, moving away from structures as the dominant focal point, creating intellectual space to work with concepts such as identity. In gender studies, the idea of identity had always been a core concept, and I was wondering if this could be a useful concept in bringing the different aspects together.

Conceptual Framework

I decided to choose the concepts of gender identity, organizational identity, and professional identity and the way they might possibly intersect as my starting points for an exploration of their usefulness for further research. The choice of these concepts posed several challenges. In the first place, I was aware of the many other identities—based on categories such as class, rural or urban location, race, ethnicity, geographic territory, education, or political party—that could be mentioned in addition to the three categories I singled out. However, my initial focus was a manageable starting point to begin the exploration of the social dynamics and practices that construct identities. Secondly, gender identity is a concept that still demands to be comprehensively defined, especially at the operational level. Recent Caribbean literature focusing on gender (Mohammed and Shepherd 1991; Senior 1991; Shepherd et al. 1995; Barrow 1995; Leo-Rhynie et al. 1997; Shepherd 2002; Mohammed 2002) appears to be moving toward such a comprehensive description of what constitutes gender identity.

The need for a comprehensive conceptual treatment of gender identity may not seem so obvious, given the fact that social identities and identification processes seem so familiar and so patent. We know that they define "who we are, how we are supposed to feel, think, and act, and in doing so, making it possible for us to live as 'we' differing from 'the other(s)'" (Hogg and Terry 2001, 3). Yet it is only by breaking this concept down into recognizable experiences that we begin to be able to observe what (gender) identity means in people's daily life and work.

In trying to define these core concepts, I realized I would need to choose a theoretical position for my work. There were several options for looking at identity/identities; which was the one that I would feel most comfortable with? Would I consider identity to be a more or less static set of qualities, equal to "intrapsychic organizations (ego structures) through which one interprets and makes sense of the world" (Kroger 2000, 17), following the more structural traditions? Or would I prefer the sociocultural approach, which focuses on "the role society plays in providing (or not providing) individual identity alternatives" (Kroger 2000, 19)—a perspective in which the individual's identity is seen as the product of the surrounding context? Would I prefer to see identity as nonstatic and fluid, part of an ongoing process in which, as Kroger (citing McAdams) says, "the process of creating a self through the experience of narrating is central" (2000, 22)? Or would I choose an eclectic position and combine a narrative approach with a sociocultural approach? I decided that I would not be concerned in advance to know exactly where my approach would fit. Central in my approach was that social identities "may change priority in everyday life, according to circumstances and interests; they are subject to negotiation, they overlap, they flow or spill over" (de Bruin in press, 2).

In hindsight, the choice of a theoretical position seems to have been motivated strongly by my own life experiences. I chose what I was able to recognize in my personal life. I was born in the Netherlands, where I lived a large part of my life before moving to Jamaica. I knew how it felt to have two "homes," each with its own history, surrounded by different memories, constructing different "selves," separated by place and time. I also knew how it felt to move around, speaking a language (English in Jamaica) that was not my mother tongue (Dutch). These languages were not interchangeable. They did not seem to tap into the same memories, they did not seem to touch the same roots; they were not able to link to the same reservoirs of feelings and sentiments. Yet this disparity did not disturb, in each of the selves, a comfortable sense of coherence and continuity. I myself had, to a certain degree, lived multiple identities. I felt perfectly at home with the idea of identities being "commonly shared stereotypes" (Crisp and Hewstone 2000) and at the same time "idiosyncratic constructs" (Deaux 2000); I recognized the position that people may take on multiple social identities to serve different functions.

Social identity theory and constructivism (Gergen 1999, 2001) formed the theoretical background of my research. From these schools of thought I

> **Box 5.1: Using Theory in Qualitative Research**
>
> Most students who have had any exposure at all to scientific or social scientific research, even informally, have been taught the hypothetico-deductive method. This is the formal method most closely associated with experimental, laboratory-based science in which a certain theory, or explanation, is to be tested against evidence about a hypothesis derived (or "deduced") from that theory. If the hypothesis is rejected, there may be something wrong with the theory, but if the theory correctly predicts what happens in the experiment, it is upheld.
>
> However, not all research follows this model. Even in the natural sciences, research in many fields (a good proportion of work in astronomy, meteorology, biology, and geology, for example) is largely descriptive, not experimental. This work is concerned with explanation but often studies large-scale, systems-level processes that cannot be entirely reproduced in the laboratory. Mathematical models may be used to test predictions about these processes, but the actual system (such as a solar system or an ecosystem or a weather system) generally cannot be manipulated by experimental methods, nor can it be adequately reproduced in the laboratory.
>
> Research that develops abstract theory from available data is sometimes called "inductive," to distinguish it from the "deductive" methods of experiments that test hypotheses. In the same vein, ethnographic methods were developed to describe complex human sociocultural systems, not to test specific hypotheses. This kind of qualitative, descriptive approach is sometimes called "naturalistic" because of its concern with understanding and describing people and cultures as they exist under natural (not laboratory) conditions.
>
> One reason for the use of qualitative, ethnographic, or naturalistic methods in social science is that human social systems are so incredibly complex that some researchers reject the idea that it is meaningful to reduce them to a limited number of variables that can be accurately measured. (In fact, the very use of the term "system" to describe human social organization can be seen as an oversimplification. We are quite an amazing species in this regard!) Others may use qualitative methods to explore a new problem before proceeding with a quantitative design.
>
> Qualitative, descriptive research is still concerned with explanation (the establishment of cause and effect) and generalization (the ability of the results to predict events or conditions in a new situation). In other words, descriptive or naturalistic research also uses theory. However, these explanations and generalizations are often more conceptual (and less predictive of specific outcomes) than those that result from the kind of formal experiments that make use of the hypothetico-deductive method. Qualitative researchers certainly argue their results are no less meaningful—if anything, they see them as more so—than those obtained using numerical measurement and formal hypothesis testing.

gained some important insights that helped me focus my research and convinced me to continue on the course taken. I describe them elsewhere (de Bruin, in press, 3) as follows:

> People may actively strive for certain social identities, by claiming membership of particular social categories . . .—for example, by taking on specific professional identities. When identities—especially those based on more visible categories, for example, gender identity—are being imposed on someone . . . people may still develop strategies to minimize the socially accepted meaning attached to certain social identities. They may develop the skills of shifting one category to a lower position in their personal "identity hierarchy" while stressing other identities instead. This shifting of identities might also be seen in situations where certain identities seem to conflict with each other. . . . A third dynamic relates to identities which are the result of passive acquisition, where people happen to have taken them on, almost incidentally, en passant. This may apply to organizational identity . . . it may come with the job. In general, people fit themselves into and, at the same time, are fitted into, social categories. They "take the cue for their identity from the conduct of others, but they make the active effort to influence this conduct to begin with" (Weick 1995, 23).

Research Approach

Studying the construction of social identities in everyday life's practices may mean studying implicit processes. Given the idiosyncratic nature of social identities, any new research trying to understand their functions and dynamics would need to be done trying to see "from within." Several ways exist to try to view the subjectivities that constitute the working life of men and women journalists. The method I preferred was qualitative in-depth interviewing, which I did not combine with participant observation. I had the feeling that interviewing on the job would be skewed by the presence of influential others, by the witnessing of colleagues, and by the visibility of ongoing work. In addition, both Jamaica and Trinidad and Tobago are very small societies. Especially in Jamaica, where I live, even while I may not know every single journalist working in the media, chances are that every single one would either know me or know of me. Traditional roles and positions would influence the interaction.

My aim was to collect data—stories, accounts, narratives—that would present me with experiences in newsroom production through the eyes of professionals. The material from the interviews should be considered as descriptions of perceptions and not as descriptions of facts. It is not so important whether the interviewees' statements are actually true or false; their texts give us an insight into how interactions with colleagues at work are perceived—how their stories about these perceptions and interactions may illustrate "culturally embedded sensemaking" in media organizations.

I decided to conduct twenty in-depth interviews with female and male journalists working in newsrooms in Caribbean media and to follow these with a qualitative analysis of the interview material. I did not know yet how I would analyze the material. The interviews were open-ended, in-depth, with a minimal structure. They all covered the same general range of issues. They all focused on the interplay between the concepts chosen above: gender, organizational and professional identity, and processes of identification in the newsroom. An interesting challenge involved how I would recognize what I thought to be an indication of identity. And, even more difficult, how would I recognize the "interplay" between these concepts? I decided to postpone finding the answers to these questions to the moment I would begin reading the transcripts.

I agreed completely with Glaser's warning about not wanting to be "forcing data into perceived categories through the imposition of artificial questions" (Charmaz 2000, 514). Yet if I intended to reconstruct specific practices, I needed to provide some direction. For this reason, I gave the interviewers a short list of keywords indicating topic areas, which if necessary could be used as a checklist, rather than more extensive guidelines. Since I share the view that interviews can be seen "as negotiated accomplishments of both interviewers and respondents ... shaped by the contexts and situations in which they take place" and that interviewers are "active participants in interactions with respondents" (Fontana and Frey 2001, 663), the choice of interviewers and locations of interviews was done after careful consideration. I selected two professional journalists, neither of whom was employed full time by any of the media organizations in the Caribbean, as interviewers. One of them was a female journalist in her early thirties, and the other was a more senior male journalist.

Given the fact that the interviews were open-ended and in-depth, expected to cover certain specific aspects, although conducted with as little specific direction as possible, experience in interviewing was a first consideration. Other considerations in selecting the interviewers were gender, nationality, status, ethnicity, and familiarity with the field.

I expected the topic to be discussed more openly and genuinely in same-sex interviews. Therefore, the male interviewer interviewed the majority of male interviewees and the female interviewer dealt with the majority of women. Further, the Caribbean is a region united by history and life experiences. However, the individual countries that make up the political union of the English-speaking Caribbean (CARICOM) also show differences among themselves. Although in most CARICOM member states English is the common language, the way English is used can show vast differences. My Trinidadian interviewer

Box 5.2: Working with Transcript Materials

Many qualitative researchers tape record open-ended or depth interviews. While the researcher or interviewer inevitably filters the material from such an interaction through his or her own perceptual lense, the use of transcripts helps prevent this filtering process from short-circuiting the analysis. Human memory is notoriously unreliable, and abbreviated note taking is a process that can easily introduce new biases of its own.

Unfortunately, if anything rivals human memory in terms of unreliability, it is probably human technology—especially recording equipment. The well-known adage states that if anything can go wrong, it will. This assertion is never more true than it is in the case of recording devices.

Many communication researchers and other social scientists use both handwritten notes and a tape recorder. But researchers often make strong claims about the empirical foundations of their conclusions. Perhaps even more so than in quantitative studies, where numbers are generally taken at face value, researchers using qualitative methods are sensitive to the need to support such claims against criticism. They are also sensitive to the nuances of language itself. How a comment or characterization is expressed may be an important clue that can be overlooked or lost without a verbatim taped record.

Tape recordings should be transcribed for analysis whenever it is possible. It is much easier to assign answers to categories and identify recurrent themes when working with verbal material on paper. Notes can be taken in the margin—in pencil if necessary—and decisions reconsidered where a particular characterization is not working out.

When working with transcripts, however, the practical, logistical issues can be overwhelming. First of all, the equipment really does fail. Backup is still needed in the form of notes or even a second recording. Second, transcription can be tedious, time-consuming, and expensive. Natural conversation—the kind of ebb and flow of natural thought and spontaneous expression that interviewing is specifically intended to produce—is often ungrammatical and contains many fragments of words, incomplete sentences, false starts and hesitations, points where the topic takes an abrupt and unexpected turn, long pauses, slang, jargon, places where the interview is interrupted by an external event, and segments where both interviewer and interviewee are talking at once. It also contains laughter, coughs and sneezes, and assorted expressive noises!

Most of the time, however, it is just not worth listening to the same tiny section of tape ten or twenty times to figure out a word or phrase that is not clear. Transcribers, who are occasionally taken from the ranks of office workers trained to record business letters and reports word for word from crisply articulated recitations, usually need very specific instruction on this point. Otherwise, transcribing a half-hour tape can take several hours—or even longer.

On the other hand, it is important for the transcriber to resist the temptation to edit the material on the fly or to substitute grammatical words and expressions for

(*continued*)

> **Box 5.2: Working with Transcript Materials (*continued*)**
>
> the language the person being interviewed actually used. This is a slippery slope that too easily leads to lost information, even distortion. It is easiest and best to keyboard everything as closely as possible to the way it was actually stated, but without agonizing over an isolated phrase that defies interpretation. Those isolated undecipherable segments are what the ellipsis (. . .) was invented for! Spelling and punctuation really don't matter.

was familiar with her home country, as well as with Jamaica. To avoid any language or other cultural misunderstanding, I wanted her to interview people from the Trinidadian newsrooms, in addition to the Jamaican ones. The Jamaican interviewer limited his interviews to people from the Jamaican newsrooms with which he was familiar. As far as status was concerned, the younger interviewer had the reputation of being a serious and experienced journalist, while the older one was known as one of the Caribbean veterans.

The issue of ethnicity was relevant to me in particular. Especially in the Trinidadian newsrooms, where journalists would not all know me, I would be judged on my appearance. Being white and European, I suspected I would immediately be classified as "foreign," which I assumed could trigger a different kind of interaction. For this reason the involvement of these other interviewers in the project was crucial.

All of the interviewees were practicing journalists in the Caribbean—ten women and ten men. The profile of the final sample shows that the majority were under thirty years old and had been in the profession between four and eight years, although a few were older and more senior. Most of them worked in the print media, some in broadcasting. Most of them had received some form of professional education and held at least a first degree.

All of the interviews were face to face and lasted for between one and a half and two hours; full confidentiality was assured. The interviews were held over a period of about five weeks and were conducted without any noticeable problems. The research was introduced as a Caribbean Institute of Media and Communication (CARIMAC) project, which in all instances meant immediate access and willingness to cooperate, based on the goodwill and reputation of the Institute. The interviews were tape recorded and took place outside the workplace. The recordings were transcribed by the interviewers and usually made available within two days after the interview.

Analyzing the Findings

I must admit that at that point the project became a trial-and-error exercise for me, but a very interesting and exciting trial and error. I knew that I wanted the interpretation of the findings to focus on recognizing indications of identities at work: the shifting of identifications; the preference for certain identities; the rejection of others; the denying, asserting, or ignoring of identities. But I did not know yet how these indications would manifest themselves. Of course, in all of this the interview responses were to be seen as "actively constructed 'narratives'" rather than information "giving direct access to 'experience'" (Zimmerman 2000, 825). The descriptions of experiences in the transcripts could not be interpreted as descriptions of factual interactions, but as a way of perception by the interviewees.

I found support for my approach in attribution theory. This theory postulates that people will try to explain the events in which they find themselves by attributing them to perceived causes (Forsterling 2001). These events include encounters and interactions with others. The explanations for other people's behavior will often be spontaneously implicit as well as explicit; they may be considered commonsense, irrational, and expressive of "naïve psychology," but they nevertheless form part of the process of systematically assigning meanings. In the context of media organizations, this "naïve psychology" illustrates "culturally embedded sensemaking" in work environments.

I started to first read the transcripts with a totally open mind. Whatever struck me was written down and noted as a "theme." In order to keep on track, I then looked through my themes and tried to select those that were relevant for my particular concern, relational dynamics. For the time being, I tabled the themes that were interesting but that fell outside of these parameters (such as sexual harassment, mobility, and so on).

I tried to keep focused on my major concern: to find illustrations of people taking on, or referring to, multiple identities to serve different functions, depending on circumstances and interests. I saw gender and gender identity as relational qualities and therefore expected the interviewees' accounts of relational dynamics to tell me more about how and why these relational qualities were produced. Of course, the immediate question was one of how "relational dynamics" express themselves. I decided to pay attention to anything that related to interactions and to any statement that referred to a sense of self, whether this sense of self had as its first point of reference gender, professionalism, or the organization.

Earlier that year I had bought a copy of a qualitative analysis software program, believing that I would find the time to work through the tutorials and learn how to do the computer-assisted coding of themes. It did not work that way. Instead, I went the manual route, by assigning codes (for categories or themes) to one or more paragraphs in the text and in the second instance grouping the related paragraphs. For example, I discovered that in their narratives, the interviewees made statements in which they seemed to shift their major point of reference. An emphasis on professionalism ("get the job done," "deadlines are sacred")—evidence of professional identification—sometimes seemed to be used as a strategy for resolving gender conflicts. When they needed to bargain, female journalists were sometimes unwilling to negotiate with male editors. Instead, they manifested a shift in priorities. The disadvantages of receiving no payment were placed second to a higher, professional goal: "As long as it's to get the job done, even though I'm not getting reimbursed [for expenses incurred], I go ahead and do it anyway."

This kind of shift in identity priority occurred often. Some women journalists who felt their lack of status in the newsroom was attributable to their sex emphasized professional prestige and satisfaction: "I'll get the praise from outside if it boils down to that." Others, who when working on a special publication were paid less than their male colleagues or received no payment at all, showed a similar shift. They emphasized their professional payoff: "I get to show my stuff, my work. I can do it my way." This underscored their professional identity, pushing their gender identity to a lower position.

In some male-dominated newsroom cultures some women felt it could be risky for them to show vulnerability or to express doubt or uncertainty. As they explained, "If you say you can't go there or you can't do this because you are a woman, ... or if you are afraid that something will happen to you, then you will never get the [big] story." These women were ready to suppress their gender identity to protect their professional identity.

In developing my analysis, I decided to first take a part of the transcripts and see if a first analysis would contribute to finding "sensitizing concepts" or background ideas that would help inform the overall project. And I was reminded of a statement by Charmaz: "Sensitizing concepts offer ways of seeing, organizing, and understanding experience; they are embedded in our disciplinary emphases and perspectival proclivities" (2000, 515).

I decided to elaborate on the results of this first part before completing the entire analysis (see de Bruin and Ross, in press). In the examples given above, I seemed to recognize some clearly developed strategies to minimize or inflate certain identities. Other strategies focused on the shifting of identities—claiming certain identities and ignoring others. Identification with a traditional male work ethos and set of professional values seemed to be useful in avoiding gender tensions and polarization. Emphasizing professional identity and playing down gender identity, in certain instances, seemed to have been a deliberate choice, diminishing the potential for gender tension that comes with gender relations—professional identity used as a shield.

This stage of my work in progress may be seen as memo writing, which has been called "the intermediate step between coding and the first draft of the completed analysis ... [that] helps to spark our thinking and encourages us to look at our data and codes in new ways" (Charmaz 2000, 517). It has provided a useful framework for me to continue with the remainder of the analysis, as well as some initial insights into my chosen problem.

Questions for Reflection

Are there other cases where gender issues might be set aside under the influence of professional norms or organizational demands? Why might this be a problem?

As a news consumer, does it matter to you whether the journalist is male or female, or of your ethnic group or a different one? Why or why not?

What do you think this author means by the phrase "culturally embedded sense making"?

What would have been the effect of the researcher in this study doing the interviews herself? Would there be possible advantages, as well as disadvantages, to this approach?

References

Allan, S. 1998. "(En)gendering the Truth: Politics of News Discourse." Pp. 121–37 in *News, Gender and Power*, eds. C. Carter, G. Branston, and S. Allan. London: Routledge.

Barrow, C., ed. 1995. *Caribbean Portraits, Essays on Gender Ideologies and Identities*. Kingston, Jamaica: Ian Randle Publishers.

Berkowitz, D. 1990. "Refining the Gatekeeping Metaphor for Local Television News." *Journal of Broadcasting & Electronic Media* 34: 55–68.

Capozza, D., and R. Brown, eds. 2000. *Social Identity Processes, Trends in Theory and Research*. Thousand Oaks, CA: Sage.

Carter, C., G. Branston, and S. Allan, eds. 1998. *News, Gender and Power*. London: Routledge.

Charmaz, K. "Grounded Theory, Objectivist and Constructivist Methods." 2000. Pp. 509–35 in *Handbook of Qualitative Research*, eds. N. K. Denzin and Y. S. Lincoln. Thousand Oaks, CA: Sage.

Crisp, R. J., and M. Hewstone. 2000. "Multiple Categorization and Social Identity." Pp. 149–66 in *Social Identity Processes, Trends in Theory and Research*, eds. D. Capozza and R. Brown. Thousand Oaks, CA: Sage.

Curran, J. 1990a. "The New Revisionism in Mass Communication Research: A Reappraisal." *European Journal of Communication* 5 (2–3): 135–64.

Curran, J. 1990b. "Culturalist Perspectives of News Organizations: A Reappraisal and a Case Study." Pp. 114–34 in *Public Communication: The New Imperatives*, ed. M. Ferguson. London: Sage.

Deaux, K. 2000. "Models, Meanings and Motivations." Pp. 1–14 in *Social Identity Processes, Trends in Theory and Research*, ed. D. Capozza and R. Brown. Thousand Oaks, CA: Sage.

de Bruin, Marjan, ed. 1994. "Women and Caribbean Media." Occasional Paper (3). Kingston, Jamaica: CARIMAC 1994.

de Bruin, M. In press. "Organizational, Professional and Gender Identities; Overlapping, Coinciding and Contradicting Realities." In *Identities at Work*, eds. M. de Bruin and K. Ross. Cresskill, NJ: Hampton Press.

de Bruin, M., and K. Ross, eds. In press. *Identities at Work*. Cresskill, NJ: Hampton Press.

Fontana A., and J. H. Frey. 2000. "The Interview: From Structured Questions to Negotiated Text." Pp. 645–72 in *Handbook of Qualitative Research*, eds. N. K. Denzin and Y. S. Lincoln. Thousand Oaks, CA: Sage.

Forsterling, F. 2001. *Attribution: An Introduction to Theories, Research and Applications*. Philadelphia: Taylor and Francis.

Gergen, K. J. 1999. *An Invitation to Social Construction*. Thousand Oaks, CA: Sage.

Gergen, K. J. 2001. *Social Construction in Context*. Thousand Oaks, CA: Sage.

Hogg, M., and D. Terry. 2001. "Social Identity Theory and Organizational Processes." Pp. 1–12 in *Social Identity Processes in Organizational Contexts*, eds. M. Hogg and D. Terry. Philadelphia: Taylor and Francis.

Kroger, J. 2000. *Identity Development: from Adolescence through Adulthood*. Thousand Oaks, CA: Sage 2000.

Leo-Rhynie, E., B. Bailey, and C. Barrow, eds. 1997. *Gender, A Caribbean Multi-Disciplinary Perspective*. Kingston, Jamaica: Ian Randle Publishers.

Mills, K. 1997 "What Difference Do Women Journalists Make?" Pp. 41–55 in *Women, Media and Politics*, ed. P. Norris. New York: Oxford University Press.

Mohammed, P., and V. Shepherd, eds. 1991. *Gender in Caribbean Development*. Mona, Jamaica; St. Augustine, Trinidad and Tobago; and Cave Hill, Barbados: The University of the West Indies, Women and Development Studies Project.

Mohammed P., ed. 2002. *Gendered Realities: An Anthology of Essays in Caribbean Feminist Thought*. Kingston, Jamaica: University of the West Indies Press.

Schlesinger, P. 1990. "Rethinking the Sociology of Journalism: Source Strategies and the Limits of Media-Centrism." Pp. 61–83 in *Public Communication: The New Imperatives*, ed. M. Ferguson. Thousand Oaks, CA: Sage.

Schudson, M. 1991. "The Sociology of News Production Revisited." Pp. 141–59 in *Mass Media and Society*, eds. J. Curran and M. Gurevitch. London: Edward Arnold.

Shoemaker, P. J. 1997. "A New Gatekeeping Model." Pp. 57–71 in *Social Meanings of News*, ed. D. Berkowitz. Thousand Oaks, CA: Sage.

Senior, O. 1991. *Working Miracles: Women's Lives in the English-Speaking Caribbean*. Bloomington: Indiana University Press.

Shepherd, V. 2002. "Challenging Masculine Myths: Gender, History Education and Development in Jamaica." Dialogue for Development, Lecture, November 19, 2002. Kingston, Jamaica: Planning Institute of Jamaica.

Shepherd, V., B. Brereton, and B. Bailey, eds. 1995. *Engendering History, Caribbean Women in Historical Perspective*. New York: Palgrave Macmillan.

Skidmore, P. 1998. "Gender and the Agenda: News Reporting of Child Sexual Abuse." Pp. 204–18 in *News, Gender and Power*, eds. C. Carter, G. Branston, and S. Allan. London: Routledge.

Steiner, L. 1998. "Newsroom Accounts of Power at Work." Pp. 149–59 in *News, Gender and Power*, eds. C. Carter, G. Branston, and S. Allan. London: Routledge.

Van Zoonen, L. 1994. *Feminist Media Studies.* London, Thousand Oaks, CA: Sage.
Van Zoonen, L. 1998. "One of the Girls?: The Changing Gender of Journalism." Pp. 33–46 in *News, Gender and Power,* eds. C. Carter, G. Branston, and S. Allan. London: Routledge.
Weaver, D., ed. 1998. *The Global Journalist: News People around the World.* Cresskill, NJ: Hampton Press.
Weaver, D., and G. Wilhoit. 1996. *The American Journalist in the 1990s: U.S. News People at the End of an Era.* Mahwah, NJ: Erlbaum.
Weick, K. 1995. *Sensemaking in Organizations.* London, Thousand Oaks, CA: Sage.
Zimmerman, D. 2000. "Analyzing Talk and Text." Pp. 821–34 in *Handbook of Qualitative Research,* eds. N. K. Denzin and Y. S. Lincoln. Thousand Oaks, CA: Sage.

6
Patient Satisfaction in a Medical Setting: An Emergent Design Approach

Robert L. Krizek and Paaige K. Turner

In this chapter Krizek and Turner describe their experience studying a medical organization, at its own request, with an eye to the organization's declining patient satisfaction ratings. The authors note that what are sometimes called "key informant" interviews—interviews with people with "insider" knowledge, in this case knowledge about the organization being studied—were especially useful, even though they say that they dislike the word "informant" itself (which may simply sound too much like a police "informer").

Experimentalists tend to call the people who volunteer for their experiments "research subjects"; survey researchers call those who answer their survey questions "respondents." Generally speaking, "informant" is the most common term for ethnographic interviewees. Informants know things about their own culture, about groups to which they belong, and about organizations in which they participate that outsiders may never realize without asking. To the "insider" these things may be obvious, but not to the "outsider" doing research.

These researchers also gain insights from simple observations of clinic practices. We have already met the term "participant observation" in chapter 1 of this book, Rakow's study of a North Dakota community. Not all observers are participants, however, and some are participants only to a limited degree. A participant observer becomes, to some degree, a member of the community being studied— one way to really grasp the "insider" point of view. The reader of this chapter can imagine how just sitting in a clinic waiting room alongside real patients, while it might not be quite the same thing as actually coming to the clinic as a patient, provides a sense of perspective hard to duplicate by other methods. Krizek and Turner used both approaches in this study.

THIS CHAPTER IS ABOUT THE METHODOLOGICAL CHOICES we made as we attempted to answer a simple question: why was patient satisfaction declining at the Metropolitan Medical Group[1] (MMG)? In particular, we sought to minimize our blind spots by employing an emergent research design that incorporated multiple data collection and analysis techniques. We will discuss this project in five stages, from the time MMG contacted us about the possibility of our examining the question of patient satisfaction (orienting to the problem) until we provided it with our understandings in both written and oral presentations (analyzing and reporting).

For us, doing research has always been about maximizing payoffs and minimizing costs. By this we mean that whatever choices a researcher makes during a project, each selected option "gets you something" and, in turn, each forces you to "give something up." Students learn in graduate methods courses that various experimental research designs sacrifice mundane realism for the sake of gaining control. Scholars writing about qualitative methods (Krueger 1988; Lindloff and Taylor 2002) tell us that focus groups encourage participants to build upon others' comments while, at the same time, creating the risk that people may not be as forthcoming about sensitive issues or behaviors in front of others (often strangers) as they would be in a one-on-one interview.

Much in the same way that theoretical frameworks can act as conceptual blinders, methodological choices act as perceptual blinders. Each distinct data gathering or analysis technique affords researchers one view or interpretation of a problem or issue, while that same technique precludes the researcher from seeing another, perhaps equally important view. We hope that telling about our research experience will help make this clear.

Stage One: Orienting to the Problem

We should begin our story by explaining that we undertook this particular project as an applied rather than a basic research endeavor (see Frey et al. 2000). The MMG contracted us to help solve a specific organizational problem. As we have described in some detail elsewhere (Turner and Krizek 2004), the MMG is the practice arm of the medical school of a private Midwestern university. Following the fiscal year 2000, a year in which MMG had posted its first significant financial loss, the Dean of the Medical School and the Chief Executive Officer (CEO) of the MMG put out a call through their liaisons for "research/consulting proposals" to examine declining patient satisfaction. Intrigued by the both the communicative aspects of the issue of patient satisfaction and the financial benefit we might accrue if selected, we submitted a

Box 6.1: Organizational Research Tips

Chapter authors Krizek and Turner offer the following fourteen suggestions for designing effective organizational research projects:

Suggestion #1: When designing research projects, researchers should maximize payoffs (the "gets") and minimize costs (the "gives") by employing, whenever possible, multiple data collection and analysis techniques.

Suggestion #2: In many research projects it helps to maximize payoffs and minimize costs by utilizing the unique talents, theoretical sensitivities, and methodological expertise of more than one researcher. In this way we should minimize the effects of our "trained incapacities" (Burke 1984).

Suggestion #3: When doing organizational work, researchers should try to get a feel for the organization, its culture(s), and the issues relevant to its membership by interviewing key organizational members before entering the organization on a broader scale. (This action could also assist the researcher in deciding whether or not the project coincides with his or her personal ethics.)

Suggestion #4: When conducting "for-profit" applied projects, a researcher should ask for written permission to use the data and findings in his scholarly work as part of his compensation. The researcher should also write the agreement in consideration of anticipated Institutional Review Board (IRB) issues.

Suggestion #5: Before creating new data (and knowledge), a researcher should acquire and review any existing data (and prior knowledge) relevant to his or her research focus, interest, or question.

Suggestion #6: When conducting research projects, in order to insure the maximizing of payoffs (the "gets") and the minimizing of costs (the "gives"), the researchers should frame any research plan as tentative and be willing to make changes to their plan as new understandings emerge.

Suggestion #7: Researchers should consider using ethnographic techniques (participant observation and informal interviewing) in order to understand any process from the perspective of someone actually immersed in it.

Suggestion #8: When using audio recording equipment, assume that there will be some sort of technological malfunction and come equipped with a second—and third—alternative for capturing interview data!

Suggestion #9: When issues of credibility and confidentiality are important in interview settings, ask interviewees to introduce you to other potential participants. If those individuals have had a satisfactory interaction with you, their introduction will provide you with instant credibility.

Suggestion #10: Researchers should consider the inconvenience attending a focus group session creates for people (especially the elderly and infirm) and focus more on using a convenience sample (people who are already on site) for recruiting participants. Also, remember that money and food are powerful enticements for attracting focus group participants.

(continued)

> **Box 6.1: Organizational Research Tips (*continued*)**
>
> *Suggestion #11:* When collecting data as a participant observer in a medical facility, a researcher should accept the real possibility of getting sick. Take plenty of vitamins and try not to breathe!
>
> *Suggestion #12:* Researchers should write their field notes in ways that will avoid attracting attention. Consider using dayminders, crossword puzzle pages, or some other artifact indigenous to the setting. For example, we've used bar napkins in bars and scorebooks at baseball games.
>
> *Suggestion #13:* When conducting focus group interviews, consider employing court or legal transcribers in addition to audio recording the interactions. Have these individuals transcribe the actual conversations and use the tapes to fill in any gaps or to clarify any ambiguities in the transcriptions.
>
> *Suggestion #14:* Whenever possible, use a narrative case approach to present to the various organizational constituencies the often disjointed understandings that emerge from your field observations and notes.

proposal in which we detailed our plan. Put simply, we proposed to interview a limited number of MMG personnel (between four and eight) in order to better contextualize the problem and then, as the bulk of the project, to interview upwards of fifty patients of the MMG in both focus group and individual settings.

Our rationale for interviewing patients was obvious. We wanted to hear in their words their experiences with the MMG. We believed that in these interviews we would capture nuances not available in survey responses. Our desire to interview MMG personnel, however, may not have been as clear. In our proposal we explained that as part of our approach to organizational interventions ranging from training programs to needs analysis, we attempt to understand any problem or issue within the organizational context and through the eyes of various organizational members. Our plan as conceived was simple—gather the data and analyze narratives, themes, and metaphors to uncover the factors underlying the decline in patient satisfaction.

In presenting our proposal at our initial interview with the dean and the CEO, we began to gain insight into the organizational context we would be confronting if the MMG accepted our plan. First, we learned that this revenue loss, interestingly enough, had followed three-plus years of declining levels of patient satisfaction. And although they didn't know exactly how they were related, the dean and her associate realized that falling revenues and declining patient satisfaction must somehow be linked. So while the dean was contemplating hiring us (or someone else) to discover the reasons for declining patient satisfaction, from this informational interview we were well aware that the "bottom-line" reason that MMG would turn to an outside researcher or consultant would be to help stop the financial bleeding. After brief negotiations they hired us at a rate somewhat less than the windfall for which we had hoped. We did, however, manage to receive approval to write one or more research reports based on our data and findings.

In our first meeting following the signing of a formal consulting agreement, a few of the medical school's "inner-circle" staff provided us with bits and pieces of information that they thought would be important for us to know about MMG and its recent past. For example, they told us that the university had sold its hospital to a private health care conglomerate in 1998 (a matter of public record), resulting in a rather strange association among the medical school, the MMG, and the hospital (a matter not for public consumption). While the faculty of the medical school treated patients at both the MMG and the hospital, and used both locations to train and mentor their students, each of the three enterprises retained its own hierarchical structure and somewhat autonomous set of practices.

In addition to discovering information about this unique structural arrangement, we learned that copious amounts of data regarding patient satisfaction existed in various pockets throughout the MMG, the hospital, and the various departments of the medical school. Through what was not said, we surmised that little, if anything, had ever been done to analyze either the quantitative or qualitative aspects of these already existing data. We decided to tackle this first.

Stage Two: Framing the Problem

As part of our self-orientation to the problem, we set about collecting, analyzing, and interpreting the existing data. We accomplished this in part by reviewing past patient satisfaction surveys and the narrative reports of the results of those surveys, and by interviewing four key MMG administrative personnel. From the quantitative survey data given us that tracked patient satisfaction, we discovered (among a variety of other things) that patient satisfaction had dropped substantially from 1996–1997 to 1997–1998, around the time of the separation of the medical school and the hospital. The four individuals we interviewed and assorted documents we reviewed attributed the reduced levels of overall satisfaction in the year 1998–1999, following the split, to the lingering confusion that had been created for the patients of the MMG. Our informants found this to be understandable and even somewhat acceptable, especially in light of the fact that revenue had remained relatively consistent. What their survey results indicated and internal sense-making processes couldn't explain, however, was that levels of patient satisfaction continued to decline through the second quarter of 2000–2001. The pre- and postsplit "trauma related to the sale" rationale could not explain this continued and steady decline in patient satisfaction for the period from 1999 on into 2001.

During our meetings with the four key MMG administrative personnel, we also heard an important phrase repeated several times and uttered at least once by each person. The phrase was "a seamless experience." And yet, although we encountered the phrase several times—mostly in terms of the organization's vision for its patients—we never heard it defined in exactly the same way. In reflecting upon this apparent ambiguity surrounding the goal of creating a "seamless experience" for patients, one of us (Turner) suggested that we reframe our task. Given the incongruencies we had heard from these key employees in regard to a "seamless experience" for patients, she posited that it might be implausible to think that other MMG personnel would have any clearer idea of what a seamless experience would be. She suggested that perhaps we should forego simply looking for the causes of declining patient satisfaction and adopt an alternative, although not entirely different, focus.

As a discourse analyst, one of the primary assumptions that guide Turner in her work is that problems arise not because people are "misinterpreting" a situation, but because they have different interpretations of the same event. We moved, therefore, from attempting to identify and label patient issues to attempting to understand the differing interpretations that exist among various organizational members and MMG patients in regard to patient satisfaction. We set out to discover the congruencies and incongruencies that existed surrounding the meanings associated with patient satisfaction by devising a tentative research plan that would aid us in accomplishing that goal.

Stage Three: Engaging an Emergent Research Design

Given the goal of identifying and understanding the multiple perspectives that may have been contributing to the problem of declining patient satisfaction, we redesigned our research plan to incorporate three principal means of data collection. First, using a "snowball sample" (Barone and Switzer 1995, 188), we conducted extended interviews (thirty to seventy-five minutes each) with fourteen additional employees of MMG, from doctors to patient coordinators to facilities managers and customer relations specialists. Second, we conducted eight focus group interviews of at least two hours with eight to fifteen participants each. We also conducted one-on-one interviews, either over the telephone or face to face, with nine patients who could not or did not want to attend a focus group session. Third, we conducted over twenty hours of observation at the main facility of the MMG, both in the role of observer and that of patient.

Our observations transpired in high-traffic areas such as waiting rooms and patient intake areas. We attempted to focus as much as possible on staff/patient interactions as individual patients navigated the health care system offered by the MMG. This third and final data collection technique utilized the methodological strengths of one of the researchers (Krizek). In addition, this technique coincides with our belief that in examining any process (such as the process of being a patient at the MMG), in addition to uncovering stakeholders' perceptions of that process through interviews or surveys, it is advisable to actually observe or participate in that process.

In the remainder of this section we will discuss some aspects of each phase of our data collection and a few of the unique challenges that continually forced us to rethink and revise our procedures. We should note, however, that although we present these three data collection strategies in a linear fashion, considerable overlap existed in the time frames in which we employed them. For example, even before we completed interviewing the MMG personnel, Krizek had commenced his participant observations and Turner had begun making arrangements for the focus group interviews.

Interviews with MMG Personnel

The initial data collection efforts following our interviews of the four key administrators consisted of one-on-one qualitative interviews (Kvale 1996; Rubin and Rubin 1995), also called ethnographic interviewing (Spradley 1979), with middle management and other personnel of MMG. Our primary goal for these moderately scheduled interviews (Barone and Switzer 1995) was to discover from the interviewee's perspective what it meant for a patient to have a "seamless experience." During this phase of our data collection we encountered some surprises, both with the data we collected and with the procedures we employed. Most significantly, during our interviews with MMG employees, we were struck by the seeming inability of many of them to take and maintain a patient's perspective on satisfaction. By this we mean that although we asked no questions delving into employee satisfaction, when we asked them about patient satisfaction, most MMG personnel moved the conversation with startling swiftness to issues of what it would take to make their jobs or their experiences with patients more satisfying. And while we realize that there is a relationship between employee satisfaction and patient satisfaction, most employees did not explicitly or even implicitly address this connection. We heard numerous comments like "they [the patients] need to understand how we operate and then they won't have any problems" or "it's a matter of educating them." In making sense of these responses, we agreed that if a person was assuming a patient's perspective, he or she would more than likely say just the opposite, something beginning with "we need to understand" or "from the patient's perspective I could see that . . . ." We concluded, therefore, that this propensity to move quickly to issues of employee satisfaction might be evidence that customer satisfaction is not a core value for many MMG employees.

While we will discuss this conclusion in more detail below, it is also important to note at this point that this unexpected pattern of responses necessitated a change in our interviewing strategies. One of the major challenges we faced in our conversations with MMG personnel was redirecting them to the topic of patient satisfaction. After each interview the two of us reviewed what questions or comments seemed to work better (although nothing worked well) in getting our interviewees to discuss patient concerns. For example, we began to ask questions that required interviewees to put themselves in the role of a patient, like this one: "If you were a patient, what would be the most significant aspects of the MMG that would affect your overall satisfaction with your care?"

In addition to continually adapting the interviewing protocol, we also faced two other issues—maintaining confidentiality and finding appropriate places for conducting interviews. Once our interviews began, we quickly discovered that somewhere in the recent past fact-finding missions such as this one had been used to eliminate positions or even specific personnel. People might, therefore, be understandably reluctant to talk. In contrast, we also found that people appreciated having the opportunity to air their ideas, needs, and concerns. The confluence of these two considerations led us to carefully schedule the times of our interviews and, quite often, to use space outside the organization.

In order to reduce interviewee anxiety, we also strove to be very clear with our assurances of confidentiality. For example, prior to beginning the recording of each interview, we informed the participant that we would destroy the tapes after they were transcribed. In addition, we waited to turn on our recorders until after we received the signed permission of the participant and we had addressed any concerns or questions they might have. We both audio recorded these interviews (no participant objected to having their interview audio recorded, although a few spoke "off the record" after the interviewer had packed the audio recorder away) and took notes as a precaution in case of a technological malfunction. As an additional safeguard we brought two tape recorders to each interview, starting one about five minutes into the interview. We did this so that if one tape ended we would not miss any of the conversation, as well as to provide another precaution in case of a technological malfunction.

Finally, we should mention that the snowball technique we used in this phase of data collection worked well. Following our interviews, we asked people to e-mail or call us with a name and contact information of one or two other people with whom we might talk. We asked them to do this only if they felt their experience with us had been positive, so they would feel comfortable recommending an associate, and only after they acquired the other person's permission as well. We felt that these simple considerations enhanced our credibility and rapport and that, once having established a feeling of trust with a participant, if he or she recommended us to another employee, this would also amount to "passing along" that credibility and rapport.

Focus Group Interviews with Patients

Coincidental with conducting employee interviews, one of us (Turner) began planning for our focus group interviews (Krueger 1998; Lunt and Livingstone 1996). During this process we had to consider a number of issues. We had to determine the best means for recruiting participants for our patient focus groups and for managing the recruitment process. We also had to determine an appropriate incentive or compensation for our participants. In addition, we needed to develop a method for managing the actual two-hour sessions, design interview/discussion questions and prompts, and determine the logistics for recording the participants' comments and interactions. Once again utilizing the strengths (and avoiding the weaknesses) of the researchers, Turner assumed primary responsibility for these details.

Our first big issue emerged as we attempted to recruit participants. Initially we tried sampling from the list of all MMG patients using a random number table. This strategy, however, produced such a low response rate that we requested the appointment list from the MMG and invited those individuals who had an appointment on one of the specific days when a focus group was scheduled. Even with this strategy and an offer of $25, we still experienced a low response rate. Individuals said they would attend, we reminded them the day before of their promise to participate, and still we were rarely able to attract more than half of our target number of fifteen participants. Through a process of trial and error we determined that the "magic formula" for boosting attendance was the guarantee of $50, a promise of refreshments (including sugar-free cookies and pastries for diabetics), and the conducting of the focus group on-site in the MMG. For our focus groups the MMG closed off one of its employee lounges. Finally, even with all of these perks, we still had no-shows for almost every session and took to recruiting patients in the halls as they exited from their appointments.

The second most problematic issue we encountered in our attempts to conduct focus group interviews came, at least in part, in the form of having to overcome a misperception. Many of the focus group participants wanted to discuss their satisfaction or lack thereof with the hospital, insurance company, or the American health care system in general, not the MMG, which provided a license for others to move off target. After the first two groups we reviewed our tapes and devised an introductory statement asking participants to separate the two sets of experiences (MMG and hospital) and to describe their experiences according to what happened first, second, and third, and what satisfied and dissatisfied them at each stage.

Participant Observation of Employee/Patient Interactions

Our final data collection technique involved participant observation. One of us (Krizek) conducted over twenty hours of what has been called "smash and grab" ethnography (Sutton as cited in Martin 2002) and informal guided conversations (see Snow et al. 1982) throughout the public areas of the MMG building. He positioned himself in the waiting areas outside the various departments (internal medicine, allergies, acute care, and so on), always attempting to sit within listening distance of the intake nurse/receptionist in order to capture his or her interactions with patients. During this process he faced and solved many challenges, including how to record field notes unobtrusively, how to maintain patients' and staff members' confidentiality, how to select multiple and diverse observation points, and how to respond to MMG personnel when questioned about his presence.

If you forget for the moment that sitting in a doctor's waiting room exposes a person to a variety of common and not-so-common illnesses, perhaps the most serious issue faced in these participant observations occurred when MMG personnel challenged Krizek's presence. In very polite and routine ways they would ask him, in essence, what he was doing occupying a spot in the waiting room: "Sir, are you waiting for someone?" "Have you checked in?" After discussing this issue, we decided to alter our tactics. First, we reluctantly concluded that it would be best for Krizek to identify himself to one of the intake personnel or the department manager on duty before assuming his place in a waiting room. While knowing that they were being observed might encourage the MMG staff members to be on their best behavior, this certainly was a better alternative than having to answer questions after being discovered. We also decided to employ the tactic of changing the point of observation more frequently.

The second serious issue involved the practice of taking field notes. Krizek, in order to remain as unobtrusive as possible, took to writing his condensed field notes in a small "day minder." Although some people write letters and work on assorted business-related projects while waiting in a doctor's office, we found that the more Krizek wrote, the more attention he garnered. He turned to writing fewer notes, did away with his yellow legal pad, and periodically removed himself to a private office to write more extended notes. And yet solving these types of problems was only the beginning. Managing the multiple forms of data such as audio recordings, videos and recordings of focus groups, and copious amounts of field notes presents its own unique set of issues.

Stage Four: Managing the Data

Two challenging problems arose in relation to managing our data. The first problem surfaced when we tried to transcribe the recordings we made of the focus group interviews. The second problem centered on the issue of making our field notes and the understandings that emerged from those field experiences both accessible and compelling for the organizational members.

In regard to the former, although we had very carefully and strategically positioned two high-fidelity tape recorders on the table and two video recorders at cross-angles, we found it nearly impossible and extremely time-consuming to transcribe the recordings ourselves. There were problems identifying the speaker despite the fact that as the facilitators of the discussion we had anticipated this problem and used individuals' first names to identify them when they began to speak. People spoke over one another, spoke to one another in simultaneous conversations, and generally ignored our pleas to wait for us to call on them. People were excited (even passionate) about many of the conversational threads and burst into the discussions unannounced.

To overcome our transcribing inadequacies, we hired trained transcribers. Our problems still persisted, however. And although we hired experienced medical transcribers, the time it took to negotiate the various sets of audiotapes and videotapes proved unwieldy and was not cost-effective. It was at that point that one of our transcribers suggested that we should employ a court reporter to transcribe these tapes. A court reporter can sit at the back of the room and type verbatim comments that can be checked against an audio recording. Despite a rather hefty hourly wage, the ability to transcribe multiple and overlapping conversations would have been more cost-effective, accurate, and timely.

In regard to packaging our field data for the MMG personnel, we experienced problems as well. As is the practice of some ethnographers, in making sense of our data we turned to a few particularly insightful and self-reflective employees for feedback on both our understandings and the format in which we had elected to present those understandings—brief executive reports, bulleted lists, tables, charts, and extended patient quotes. We prefer to label these individuals as our "sounding boards" instead of using the term "informant." In the end, after our feedback sessions we decided that we would manage our field data by combining bulleted lists of patients' responses with an extended text based on our field observations. In accordance with Fisher's (1984, 1987) assertions, we believe in the narrative character of human understanding (people remember and relate to stories), and therefore, we decided to package a number of our field experiences in narrative wrapping. Below is one such example stemming from observations made of interactions at the MMG's main facility. Our purpose in writing this narrative was to give a holistic picture of one situation—what was said and what was the outcome. While the case might not be typical of most interactions at the MMG, it is representative of a number of issues surrounding the sources of patient dissatisfaction:

> The chairs in the waiting area are about 75 percent occupied. Periodically a patient's name gets called out and that person is ushered out, presumably to see a doctor.
> A female employee dressed in a colorful lab coat enters the waiting room to tell an African-American male to get "something like _____ [name of a medicine]." She says it loud enough so that everyone in the room could hear. Just then an African-American woman arrives on the scene, approaches the intake window, states her name, and says she has an appointment. The employee at the intake widow can't seem to find the woman's name on her appointment list.
> "Are you sure your appointment is today, Ms. Dillard? I can't seem to locate your name. You wouldn't happen to have your appointment card with you, would you?"
> It's 2:15 P.M.
> The woman walks over to an empty chair, sits, and places her purse in her lap. She begins to search, first her billfold, then the inner caverns of the purse itself. "I can't seem to find it. I'm sorry, but I'm sure my appointment was for today at 2:30. I hope this doesn't cause a problem, I have to get back to work."
> "I'm sure we'll get this cleared up. Just have a seat and I'll check to see if maybe your appointment got made with another department."
> I can hear the employee on the phone saying, "She's very nice; could you check and see . . . ." Just then another name gets called out: "Mr. Desantis?"
> After a few minutes, maybe ten, another employee from somewhere else in the building enters the waiting room and escorts Ms. Dillard out. "We're sorry for the confusion. I'm sure we'll get it straightened out." After about another ten minutes the two return, walk up to the window, and after a brief three-way conversation Ms. Dillard, somewhat jokingly, says to another waiting patient, "I don't want to have to get ugly today." Ms. Dillard sits back in her chair. She's now been here for over thirty minutes.
> The intake employee now slides her window shut. Ms. Dillard begins talking to other patients around her as each takes their turn telling their horror stories. Ms. Dillard says, "I'm wondering what they're talking about back there. Just get me in to my appointment. I took time off work to get here today."

"This is a big problem. I ain't gonna deal with this no more," she says to anyone who will listen. "I don't need no doctor I can't get to see. If she doesn't see me today...."

Just then she gets called to the window. I can't hear everything that is being said; however, it seems this woman's doctor doesn't ever see patients on this day of the week. I think to myself, how could they not have known that forty minutes ago.

"So what can be done? I took off from work today and someone gave me an appointment."

"Again, I apologize for the confusion," says the intake employee. "Let me give you a couple of options. The doctor is in clinic with her residents, and as I said she doesn't see patients when she's with her residents. Clinic is done at 5:00 and she can see you then."

Ms. Dillard has been here for almost an hour. "I can't wait until then. I have to get back to work."

"We could schedule you for another day."

"Can I get another doctor? Is there another doctor I can see? She seems real good but if I can't see her...." Ms. Dillard turns to another patient, one of her complaint group. "I had to wait to see her the first time I came here. Now this for my second visit."

"Again, I apologize for your inconvenience."

"I've had a lot of problems with this place. Today I left work to get here. I guess I'll go back to my private doctor. I have a doctor my family members go to. I'll just go back to private practice."

She grabbed her purse and stormed off.

The next day I discovered from the intake employee that Ms. Dillard actually had an appointment scheduled for the same time and date the next month.

"It was her fault. We weren't wrong here. It wasn't our mistake."

I also discovered that no one was informed that MMG lost a patient yesterday.

Stage Five: Analyzing and Reporting

In this project we employed multiple researchers, multiple data collection techniques, multiple and at times creative data management techniques, and an emergent research design—all so that we could fulfill our contractual obligations with the MMG to provide it with a clear picture of patient satisfaction. As the final step in this process, we analyzed our data by focusing on both congruencies and incongruencies in the themes and stories that emerged from our contact with all organizational stakeholders. This yielded two interrelated findings.

First, we reported that while MMG faces many challenges, the key issue for increasing overall patient satisfaction was minimizing new patient "dissatisfiers" long enough for them to experience "satisfiers." We explained that while most people imagine that individuals are either satisfied or dissatisfied, we found that overwhelmingly most MMG patients were both satisfied and dissatisfied at the same time. This suggested to us that patients evaluate different experiences with the MMG along differing continuums, with some experiences decreasing and increasing satisfaction and some experiences decreasing and increasing dissatisfaction. For example, individuals may be very satisfied because of their doctor's knowledge but dissatisfied because they are unable to get referrals. Below is a summary of the major factors that we believe were contributing to the reporting of reduced levels of overall patient satisfaction.

Many patients, particularly new patients, experience dissatisfiers (such as the referral process) more strongly than satisfiers (such as interactions with doctors). In our interviews, observations, and focus groups it became very clear that when individuals had high amounts of satisfaction they would tolerate high amounts of dissatisfaction as well. If, however, they had low amounts of satisfaction, they would not tolerate the same amount of dissatisfaction. What appears to be a deciding factor in determining whether an individual will leave or stay is the relationship between the amount of satisfaction and the amount of dissatisfaction. Dissatisfiers included (in addition to the referral system) the scheduling of appointments, the phone system, waiting for long periods of time in an examination room, confusion with billing statements, lack of toys and current reading materials in the waiting rooms of some departments, the use of residents, parking and parking validation, registration procedures, and the physical features of the MMG Building. Satisfiers centered on the doctors—their knowledge, genuine concern, and overall demeanor; the patient's individual ability to bypass the formal system of the MMG (for example, in getting references or making appointments); and the overall mission of MMG as a teaching institution.

Our second finding was the congruence and incongruence in the beliefs of the MMG personnel about what created satisfaction and dissatisfaction for patients. In addition, in our final reports we also outlined various issues related to the beliefs and behaviors of the MMG personnel. However, given the contractual nature of our relationship with the MMG and the open and honest nature of our interactions with its employees, we have elected to keep those specific understandings confidential.

For us, research is always about choices. In this chapter we have included various suggestions for helping you to make those choices.

Questions for Reflection

What ethical issues might be associated with unobtrusive (anonymous, unannounced) observation in a medical clinic, under some circumstances?

Think of a particular organization or group to which you belong. What knowledge would an "outsider" need to know to understand this group that you, as an "insider," could provide?

Why do you think patients were becoming less satisfied with their experiences at this clinic?

How would you best communicate these conclusions to the managers who commissioned this study?

What are some of the advantages of doing applied research that is paid for by the organization being studied? Disadvantages? How could this create a conflict of interest for the researcher?

Note

1. This name is a pseudonym for the actual organization that was studied.

References

Barone, J. T., and J. Y. Switzer. 1995. *Interviewing: Art and Skill.* Boston, MA: Allyn & Bacon.
Burke, K. 1984. *Permanence and Change: An Anatomy of Purpose.* 3rd ed. Berkeley, CA: University of California Press.
Fisher, W. R. 1984. "Narration as a Human Communication Paradigm: The Case of Public Moral Argument." *Communication Monographs* 51: 1–22.
Fisher, W. R. 1987. *Human Communication as Narration: Toward a Philosophy of Reason, Value, and Action.* Columbia, SC: University of South Carolina Press.
Frey, L. R., C. H. Botan, and G. L. Kreps. 2000. *Investigating Communication: An Introduction to Research Methods.* 2nd ed. Englewood Cliffs, NJ: Prentice Hall.
Krueger, R. A. 1998. *Focus Groups: A Practical Guide for Applied Research.* Thousand Oaks, CA: Sage.
Kvale, S. 1996. *Interviews: An Introduction to Qualitative Research Interviewing.* Thousand Oaks, CA: Sage.
Lindloff, T. R., and B. C. Taylor. 2002. *Qualitative Communication Research Methods.* Thousand Oaks, CA: Sage.
Lunt, P. K., and S. M. Livingstone. 1996. "Rethinking the Focus Group in Media and Communication Research." *Journal of Communication* 46 (2): 79–98.
Martin, J. 2002. *Organizational Culture: Mapping the Terrain.* Thousand Oaks, CA: Sage.
Rubin, H. J., and I. S. Rubin. 1996. *Qualitative Interviwing.* Thousand Oaks, CA: Sage.
Snow, D. A., L. A. Zurcher, and G. Sjoberg. 1982. "Interviewing by Comment: An Adjunct to the Direct Question." *Qualitative Sociology* 5 (4): 285–311.
Spradley, J. P. 1979. *The Ethnographic Interview.* New York: Holt, Rinehart, & Winston.
Turner, P. K., and R. L. Krizek. 2004. "Patient Satisfaction at MMG: A Matter of Perspective." In *Case Studies for Organizational Communication: Understanding Communication Processes,* ed. P. Shockley-Zalabak and J. Keyton, 219–29. Los Angeles: Roxbury Publishing.

7
Interpreting Signs: Reflections on Research Design in Context

Robert J. Balfour

When, in the planning phase of this book project, the call went out for submissions of narrative descriptions of research projects for use in this book, potential authors responded in many different ways. Some were confused about what to do. Most had to struggle to give up the rigid formalities traditionally associated with journal articles about research and to write effectively in first person about their personal experiences. It was difficult to provide potential authors with examples because few books like this have ever been produced—perhaps none at all!

One author stood out, among all those who responded, as the author contributing the most stunning literary narrative. This chapter is as effective as a piece of literature as it is as an instructional example in a research book. It also provides the ideal example to force us to think about the limitations (and some of the advantages) of field experiments.

Slater's complex, multimillion dollar field experiment on a community drug use prevention campaign introduced in Part I was challenging, but he made it work. Balfour's much smaller scale dissertation project in rural South African schools was challenging in very different ways, but he certainly made it work as well. Here, Balfour shares the lessons he learned in gathering data he really couldn't use at all to test his original hypotheses. But this "failed" portion of the larger experiment teaches us at least as much as anything possibly could about the social organization of a particular South African secondary school and the reasons why introducing new educational material or techniques into such a school might or might not have the envisioned impact.

"**D**ON'T BE THE KIND OF RESEARCHER who rushes in, extracts the data, and pulls out; don't leave them to pick up the pieces after you've gone. Be responsible." Slivers of winter sunlight pour into her rooms off Trumpington Street. The walls of the colleges loom grimly outside; their stained glass windows turn from mirrored gloom to glowing colours rich against the fading of light. Professor Yvonne Dunoit's[1] admonishment seems alien here, my purposefully designed language textbooks in hand, the specially selected anthology of short stories lying on her desk awaiting final scrutiny. I'm edgy and pace the length of the room before replying.

"I'm going home prepared," I respond. But this is not quite right. I feel less prepared than I might, and sound more defiant than is necessary. She smiles, looks toward previous drafts of my methods chapter, and shuffles the papers around, distractedly brushing a wave of thick red hair from her eyes. The smile is rueful, restrained: "Yes, yes . . . but the research context can 'fix' your careful plans. You'll need to 'interpret the signs' and adapt carefully—with sensitivity, Robert—to the context." Outside, the darkness and damp congeal on cycle spokes, walls, and the coats of people passing by. Veins of water trickle down the walls of buildings. I leave her office, trundle down the stairs and think already of sun and my work in African schools. I imagine the delight of children as they touch and page through the textbooks under my arm, specially illustrated and color coded in bright pastel shades for easy reference. Already I can see smiling teachers to work with, and all this glows with the general "good" of the work I want to do. They won't even know research is being done in the school; the design is seamless and complete, and I'll work to make it seem like part of the existing curriculum for English. The project materials are designed to expedite the learning of English by choosing narratives that reflect diverse communities and experiences in South Africa. The seeming alienness of these stories from the communities in which I want to work will also serve to "enlighten" the children about the cultural diversity and challenges still to be addressed in the new South Africa—challenges like the harassment of women by men in what is still a very patriarchal society. By the time I get back to my rooms, the pages of the printed textbooks have already begun to curl in the evening moisture.

Back at my desk, in No. 7 Selwyn Gardens, I set out the project design before me. There are to be four groups of children, each of which will receive the project materials in turn so that, by the end of the ten months, I'll have a picture of the differential effects of teaching, materials, and ability on their progress towards learning to write better in English. "What will you do if you can only get two groups, not four? Have you thought about the ethical issues involved in exposing some groups more to the new work? What if the teachers feel that your materials aren't appropriate?" The questions recede, are muffled in the sound of rain on the windows and the warmth of the coffee mug in my hands. I have answers for the unforeseen and, yes, I convince myself that the schools will be so grateful for the intervention that they will not mind my choice of stories dealing with the abuse of women by men in South Africa. Moral right will overshadow other sensitivities.

Away from Cambridge and in KwaZulu-Natal, the distances from city to countryside are long and tropical. The drive is in two stages. The first is along the coastal towns, their empty holiday apartments awaiting the season, with the vegetable patches of market gardens shaded a little by lines of planted palm trees. The further from the city I get, the less formal the gardens become. The second stage of the journey takes me inland. The sea disappears in the rearview mirror, almost an hour and a half by car into a hinterland that, unfolding initially in lush green, becomes dry and then the victim of "scorched earth"—sugar fields burned to gather the harvest, the seemingly abandoned mud huts, churches and clinics baking in the sun, the children walking dangerously close to oncoming cars. I'm not worried; this is the way I wanted it to be. The area is in need of help, and the people dawdling under the shade of a tree outside a dusty general store appear to watch with resignation. Cars fly past with no intention but reaching the wealthier towns further inland as quickly as possible. I am in one such car, but I will stop because here is where my journey ends and the project begins.

I know the academic technology of my project must be hidden; high-flown terms like "quasi-experimental" design, pedagogy, contrast groups, variables, and differential exposure would all require reinterpretation or mediation. The context will need a simplified model that the teachers and children will understand. In my mind I imagine this to be the only accommodation necessary—time will reveal the foolishness of my assumption.

In the meantime, that same "do-good" energy that infused the design of this "quasi-experimental" project (intended to improve the communicative skills of young Black adolescents) drives my selection of the project schools. Even with the hypercomplexity of my design, attempting to control three variables (innovative materials, innovative teaching methods, innovative communicative strategies) over four groups, I don't stop to consider the subtleties; I'm rushing to the schools daily, eager to record, to collaborate, to "get done."

The teachers seem very happy and hopeful about the work. "Yes, we really want you to come to visit us—to work with our children and improve their language," said Mrs. Zondo. Later I learn that she is both a principal herself and the wife of the principal of the school that had originally assented to collaborate with me. I nod enthusiastically: "I've always wanted to work here. This is where the transformation of education is really needed." It sounds like I'm assuring her. Her husband, Alfred Zondo, the principal of Sibongile High, looks quizzically at me and then at his wife, who is wearing a Java print caftan and headwrap. Something is missing; there is a pause and I'm momentarily confused. Mrs. Zondo, looking at me warily, says, "I'd like you to work in my school as well." Without thinking it through, and only with the end point in mind, I smile broadly. I can't believe my luck! His school has only three groups of children in the grade I wish to work with—so I will need at least two schools in this area in order to compare the learning experience of four groups of children using the intervention materials. Any unease about Mrs. Zondo's wariness I brush aside for now. Her school is close to his; the catchment area is the same, and their being married means that access to a second school is no longer a source of anxiety. In the rush to get acquainted I overlook the possible problems this situation might pose. We visit her school, named Nkostintaba Secondary, perched atop hills that overlook a valley verdant with tropical vegetation, vines entangling trees, pumpkin flowers wilting in clumps between long grass; the clouds are low and heavy. The teachers stroll out to meet us; they seem shy and almost reluctant in the presence of Mrs. Zondo.

Months pass, but my energy does not flag. I watch the sea recede every week and I am at home. I'm in each school at least three times a week, working with teachers, talking, sitting in classrooms with nervous and excited children. When it rains children rush to greet me at the car. One will hold an umbrella above my head; another will carry my books. In time I realize that the school administered by Mrs. Zondo is far less organized than the other one managed by her husband. She is often ill and the teachers, who appear to efface themselves in her presence, disappear in her absence. Her illness, as it turns out, is as a consequence of her gift for mediation between people and their ancestors. In the Zulu language she is called a *sangoma:* in English, a traditional healer, or psychic. On the days on which she is absent, we understand that the spirits of the ancestors have conveyed messages to her. This process occasions illness and stress. And there are other, more disconcerting truths to learn. Toward the end of the quarter I find out that there is only one qualified teacher in the school; the rest are all former primary school teachers. I know that this kind of information, to be taken for granted in schools in England, has nevertheless to be determined from scratch in rural South Africa. If the project seeks to understand the effect of a teacher's preparedness on the pupils' learning, does it matter whether the teacher is not adequately qualified to teach beyond primary school? Is this a problem, and how will it affect the comparability of results and data obtained from both schools?

Another week. Mrs. Zondo is dressed today in a white caftan printed with large pineapples, sliced watermelon, and pink hibiscus that seem to radiate a heat of their own. "You see, when we started this school here, the Chief of this area wanted it somewhere else, down there in the valley in the bushes; but I had it built here," she explains. "He threatened us, but what could he do? The community needed a school so we moved here. All my teachers moved from that primary school and started this secondary school." At a loss I ask, "Surely the department would have sent qualified teachers?" She laughs, leans back from her desk, and smiles expansively; she shrugs her shoulders. "These Zulus are all the same. It's a kind of arrogance. They think that because you are foreign that you are a lesser human. I'm a Sotho woman and I would never have come to this place were it not for my husband." While she says this to me her sandals click-clack under the desk.

The sandals look Italian; long and elegant strips of leather arch and crisscross over her graceful feet. "This Chief is the only authority here; we don't see inspectors often, and who wants to teach in a place where the Chief is in conflict with the principal? This is my school; I built it with my hands." Click-clack, click-clack. She smiles. I smile too: "I wish I had known about this earlier." Mrs. Zondo shrugs her shoulders. "We're happy you are here. The children will learn more from you than from their teachers. Perhaps had you known these things you might not have wanted to work with us, and we would have been very unhappy about that." I'm sweating. Outside the sun wilts even the weeds, and the earth is dry where the footsteps of the children have etched pathways that cross each other at seemingly arbitrary points. Lizards scatter when I leave her office. I leave the school and walk along the corridor towards the car.

Some classrooms are full of children sharing pencils and paper. In others there is a scattering of six or ten, and the teachers fan themselves outside. The children's voices are like the murmuring of bees. The teachers', when you hear them, are staccato. Though the children are of mixed ability and seemingly equivalent to the children at Sibongile High, the teaching is evidently not of an equal standard. In one class the teacher gives up midway through the lesson and asks me to take over; she does not feel competent to teach my materials. I take up the lesson, leaving my observation book at the back of the classroom. The pupils and I get along very well; they seem more fascinated with me than with the language lesson at hand, but it's a useful way to get them to use and learn more words. If they learn well, I promise a "question-for-answer" session in the last ten minutes. Children love this.

"Are you married?"

"No; not yet. Where are your parents?"

"Not here, I have no father. My granny looks after me. My mother works in the town. When are you going back to England?"

"Not until December. What do you want to do with your life?"

"I want you to take me back to England with you. I can work in your garden. Will you take me?"

"No. You are worth much more than that. Why not become a teacher, a lawyer, a doctor?"

"We have no money. No one from this school goes away. We stay and work in the sugar fields. Have you seen snow?"

And so it goes on.

I had not noticed that the teacher left the classroom, and after the lesson I am not able to find her for the rest of the day. When I leave the school the heat is at its worst; flies and birds make for the shadows and everything seems to slow down. Even the little green snake, slithering across the road before my car, stops momentarily to look at me before easing its way into the grass on the other side. At home, lying beneath the rotating arms of the fan, I think about the data to be gathered from Mrs. Zondo's school. If I am to teach the children, as was the case throughout this past week, then the data will be compromised. My project at this school will be assessed on how well I was able to implement my own work. It's not research anymore; it's relief teaching.

The quarter comes to an end and it's time for a visit from my field supervisor, Valery Coton. We visit Mrs. Zondo's school first. The lesson, which the teacher has prepared, is on how to examine the functions of language in context—a discourse approach to speech as a function of human need. Val Coton and I arrive ready to observe, but the children are streaming out of classrooms, released too early for break. I wonder if I mistook the scheduled time. "What's going on?" I ask a teacher. She smiles at me. "Ma'am Zondo has released the pupils early today; they are going to practice for their traditional dance competition." I look at the children, now running with evident joy to the sports field—a patch of earth with short dry scrub emerging in tufts between the dust. Val and I stroll towards the staffroom. Mrs. Zondo is seated with her teachers in a circle on the floor. They are surrounded by yards of fabric. "Mrs. Zondo, this is my supervisor, Valery Coton. I told you about her on Monday and now she's come to observe a class today," I say. I sound calm, but I'm furious; the collar around my neck has grown tight. She looks at me and, waving the scissors in her hand, says with indifference, "She's not going to see anything today. The children must practice for the dance." Val reddens, smiles, and asks what the women are doing. Mrs. Zondo answers for them. "They are cutting out dresses from patterns for the dance." I show my supervisor around the school: empty desks, broken windows, dust, the male teachers sitting in the sun, regarding us with amusement. No class today, nor for the next two weeks.

My visits become as unwelcome as those of the inspectorate. The teachers, taking their cue from the principal, greet me with nonchalance; only the pupils seem genuinely happy when I'm there. I feel the dimensions of my entrapment, not as evident before today. Wish as I might, I cannot withdraw from the school for fear of offending Mrs. Zondo, who might then influence her husband. Half my sample is compromised and it is too late to start somewhere else. The alternatives are few. To keep her "sweet" and to avoid confrontation, I decide to simply work with what exists, not with what I want. So,

I become an enthusiastic photographer of the children's dances. We travel together to the regional competition and I'm given a seat with the local dignitaries. We're all enthralled with the dance, the traditional gospel, the Zulu choruses, and most of all, with the oral poetry. The children are engaged; on display, their bodies gleam with sweat and the hours of effort pay off. Nkosintaba Secondary walks away with most of the prizes, again. I'm learning to accommodate, to survive.

Another week. I am at the school and sheets of rain pour across the valley. Even though the research is now nothing more than a conceit, I continue to teach the children. Today another lesson is cancelled because too few children came to school. I look out over the valley; large globes of water pour from the edge of the corrugated roof and have washed away the soil close to the foundations. All that remains are pebbles and stones, rounded after seasons of rain. That explains the damp patches and cracks on this side of the wall, I think to myself. My eyes roam the edge of the veranda. Further along, in a puddle of water, is one of my textbooks, the crest of the university barely submerged, the print running in streams across the page. I cry into the rain.

Towards the end of the year Val and I visit the "better school" on another day and observe a lesson. The teacher, Mrs. Zulu, asks about the story. The children respond in chorus, half of one opinion and half of another. We can't understand anything. The story (*F-u-d-u-u-a!!* from Tlali 1989) is about the harassment of a young woman on a train and the complicity of men and women in "covering" for the perpetrator. During groupwork, the story engages attention, but the topic of sexual harassment in an African context—though relevant to all—has an effect best conveyed in pupils' own words. Samuel, a bright and vociferous young boy, says,

> Although it is talking about young ladies, that lady what she is talking about is connected to us, we are a man, because that problem happened in the train. . . . But it is also for us, the Black community. . . . It gives us some more knowledge to know about what is happening in this world where we are living.

His friend, Excellent, is determined to be recorded on the machine also:

> That thing that I don't like is that it tell us about how . . . how women is hurt in the train. It affect me. Because the womens . . . the womens is like . . . soft people. That is why I don't like to offend him . . . them."

I'm not sure what he means by soft people and ask, "Okay, so you say women are soft people. Could you tell me why this is not a good thing to hear about, or read about?" Excellent replies with confidence, "Yes. That is wrong to hurt their women."

At this point, Cynthia, a quiet but highly intelligent pupil, speaks up:

I did not like the story because it made us to be alert about people who did . . . do sexual harassment. Because *F-u-d-u-u-a!!* it did the sexual harassment . . . it was too open."

"Cynthia, what do you mean by 'too open'?" I ask. She replies, "It's like . . . it's like the story it does the harassment. It is too open for us."

Val and I leave the class at break time. Amid the noise of games a disturbed adolescent runs through the open gates. Unbelievably, he is naked and chasing the girls. Mrs. Zulu, chatting amiably to Val, sees him and within seconds bolts to the staffroom where she locks herself inside with the other female teachers. Val and I stand and are at a loss for words; we are at sea, exposed in an open quadrangle. He sees us and runs around us in circles. "Give me money, give me land; you White people stole my money, stealing my land." This must last no more than a minute, but it feels like forever. Then the male teachers and boys group themselves around the naked young man, murmuring. The girls, excluded, taunt them from a distance. Moving en masse to the school gates, the boys make the young man resume his clothes. Propriety forbids women to deal directly with such matters.

Reading the signs, I connect the classroom discussion (open and aware of issues) and the story and playground action (hidden and taboo). Val and I drive back to the city in hot silence. Halfway home she turns to me, light reflecting off her one-way lenses. "That was a great day, Robert; you're doing really well with their English." I nod. What happened this morning has left me floundering. It is clear to me that the distance between awareness and belief is great. This ten-month intervention, attempting to increase the acquisition of English, and simultaneously to encourage awareness and dialogue, has dimensions and implications I had not anticipated. We drive on, and I deliver Val to the university. In the English Department common room I tell this story to my friend Margaret. "You really must write this up, Robert. People will be so interested in what you're finding." But I can't. Not yet. Like a wound, it must close before I carry on. Sometime during the next day I see Val in her office; she's sipping tea and the air conditioning flutters above us. The tropical landscape and burned land around my schools is another place, far from here. We discuss the project in a desultory fashion and then Val looks at me directly. "It was great being with you in the schools yesterday; you're making a difference . . . besides . . . that was a fine figure of a man." In the ensuing silence I look away and remember the landscape, its lush vegetation, burned remains, and tropical decay. The plans made in Trumpington Street adjust; I read the signs, learning more from this process than the design could ever yield.

The project ends with final examinations that both schools write. I remember Dunoit's admonition and in the last days of November my mind is already uncomfortably back in England. With fatigue and no will, I prepare two reports for the schools. In the first one I write about the children and the dedication of the teachers. I describe their results based upon the data, recording increasing levels of competence and evident progress as a result of this writing project. I do not touch on the incident in the classroom or on the playground—simply put, I have not yet found a way of telling that story, of constructing its laden and ambiguous meanings. Though the project was intended to explore such meanings, I realize that the methodology, with its emphasis on "progress and achievement," did not allow me to deal with anomalies effectively. I had no framework to make sense of the rich veins of experience and learning yielded in the children's responses. Oddly, I feel again that same sensation of standing vulnerable in the quadrangle, alone and unable to respond to what is going on around me.

For the second school I write a different report, and this one, because the data are so irregularly described and generally unavailable, is more of a story. I tell of how the school started, its problems and challenges; I speculate on the reasons why the pupils performed so weakly in the project. Here, too, I cannot write about the principal, the teachers, and the lack of interest displayed by both in the academic education of the children. This story has few ambiguities in my mind because, unlike the classroom and playground incidents at the first school, I have learned my lessons on-site and as I went along. Of the second school I can construct only narratives of its failure; the data reveals as much by its very incohesiveness.

I return to Cambridge in the following January, during another winter. As before, the moisture condenses on everything, and when it rains and the wind blows, it is difficult to get up in the morning, difficult to know where to start the writing-up. My head pounds and the heated air is overwhelmingly dry. But I think to myself, with some bitterness, "At least I no longer fry in my own fat as I did in the tropics." Listening to the recordings of the children's voices on the machine makes me grieve; I wonder what will become of Samuel, and it's difficult to think of the future for Cynthia. Their lives and futures seem so limited. In that context, with its crushing limitations, their talent and spirit are cast into relief and I fear for them. Perhaps I have left the children and schools to pick up the pieces; perhaps they'll be fine without me. I'll never know, and as the rain trickles down the windows and I catch the glimmer of reflected droplets off the cyprus trees, I sense my limitations. Anxious that I might well be the kind of researcher who turns away from his subject without doing it justice, I sit down and begin rewriting—but without confidence. Yvonne tells me that the data from the second school cannot be used and, barring what I have written here for this book, I know that I can never return to it, in writing or even in memory.

Questions for Reflection

When did Balfour stop being an "objective" researcher and become a participant in the daily life of the institution he was studying? Why?

What were some of the "lessons learned" from Balfour's experience with the second, less well-organized school that would never have been learned without his experiences there?

Why would these lessons probably not have been learned without departing from the original quasi-experimental design?

Do you agree that Balfour should drop the data from the second, dysfunctional school from his analysis? Why or why not?

Note

1. All names used in this text are pseudonyms in order to protect the identity of the subjects.

Reference

Tlali, M. 1989. *Footprints in the Quag.* Cape Town: David Philip.

Part III
PROBLEM-FOCUSED RESEARCH

COMMUNICATION RESEARCH IS OFTEN divided into concentric levels of analysis—researchers are often trained as specialists in interpersonal, organizational, or mass communication and then tend to choose research topics at the appropriate level. However, important research questions are often generated by a focus on an identified problem or issue rather than the level or type of communication most directly involved. This section presents four such studies, which ask questions about peer pressure among young people, health advertisement effects, communication in a hospice care setting, and the dynamics of domestic violence. As it turns out, three of these four studies are primarily concerned with interpersonal communication dynamics, but it is their focus on real-world problems that unites them.

In each case, the issue being addressed is clearly driving the choice of research method. The goal is not so much to understand a particular type of communication in the abstract as it is to understand how that type of communication influences people's everyday lives in both negative and positive ways. Possibly as a result, the studies in this section are especially diverse in their choice of methods, which represent the full range of designs from qualitative to quantitative. Each author in this section also devotes particular attention to the choice of design, and these choices (explicitly driven by the shared objective of answering a real-world question) are in each case unique.

Timothy Meyer and Thomas Donohue, for example, provide us with a glimpse of an entire program of research centered on the question of peer influence on both negative or antisocial and positive or "prosocial" behavior. As they developed their research program in this area, they have experimented with a variety of quantitative and qualitative methods, and they provide us with an extended discussion of how they found each of these of value to answering their research question—as well as their eventual method of choice, the depth interview. Logistical as well as theoretical considerations influenced this choice. It is not easy to observe the private behavior of young people in natural settings in order to discern how they might influence one another over time. While retrospective self-reports of this influence might have their own limitations, Meyer and Donohue believe they yield the most useful information.

Brian Southwell wanted to understand the influence of health-related public service advertisements on audience members. Because he felt that both characteristics of audiences and characteristics of the ads themselves were needed for a meaningful understanding of this issue, he needed to develop a specialized design that could accommodate these different types of data into a single analysis. While his research would probably be classified as a "mass communication" study (because of its focus on advertising effects), it has much in common with the interpersonal communication studies that are also included in this section. Southwell's thinking is strongly centered on the engagement of the individual audience member with the ad material. Yet he needed to take the "macro" level characteristics of the mass communication material into account as well.

Finally, both Elissa Foster (studying communication between volunteers and patients in a hospice setting) and Loreen Olson (studying the communication dynamics of violent relationships) introduce us to a method called "autoethnography" in which the researcher's direct experience is used as a window on the problem being studied. Leaving the relative emotional and epistemological safety of the researcher's role as "objective observer" raises a number of nontrivial questions about the nature of the conclusions. Traditional social scientists, even those using ethnographic methods, might argue that the subjective experience of a single person—even one trained in research methods and fully aware of the issues involved in using one's own experience as a research tool—is not a good way to illuminate the shared experiences of others. They might argue that this approach is too dependent on the researcher's own circumstances, perceptions, personality, and values, and that it too completely sacrifices the "distance" in perspective gained by the use of more conventional approaches. Clearly, these two researchers disagree, and their reports in this section make compelling cases for their nontraditional technique.

8
Peer Influence and Prosocial Behavior: Ten Years of Study

Timothy P. Meyer and Thomas R. Donohue

Here authors Timothy Meyer and Thomas Donohue describe their pursuit of the design of research defined not so much by an interest in a specific group, organization, or setting, but by a focus on a specific social issue, that of peer influence among young people. Of course, peer influence has probably always taken place, but in today's world of gang violence, teen use of both legal and illegal drugs, and concern over early sexual activity, understanding peer influence has taken on new significance. Further, we live in a society in which neighborhoods seem weaker than in the past, the population is more mobile, and children routinely spend more time with people their own age than with family members. These factors highlight the significance of understanding peer influence.

Sociologists have long noted that what constitutes a "social problem" is often a matter of perceptions and definitions. Behavior that is seen as problematic in one culture or community might be acceptable in another; norms characteristic of one time period may be quite different from norms at another. To complicate things further, young people in many of today's societies may be expected to rebel against authority in some areas.

Regardless of variations in societal standards, however, actively harmful behaviors (the use of drugs that may be addictive, harmful violence, sexual behavior that spreads disease) are widely accepted as elements that society has some responsibility to curtail, especially among young people. Many factors probably contribute to young people's tendency to adopt behavior disapproved of by adults, of which peer influence is just one.

But rather than looking only at the negatives, Meyer and Donohue also argue in this chapter that peer influence is crucial to understanding how young people adopt positive or "prosocial" behaviors as well as negative, antisocial ones. These dynamics are too often overlooked by those seeking to explain only "bad" behaviors. Yet similar factors are at work in both cases; understanding one kind of peer influence helps us understand the other. And recognizing the value of "prosocial" peer influences helps remind us that youth culture is not all bad, as well.

In this context, the authors of this chapter discuss the usefulness to their research goals of a wide variety of methods introduced in earlier chapters, including experiments, surveys, depth interviews, and observation—simple, participant, and "unobtrusive." Throughout, their focus is on answering a single specific research question—what is the nature of peer influence among young people?

THIS CHAPTER DESCRIBES OUR ONGOING, evolving examination over the last ten years of the various dimensions of peer influence on the beliefs, attitudes, and behaviors of adolescents and young adults. We have more than three decades of experience researching the impact of media on audiences defined by characteristics such as age, cognitive developmental state, gender, socioeconomic status (individual or family), or urban versus suburban or rural settings. Media content we have studied has varied from entertainment to information to advertising. Theories and methodologies we have used also represent a wide range of perspectives with varying assumptions, strengths, and limitations (as is inherent in all theories and methods).

We have used traditional social science research methods, including laboratory and field experiments, surveys and questionnaires, content analyses, focus groups, and ethnographic research methods (such as depth interviews and participant observation). We have always been strong advocates of utilizing a rich variety of perspectives and methods to guide the development of new knowledge. Our research into the influence of peers on the beliefs, attitudes, and behaviors of adolescents and young adults clearly reflects our openness to different theories, perspectives, and methodologies.

The Early Context

As the visual media of film and television diffused throughout the United States (and, eventually, most of the world), violent content quickly became a popular ingredient of the stories told. Even news reports frequently incorporated violent themes. It was not surprising, therefore, that a focal point for research would be the impact of violent content from these media on viewers' behavior, specifically the links, if any, between violent content and violent behavior of viewers. Early research looked for a cause-and-effect relationship in which those exposed to the greatest amounts of media violence would be most likely to behave violently themselves as a direct consequence. Laboratory experiments simulating aggressive behavior were used to study viewer responses to different types of media violence (Bandura et al. 1963; Berkowitz and Rawlings 1963; Meyer 1972). A few field experiments were also implemented (Feshbach and Singer 1971). Other studies established correlation-based evidence linking the amount of exposure to media violence with viewer reports of violent behaviors (for a review see Comstock et al. 1978).

As research on violence effects evolved, it rapidly became clear that many different factors, media and nonmedia, played some kind of role in accounting for violent behavior in society. On the nonmedia side, individual personality traits were studied, along with important social context factors that described the degree to which real-life violence was present in viewers' environments and how those factors would make some viewers more or less predisposed to violent behavior. Since violence was a part of human behavior predating any of the mass media, it seemed reasonable to understand media violence in this broader context.

Violent behavior has always been influenced by interpersonal and other environmental factors. One of these factors is peer influence. Here the focus has been on group members' pressuring an individual to commit a violent act that would not have been committed by the individual acting alone. Violent behavior in group settings has also been attributed to a phenomenon commonly referred to as "contagious aggression," a process involving the violent acts of one group member triggering the violent acts of other members, sometimes overriding the misgivings of some (Berkowitz 1962). Studies of gang behavior have long been a focus of research that has documented how group norms and expectations help determine the violent behavior of group members.

Alongside an ever-growing body of media violence effects research, other researchers were motivated to look at the "prosocial" potential of film and television, that is, the capacity of these stories to have a positive influence on viewers. Just as media could affect antisocial behavior, so could they also have prosocial effects (Meyer 1978; Meyer and Hexamer 1985). In the overall context of prosocial behavior, many nonmedia factors were again identified as being crucial to the process that influences the display of prosocial acts. One of these was peer influence. Group membership could influence an individual's behavior in positive, beneficial ways, including the avoidance of antisocial behaviors that might have occurred for individuals acting alone apart from the group.

> **Box 8.1: Disentangling Variables**
>
> Creating a useful, practical, working definition of an abstract concept such as "peer influence" and then figuring out exactly how to measure such a variable is among the most difficult challenges a researcher faces. This process by which a concept or idea is translated into a measurable variable that can be incorporated into a research design is called "operationalization."
>
> Very often, the more abstract the concept, the more difficult the operationalization. For example, the concept of "intelligence" has been notoriously difficult to operationalize, to the point some researchers have questioned its usefulness as a concept. Intelligence is usually operationalized as how someone answers questions on an intelligence test, but whether this is meaningful depends on the test. Some argue that no paper-and-pencil test accurately reflects what we really mean by human intelligence.
>
> Variable definitions and their measurement are never perfect, but it is important to be as clear about this as possible. As Meyer and Donohue point out, some researchers in their area have used simple peer presence as an indicator of peer influence. While it is obviously true that the presence of peers is a generally necessary precondition to their having an influence, and it is also true that researchers cannot easily measure such an abstract item as "influence," these are not the same thing.
>
> Why does this matter? Confusing the two variables could divert researchers from recognizing the existence of other important factors that might determine (in this case) peer effects. We can think of this as a measurement issue—peer presence is not a very good measure of peer influence; direct evidence of some kind of communicative behavior would be better, evidence of the behavior's effects even better. We can also think of it as a matter of mixing up or "confounding" two or more variables that should have been treated separately.
>
> The term "confounding variable" is used to describe a situation in which a researcher thinks one factor is responsible for an observed effect, when actually another associated factor that was not taken into account (or controlled) was the actual cause. Often the two factors are closely intertwined conceptually, as is somewhat the case with presence versus influence.

Our Research on Peer Influence

While our research into peer influence was spurred by our interest in how both media and nonmedia factors functioned to affect behavior, notably among adolescents, we quickly realized the underlying complexity inherent in studying peer influence. Challenges we faced included defining the peer factor, measuring peer influence, and identifying key behaviors that might be influenced by peers.

Defining the Peer Factor

Peer presence and peer influence are not the same thing. Young people frequently find themselves in the presence of peers, such as the kids with whom a child walks or rides the bus to school. The child may or may not consider one or more of these "friends." Similarly, at school, at the locker, or in various classes, there are peers all around. Kids see what others are doing, they talk about their own and others' behavior, and they sometimes discuss their feelings and concerns with some of their peers. The mere *presence* of peers, however, does not necessarily imply peer pressure. The research literature, along with common sense and personal experience, tells us that not all peers are alike (Urberg et al. 2003). Some peers are generally more influential than others. Some peers are more influential at certain times or in certain circumstances. Moreover, some kids are more easily swayed by peers than others.

The selection of peer group members matters a great deal. Research has asked whether kids select peers who are like them or whether peer group members become alike due to group influences (Ennett and Bauman 1993, 1994; Fisher and Bauman 1988). Results have supported both selection processes. Sometimes, the proximity of peers can be misleading when evaluating their influence. A child gets to know some or maybe all of those seen day in and day out; some may be only acquaintances; others might become friends.

Other research has looked at groups admired by kids who are attracted based on members' appearance, success, popularity, "air of mystery," or other markers of being "cool" (Andrews et al. 2002; Zollo 1999). Such peer groups are generally regarded as having a lot of influence over new members because the kids who aspire to membership are usually quite willing to act, talk, and dress like the other group members.

Peer influence, when operating, can also be direct or indirect. Direct influence involves the overt urging of a member(s) to get a nonconforming member to align his or her behaviors with the rest of or at least the majority of the group (Fitzgerald and White 2003). As one teenager remarked in our research, "It was, like, do like we do or get lost." Or, as another teen put it, "If you didn't show up at the weekend parties and drink, they just stopped telling you where the next party was gonna be. You know, 'Put up or shut up,' I guess." Indirect influence is more subtle and usually much more difficult to measure. It occurs as a result of time spent with a peer group where children engage in routine social comparisons between themselves and others. Shoes, clothes, hair color and style, or other visible signs of consumption or possession may all come into play here.

Some friends might talk about having tried smoking or drinking and may continue to share their experiences with the larger group. While there may be no overt influence attempts, the familiarity factor evolving over time may indirectly affect group members who have not experimented with smoking or drinking. Of these two types, direct peer influence is clearly the most powerful and is more easily measured than indirect peer influence, but both are part of the process. Sometimes researchers make a mistake when they claim to measure peer influence and actually measure mere peer presence.

The research literature is very clear that when peer pressure is present and accounted for, the influence of peers in the initiation of young people's smoking leaps out as one of the most crucial determinants of underage smoking (Musher-Eizenman et al. 2003; Smith and Stutts 1999; Wang et al. 1997). The same is true for the perceived influence of parents and admired older siblings. Interpersonal interactions of a certain nature with real people explain why young people engage in a broad range of behaviors. And the same crucial difference between peer presence and peer influence/pressure would apply to many different behaviors where peers are a key factor.

Some of these behaviors would include underage drinking, gambling, illegal substance use, sex, or legal behaviors involving body piercings, tattoos, clothing, shoes, hairstyle, hair color, jewelry, and so on (Bahr et al. 1995; Bearden and Etzel 1982; Hardy et al. 2002; Mangelburg et al. 1997; Stice et al. 2003; Yin 2003/2004). In many instances, however, children are resistant even to intense pressure in certain areas while being apparent "pushovers" in other areas.

A second major component involved in our research has centered on drawing important distinctions among different kinds or types of peers. Some types of peers will be much more influential than others. Differences in peer influence occur between others identified as a "best friend" versus a member of a "friendship group" (Meyer et al. 2001, 2004). "Best friend" implies more intimacy and sharing of experiences and feelings than would occur with friendship group members. Those identified as members of the friendship group may be closer or more distant from the group's other members, with their ability to influence others varying accordingly (Maxwell 2002). In this sense, all members of a given peer group are not alike. Some tend to be leaders, others followers; some occasionally deviate from established group norms, while some remain in the group but appear aloof or isolated.

A third major dimension of research into peer influence involves the presence or absence of multiple peer groups. While most children have a primary peer group consisting of a small number of best or close friends and other friendship group members, a considerable number of children have multiple peer groups where membership is determined via different means (Sim and Koh 2003). Children may become members of peer groups due to participation in school or church-related activities (such as a music group like band or choir). Those who are active in extracurricular activities often participate in two or more of them on a regular basis. Peer relationships formed here are in addition to those formed on the basis of coincidence or proximity (on the school bus or in the neighborhood).

How to Measure Peer Influence

Peer influence has been measured in many different ways in several different academic disciplines over the past sixty years, using a diverse array of methods. Traditional social science procedures have long been employed to tap into the structure of peer networks, and to study how peer influence varies in different settings and for different behaviors and how relationships among peers manifest themselves in the short and long term (Mochis 1987).

Experimental methods have been used to show how the presence of peer or group norms influences the behavior of "deviant" group members, getting those who are "not on board" to go along with the group. This pressure to conform yields behaviors that would not likely have occurred if the individual were acting alone and were reluctant to act in a certain way. Experiments have the capacity to allow for cause-and-effect arguments where specific conditions of peer influence can be stated and formally operationalized. Predictions can be confirmed and explanations supported by the experimental findings.

However, many experiments suffer a lack of generalizability to what happens in the real world outside the laboratory setting (for discussion see Anderson and Meyer 1988). Experiments rarely involve actual overt behavior that is called for from participants (a response to a question on a piece of paper may or may not correspond to how that same individual would act if confronted with a similar real-life situation). Experiments control for unwanted or extraneous factors that could influence how participants respond, but in so doing they may eliminate some important factors that can and do affect the behavior in question when it might surface in a real situation. For these and other reasons, social scientists have continued to look for other research methods that overcome some of these limitations.

Using nonexperimental methods such as surveys, researchers look for factors that are related to real-world behaviors and try to measure the presence and strength of these relationships. They further look at how combinations of factors might interact to predict or account for certain behaviors. Peer presence or peer influence (direct or indirect) are among the factors that researchers measure, along with others likely to affect behavior. In our research, for example, in one study we included factors such as personal preferences, celebrity endorsers, same-sex best friends, opposite-sex best friends, advertising, and price in trying to identify those that were most important to teenagers in their purchases of brand name athletic shoes or clothing. Questionnaires elicited responses linked to actual teen behaviors in a variety of different areas, most of them related to product purchases (Meyer et al. 2001). Other researchers have focused on factors similar to those we used to see how they are related to other behaviors. Underage drinking, gambling, smoking, sex, and drug use are among the behaviors that have been studied over the past seventy-five years (Michell and West 1996; Wang et al. 1997). Through the accurate identification of the factors that affect these behaviors, researchers hope to develop policies or programs that reduce their occurrence.

When a nonexperimental method is used, the resulting evidence can suggest the existence of a cause-and-effect relationship, although the evidence does not satisfy the conditions considered necessary for a causal argument (Anderson and Meyer 1988). Only rigorous experimental procedures are capable of generating actual cause-and-effect evidence, but survey research has proven useful in documenting many relationships that can then be tested in experimental procedures. Sometimes what appears to be an almost certain candidate for a cause-and-effect relationship turns out to be something of a completely different nature. For example, in some countries that banned tobacco advertising, smoking rates actually went up after the ban was in effect, defying the suspected relationship between tobacco advertising and getting young people to start smoking (Lancaster and Lancaster 2003; Luik 1994).

While traditional survey research has been most widely used in investigating peer influence, other procedures also provide findings that have increased our understanding of how peers work to influence the behaviors of others, including procedures generally referred to as qualitative. While some of these methods do involve measuring and counting, their focus is different from that of traditional quantitative social science procedures. They are mostly descriptive in nature, involving studies of process (e.g., how peer influence actually takes place over time in a real-life group) or providing examples in rich detail that document how peer influence operates amid many other influence sources (Lindlof and Meyer 1987). We have made use of participant observation, focus groups, and individual interviews in our research to more fully inform us about how peer influence manifests itself in different ways in different circumstances and for different types of people.

Participant observation involves the use of a trained individual who immerses him- or herself into a real-world group setting, usually where his or her role is known in advance to the other group members (Lindlof and Meyer 1987; Anderson and Meyer 1988). The researcher is there to observe, to document, and generally to get a realistic feel for what group members go through over a period of time. Sometimes, the researcher is an outsider who does not fully participate like the other group members. Researchers may also create an unobtrusive way to document group activities without the researcher being physically present. This can mean setting up a videotape system where cameras record picture and sound in real time and the tapes become the data source.

Adding a new member to the group may change the behaviors of one or more group members from the responses that would have occurred without the newcomer present. How well the new member learns the membership role and adjusts to the group will also have an impact on what is observed and learned. Researchers using participant observation, commonly referred to as "ethnographers," are often committed to carrying this out over a long period of time, sometimes over a period of months or years. The extended time frame is essential to allow for the researchers to become acclimated to the members and how they operate, especially vis-à-vis one another, and for group members to adjust to their presence. Ethnographers expect that as time goes on, any changes in group behavior initially brought on by their presence will eventually disappear (Anderson and Meyer 1988). Researchers also take steps to account for such changes through individual interviews with members that include questions about whether or not behaviors have changed since the observer appeared.

On the surface, using a videotape system seems to offer a perfect solution to drawbacks posed by the presence of a researcher (either as a direct participant or simple observer). If the cameras and microphones are well placed and mostly hidden from participants (even though all members know about and have agreed to the taping process in advance), members quickly adjust to the awareness of the taping and go on about their business in a mostly normal fashion. Again, interviews can be effective in identifying any member's behavior that seems different from what was displayed before the taping system was introduced into the group setting. But the researcher still has to make sense out of what is being said and done when the group is functioning. While interviews can help to clarify some of these things, the researcher's "feel" for what is actually going on in the group is lost (Lindlof and Meyer 1987). There is no real substitute for the opportunity to observe members face to face or for the chance to do what the group does when they do it.

Depth interviews offer another research technique that can provide a wealth of richly detailed information on the role of peers in influencing behavior (Anderson and Meyer 1988; Meyer 1994; Meyer et al. 2004). A researcher talks to individuals in an interview setting, often in sessions that extend over a period of time. Certain key questions are planned in advance but many others arise from the answers given. The person being interviewed has time to think about answers and explain them.

The ability of the researcher to get the participant to feel comfortable answering the questions and to be completely candid in responding is crucial to providing reliable, useful information. The rapport between the researcher and the interviewee must be one of trust, warmth, and confidentiality. Such rapport is usually established over a period of time in which the researcher gets to know the interview subject quite well. As always, some researchers are better at this than others and can establish rapport much faster.

We have found individual depth interviews to be the most valuable qualitative procedure in learning about how peer influence operates (Meyer et al. 2004). While we do use other qualitative techniques, individual interviews provide a respondent context where individuals are very comfortable talking about how they have dealt with (or continue to deal with) their peers in many different contexts over the years. While participant observation has its merits, it is limited for studying peer influence because it only occasionally occurs in the same fixed setting (such as the basement of someone's house or a park). However, individual interviews can get kids to talk about these different contexts and how they might affect the degree to which peers are influential.

Focus groups are a commonly used technique in examining peer influence in settings where behavior is in question (Bergin, Talley, and Hamer 2003; Ioannou 2003; Michell and West 1996). A focus group usually consists of eight to twelve participants who have been recruited for the study, a moderator who will pose questions and guide the group's discussion over the one- to two-hour session, and a list of predetermined objectives that the focus group is expected to address. Generally, researchers want to elicit responses from certain individuals in their own words, often spontaneously. For some questions, all participants are expected to give an individual answer. For others, one or more participants who respond may suffice.

The upside of focus groups is at the same time the downside. Individuals may respond differently in the group setting than they would when acting alone. The good news is that a comment from another participant might trigger an enlightening response that would not have occurred to that person when questioned outside the group setting. The bad news is that another participant may "put words in others' mouths" that would not otherwise have been spoken. The group effect may thus elicit real or fictional responses. Researchers may have no clear way to tell the difference.

Focus groups are often done to assist researchers in constructing a survey questionnaire that will be administered to a much larger sample of respondents, sometimes selected by a random sampling procedure. But focus group members are not selected at random. Many who are contacted to participate decline. Those who do agree may thus differ in many important ways from those who refused. Participant responses, while useful for some purposes, would not be representative of any larger group or population.

We have found focus groups to be a useful tool for our research, in part because we are well aware of their inherent limitations. We use focus groups in conjunction with other qualitative (and quantitative) procedures to take advantage of the focus group setting's capacity to generate responses that might not ordinarily come to mind when questioning people in individual interviews. We have used some of these group responses to frame survey questions and/or to ask questions in individual depth interviews.

Which Behaviors to Measure?

While peer influence has been a topic of interest to researchers and to society for many decades, our interest in peers stemmed from our early research into the factors affecting antisocial behavior. We then looked at a variety of other behaviors that were and are affected by peers. We studied the comparative influence of peers, best friends, friendship group members, siblings, and other interpersonal factors as compared to those factors more clearly under the control of marketers, including price, advertising, promotions, celebrity endorsements, and so on (Meyer et al. 2001, 2004).

We also were intrigued with the influence of peers on behaviors that were not linked to marketing contexts. One of these was the consumption of alcohol by those not of legal drinking age. Our concern was not with which brands of beer or distilled spirits were consumed; rather, we focused on how peers and other interpersonal factors might function for teens when it came down to the decision of underage kids to start drinking alcohol as compared to the purchase of certain styles of clothes. While we found some similarities in terms of how important peers are in these two different types of behaviors, some differences did emerge.

One key difference between drinking decisions and brand name athletic shoe purchases, for example, was the role of advertising versus that of peers. For shoes, advertising was perceived to be a significantly more influential factor than it was for the decision to start drinking. Alcohol consumption represented a much more important decision to most teens we studied. Teens generally regarded the decision of whether to buy athletic shoes (versus other types or styles of footwear) as "no big deal." The specific brand purchased, however, was very important. Teens told us over and over again (via questionnaire responses and in focus groups and depth interviews) that "you had to have _____ [brand]. Nothing else was gonna make it."

When it came to drinking, however, there were other things to consider that made advertising essentially irrelevant. In this regard, what parents would think and the potential ramifications of being caught had to be weighed against the need to "be cool" in the eyes of their friends and friendship group.

Often weighing in heavily was appearing "cool" or mature to the opposite sex. As one teen put it, "I figured if she thought I was an experienced drinker, she'd want to hang out with me. Besides, I wanted to get in on the fun." Still, the decision was not easily made for many of the teens in our research.

In the context of studying factors that teens identified as being influential in their decisions to drink, smoke, or gamble, we began to see an often forgotten role for peer influence that was positive, not negative (Jacobs et al. 2004; Powell 1993). Some teens mentioned in passing about how a best friend kept them from smoking or drinking, even to the point where they are convinced to this day that without the persistence of a friend, they would have started drinking or smoking (or done so at an earlier age). This led us directly to the area of prosocial behavior and how peers operated as a highly influential factor. Here we saw two types of prosocial influence: (1) peer encouragement of positive behaviors such as participating in a constructive extracurricular activity (such as music, drama, or athletics), helping to raise money for a cause, joining a cleanup project, or helping out senior citizens; and (2) peer discouragement of negative or antisocial behaviors such as smoking, drinking, gambling, using illegal drugs, or having sex.

We found the research literature filled with studies on how peers who smoked encouraged nonsmokers to start smoking. References to peers discouraging kids from smoking were few and far between. Interestingly, despite this, programs to prevent youth smoking have frequently included components that fostered antismoking or antidrinking activities to reinforce abstinence or for nonsmokers or nondrinkers to encourage their smoking or drinking friends to quit. Our research has revealed many interesting examples of peer encouragement of prosocial behaviors, such as the following:

> The tennis and band people could be really, really fun and still had goals and knew what they wanted from their lives. Like me. The band and tennis people all pretty much wanted to go to college and try their hand and making something more outta the hand they were dealt. They always had a 'bigger world' perspective, which is something I had and discovered that with them.

> I played football . . . ain't very good, but I gave it a shot. I went out for football because all my friends said they were, too. We helped each other eat good stuff and work out and keep up our grades so we could stay on the team and do good.

> If I didn't have the same friends as I did in high school, I probably would have never had the grades to go to college. They all studied a lot and we were in the same classes so we studied together for tests and stuff. And, when they joined activities at school, I did, too. You know, it, like, seemed like fun. And some of it was fun.

Examples of peers deterring negative behaviors include these:

> Well, the one or two times I did go out . . . if my friends would see me with a smoke in my hand or a drink they would physically take the beer away and knock the smoke outta my mouth. There weren't many words exchanged. They knew I knew where they stood on the whole "being bad" thing.

> I'd say in high school, probably 75 percent of all my decisions were based on what my friends would think. Drinking and smoking were not accepted by my friends. I tried both, but I just didn't want to have to deal with them if they found out.

> We helped each other stay outta trouble, you know, like avoiding drinking parties 'cuz if you got caught, you were off the team. I never said it out loud, but when I'd hear about kids getting nailed for underage drinking or driving after drinking at a party, I was so glad that my teammates stayed together in not goin' to stuff like that. I dunno, it probably saved me from lots a trouble.

Current Research

We continue to locate and document the different ways in which peers have a positive social influence on individual behavior. We are currently doing research on how teens connect with peers via the Internet and how the new "cyber networks" function, both independently of conventional face-to-face peer groups and with them. We have a particular interest in the effects of interactions with peers not only from other U.S. communities, but from other countries as well.

While the Internet as a source of contact and interactions still presents some substantial risks, especially for unsuspecting young people, kids nonetheless are using it with greater and greater frequency as an interactive communications medium. They search for and make use of Internet information sources. More and more are shopping on the Internet. But it is the "connection" with other kids, their peers, that has sparked a tremendous amount of interest. The capacity to remain anonymous to others while sharing information is an appealing attribute of the Internet as a means of interactive communication for young people.

In our future work, we anticipate using the full range of research methodologies and tools described in this chapter. We remain convinced that researchers should avail themselves of any and all tools that provide insights— confirming some, modifying others, and adding new ones.

Questions for Reflection

Do you agree with the authors that depth interviews are the best qualitative method to pursue the answers to peer influence questions? What are some of the advantages and disadvantages of relying on interviews for this purpose?

Will young people be able to give accurate and candid answers to questions about what has influenced them? How might triangulation (the use of multiple research methods) help overcome this limitation?

Meyer and Donohue note that ethically, research participants must agree to unobtrusive observation. Exactly what changes will this introduce in the behavior of these individuals?

Could anonymous participant observation—joining a group for the purpose of studying group members' behavior without identifying oneself as a researcher—ever be ethically justified, in your opinion?

What other kinds of behaviors (prosocial or antisocial) not specifically mentioned by these authors might also be influenced by young people's communication with their peers? Your own experiences growing up might be helpful in thinking this question through.

References

Anderson, J., and T. Meyer. 1988. *Mediated Communication: A Social Action Perspective.* Beverly Hills, CA: Sage.
Andrews, J., E. Tildesley, H. Hops, and F. Li. 2002. "The Influence of Peers on Young Adult Substance Abuse." *Health Psychology* 21: 349–57.
Bahr, S., A. Marcos, and S. Maughan. 1995. "Family, Educational and Peer Influences on the Alcohol Use of Female and Male Adolescents." *Journal of Studies on Alcohol* 56: 457–69.
Bandura, A., D. Ross, and S. Ross. 1963 "Imitation of Film-mediated Aggressive Models." *Journal of Abnormal and Social Psychology* 66: 3–11.
Bearden, W., and M. Etzel. 1982. "Reference Group Influences on Product and Brand Purchase Decisions. *Journal of Consumer Research* 9: 183–94.
Bergin, C., S. Talley, and L. Hamer. 2003. "Prosocial Behaviours of Young Adolescents: A Focus Group Study." *Journal of Adolescence* 26: 13–32.
Berkowitz, L. 1962. *Aggression: A Social Learning Analysis.* New York: McGraw-Hill.
Berkowitz, L., and E. Rawlings. 1963. "Effects of Film Violence on Inhibitions against Subsequent Aggression." *Journal of Abnormal and Social Psychology* 66: 405–12.
Comstock, G., S. Chaffee, N. Katzman, M. McCombs, and D. Roberts. 1978. *Television and Human Behavior.* New York: Columbia University Press.

Ennett, S., and K. Bauman. 1993. "Peer Group Structure and Adolescent Cigarette Smoking: A Social Network Analysis." *Journal of Health and Social Behavior* 34: 226–36.

Ennett, S., and K. Bauman. 1994. "The Contribution of Influence and Selection to Adolescent Peer Group Homogeneity: The Case of Adolescent Smoking." *Journal of Personality and Social Psychology* 67: 653–63.

Feshbach, S., and J. Singer. 1971. *Television and Aggression.* San Francisco, CA: Jossey-Bass.

Fisher, L., and K. Bauman. 1988. "Influence and Selection in the Friend-Adolescent Relationship: Findings from Studies of Adolescent Smoking and Drinking. *Journal of Applied Social Psychology* 18: 289–314.

Fitzgerald, D., and K. White. 2003. "Linking Children's Social Worlds: Perspective-taking in Parent-child and Peer Contexts." *Social Behavior and Personality* 31: 509–22.

Hardy, C., W. Bukowski, and L. Sippola. 2002. "Stability and Change in Peer Relationships during the Transition to Middle-Level School." *Journal of Early Adolescence* 22: 117–42.

Ioannou, S. 2003. "Young People's Accounts of Smoking, Exercising, Eating and Drinking Alcohol: Being Cool or Being Unhealthy?" *Critical Public Health* 13: 357–71.

Jacobs, J., M. Vernon, and J. Eccles. 2004 "Relations between Social Self-perceptions, Time Use, and Prosocial or Problem Behaviors during Adolescence." *Journal of Adolescent Research* 19: 45–62.

Lancaster, K., and A. Lancaster. 2003. "The Economics of Tobacco Advertising: Spending, Demand, and the Effects of Bans." *International Journal of Advertising* 22: 41–65.

Lindlof, T., and T. Meyer. 1987. "Mediated Communication as Ways of Seeing, Acting, and Constructing Culture: The Tools and Foundations of Qualitative Research." Pp. 3–24 in *Natural Audiences: Qualitative Research of Media Uses and Effects*, ed. T. Lindlof. Norwood, NJ: Ablex.

Luik, J. 1994. *Do Tobacco Advertising Bans Really Work? A Review of the Evidence.* Ontario, Canada: Niagara Institute.

Mangelburg, T., D. Grewal, and T. Bristol. 1997. "Socialization, Gender, and Adolescents' Self-reports on Their Generalized Use of Product Labels." *Journal of Consumer Affairs* 31: 255–79.

Maxwell, K. 2002. "Friends: The Role of Peer Influence across Adolescent Risk Behaviors." *Journal of Youth and Adolescence* 31: 267–77.

Meyer, T. 1972. "Effects of Viewing Justified and Unjustified Real Film Violence on Aggressive Behavior." *Journal of Personality and Social Psychology* 23: 21–29.

Meyer, T. 1978. "Television and Prosocial Behavior: Alternatives to Antisocial Television Programs." *Discovery* 17: 20–23.

Meyer, T. 1994. "Tobacco Advertising on Trial: An Assessment of Recent Attempts to Reconstruct the Past and an Agenda to Improve the Quality of Evidence Presented." Pp. 205–20 in *Explorations in the History of Marketing*, ed. R. Fullerton. Greenwich, CN: JAI Press.

Meyer, T., and E. Hexamer. 1985. "Assessing Impacts on Children." Pp. 144–57 in *Methods for Research in Broadcasting*, eds. J. Dominick and J. Fletcher. Boston: Allyn-Bacon.

Meyer, T., K. Gettelman and T. Donohue. 2001. "College Students' Perceptions of Advertising and Price Versus Non-marketer-controlled Factors on Their Purchases of Brand-name Athletic Shoes and Clothing." Pp. 47–52 in *Developments in Marketing Science*, eds. M. Moore and R. Moore. San Diego, CA: Academy of Marketing Science.

Meyer, T., K. Meyer and T. Dohonue. 2004. "Teenagers' Perceptions of the Influence of Advertising and Price Versus Peers, Parents, and Personal Choice on Their Purchases of Brand Name Athletic Shoes and Clothing." Pp. 365–80 in *Sports Marketing and the Psychology of Marketing Communication*, eds. L. Kahle and C. Riley. Mahwah, NJ: Erlbaum Associates.

Michell, L., and P. West. 1996. "Peer Pressure to Smoke: The Meaning Depends on the Method." *Health Education Research, Theory, and Practice* 11: 39–49.

Midlarsky, E., and M. Hannah. 1995. "Assessing Adolescents' Prosocial Behavior: The Family Helping Inventory." *Adolescence* 30: 141–55.

Mochis, G. 1987. *Consumer Socialization: A Life-cycle Perspective*. Boston, MA: Lexington Books.

Musher-Eizenman, D., S. Holub, and M. Arnett. 2003. "Attitude and Peer Influences on Adolescent Substance Abuse: The Moderating Effect of Age, Sex, and Substance." *Journal of Drug Education* 33: 1–23.

Powell, S. 1993. "The Power of Positive Peer Influence: Leadership Training for Today's Teens." *Special Services in the Schools* 8: 119–36.

Sim, T., and S. Koh. 2003. "Domain Conceptualization of Adolescent Susceptibility to Peer Pressure." *Journal of Research on Adolescence* 13: 58–80.

Smith, K., and M. Stutts. 1999. "Factors That Influence Adolescents to Smoke." *Journal of Consumer Affairs* 33: 321–57.

Stice, E., J. Maxfield, and T. Wells. 2003. "Adverse Effects of Social Pressure to Be Thin on Young Women: An Experimental Investigation of the Effects of 'Fat Talk.'" *International Journal of Eating Disorders* 34: 108–17.

Urberg, K., Q. Luo, C. Pilgrim, and S. Degirmencioglu. 2003. "A Two-stage Model of Peer Influence in Adolescent Substance Use: Individual and Relationship-specific Differences in Susceptibility to Influence." *Addictive Behaviors* 28: 1243–56.

Wang, M., E. Fitzhugh, J. Eddy, Q. Fu, and L. Turner. 1997. "Social Influences on Adolescents' Smoking Progress: A Longitudinal Analysis." *American Journal of Health Behavior* 21: 111–17.

Yin, S. 2003/2004. "Kids' Hot Spots." *American Demographics* 12: 16.

Zollo, P. 1999. *Wise Up to Teens: Insights into Marketing and Advertising to Teenagers*. Ithaca, NY: New Strategist Publications.

# 9

Adolescent Memory for Health Information: Mixing "Micro" and "Macro" Variables

Brian G. Southwell

In this contribution Brian Southwell provides us with an interesting discussion of the interface between the psychological "micro" or individual level of analysis and the sociological or "macro" level that takes into account characteristics of the broader environment—in this case, the broader environment of available media messages. Media research is a unique field in that it often concerns itself with data about both of these things simultaneously. Media effects cannot exist without both media messages and the audience members who may read or hear them.

But this seemingly simplistic statement belies the complexity of formally combining statistical data about these different types of units. The concept of "unit of analysis," which we saw used in Slater's community drug prevention project to describe the difference between comparisons involving individuals and comparisons involving entire communities, is used here to describe the distinction between data about people and data about available messages. Audience members are individual human beings with unique cognitive and personality characteristics; these interact in complex ways with a media environment that offers a particular distribution of messages with particular traits. We can study those messages through various forms of media content analysis, but combining audience data with media data is not simple.

Southwell's study also provides us with a good example of how valuable research can make use of data originally collected for another purpose. Large-scale studies like the laptop-based media effects project described here are very expensive, and it is not easy to get people to participate. This project serves as a useful reminder that valid research can "piggyback" on existing data sets or larger studies designed to meet other goals. It is not always essential to design a separate new study to answer important research questions.

— 129 —

MANY PEOPLE AGREE THAT COMMUNICATION inherently involves multiple entities. Beyond the simple example of two human beings conversing and interpreting each other's comments, situations abound in which people (who represent one type of entity to be studied) engage external stimuli (such as television shows, which represent a different type of entity) in a variety of different settings (which represent yet another entity type). To explain communication outcomes from a social science perspective, then, it follows that description of not only individuals but also of stimuli and settings should be a crucial part of research. Understanding teenagers' reactions to music videos, for example, probably requires that we know something about not only teenagers as individuals, but also about exactly what they are watching, where they are watching, and with whom they are discussing such content. That simple idea suggests that researchers should pursue the simultaneous use of multiple types of data that arise from samples of various entities, such as people, news articles, advertisements, or physical locations. When researchers fail to take advantage of this possibility, important opportunities can be missed. Admittedly, organizing various types of data into a single study can be a daunting challenge. We explore some such difficulties here. I also will argue, nonetheless, that the rewards of multilevel research using multiple information sources can dramatically outweigh the costs.

One general communication research problem that calls for studies employing multiple data sources involves the fundamental concept of human memory for mass media content. If we seriously ask what predicts individual memory for exposure to mass media content, an array of candidate predictors and explanations arises that reside on different conceptual planes: for example, individual-level explanations versus explanations that have to do with some formal aspect of the media content itself. On one level, Cappella (1996) has argued that investigation about possible media effects would be well served to begin with consideration of the mental processes and structures that constrain audience member responses. Studying memory among humans, after all, means that biological and cognitive constraints bound what is possible. While such individual-level consideration is undoubtedly relevant and useful, all individual engagement with electronic media also occurs in a social, cultural, institutional, and organizational context (Pan and McLeod 1991; Wright 1986). And individual memory for a particular type of media content logically depends on content availability, as well.

In other words, then, a study of individual people alone might be insufficient to answer questions about memory for mediated images or sound. Studying different variables at different levels of conceptualization at the same time, though, requires careful thought. I faced just such a challenge when I began my investigation of memory for health advertisements among adolescents and will recount some of that experience here. Before discussing some of the details of that experience, though, I would like to address a larger question: Is memory for media content a communication impact that matters? Is prediction of memory an outcome worth the potential trouble of organizing disparate data sets?

Memory as an Impact That Matters

Memory is a multidimensional construct encompassing an array of different conceptual systems and variables (Bower 2000). In my research, I have studied a specific aspect of memory characterized by a person's recognition ability and retrieval of what is called "encoded exposure" to health advertisements (see Southwell et al. 2002, for discussion). While much time and effort is spent debating the impact of persuasion efforts on wholesale belief change, what is (or should be) often of more immediate interest to campaign planners and evaluators is whether efforts to present campaign content first generate at least a minimal "memory trace" in individuals. Knowing that a public service announcement aired on thirty different television stations across the country is different than knowing that anyone noticed, processed, or remembered the material from the ad. Only at the point of memory trace generation can a researcher begin to suggest that a potential audience member's response to a presentation might possibly affect their beliefs or behavior change.

Here it is useful to draw on Lang's (1995) notion of encoding, which is a basic outcome resulting in cognitive storage. What we will call encoded exposure, then, is the outcome of a process that results in a minimal memory trace in an individual. We should be able to measure it using recognition-based procedures—as opposed to other memory tasks, such as unaided recall—that offer prompting to respondents and are believed to tap the existence of a memory trace. Unaided recall is the ability to offer detail about a particular content when asked an open-ended question at some point after an initial opportunity to engage the content. Recognition, in contrast, is a more basic ability to respond to a closed-ended question about past engagement with specific content when presented with that content once again. While recall suggests a relatively high degree of current information salience and accessibility, recognition involves a somewhat more basic standard of past cognitive engagement (Shoemaker et al. 1989; Singh et al. 1988).

Is simple encoded exposure likely to be a useful variable in predicting campaign success or failure? After all, some theories of behavior change, such as the Theory of Reasoned Action (Ajzen and Fishbein 1980), involve systems of attitudinal beliefs that may seem vulnerable to change only through more comprehensive engagement with particular content than simple encoding would seem to measure. But insofar as behavior change arises through perceptions of social norms (Ajzen and Fishbein 1980; Hornik 1997) or consistent arousal of preexisting beliefs (Jo and Berkowitz 1994), knowing persons have an image of particular content they can draw upon when asked is indicative of direct influence possibilities. If I can remember seeing an advertisement that depicts people voting, for example, then this suggests that both my mental idea of the number of people who vote and the entire system of beliefs I have surrounding voting could have been affected or aroused by that media content.

Encoded exposure is also worthy of investigation for another, perhaps more controversial, reason. Insofar as people have a limited capacity for processing and storing information (see Lang 2000 for discussion), encoded exposure signals the use of mental resources. Encoded images of advertisements, for example, might be viewed as occupying space that might otherwise be used for other information. Encoded exposure itself, then, reflects an effect that is keenly relevant given the current media-saturated era in which we live. As Cooley noted almost a century ago, we might see communication as having an impact on a society by "fixing certain thoughts at the expense of others to which no awakening suggestion comes" (1909, 64). If this is so, what predicts whether certain thoughts will become fixed and others will not?

Studying Memory for a National Health Campaign

My investigation of memory for mass media content relied in important ways on an independent evaluation of national mass media efforts conducted for the U.S. Office of National Drug Control Policy (ONDCP). (See Hornik et al. 2000, for an overview of that evaluation effort.) Various aspects of the project made it an appealing opportunity to investigate memory questions—including its national scope, the fact that survey responses were recorded in everyday settings rather than in a laboratory, and the diversity of related but essentially independent data sources it made available for public use.

Such a study likely would have been prohibitively expensive and difficult to conduct by a lone investigator unaffiliated with an ongoing major research project or unwilling to make use of preexisting data. The cost of nationally representative surveys, especially one like this making use of laptops for data collection, is high, and the corresponding logistics are daunting. By designing my investigation in conjunction with this preexisting evaluation effort, however, I was able to complete the study. While some aspects of theory might usefully be constructed in an isolated ivory tower, opportunities for meaningful empirical investigation sometimes need to be sought elsewhere. Finding ways to leverage the resources of existing projects to answer theoretically important questions is a skill that will be increasingly important to scholars in the future.

The campaign being evaluated by the larger project was designed to discourage adolescents from trying marijuana and other drugs. In 1999, ONDCP began efforts in which campaign partners developed antidrug advertisements for a variety of media and then purchased airtime and space for those advertisements (Hornik et al. 2000; Hornik et al. 2001). In cooperation with ONDCP, the National Institute on Drug Abuse funded efforts to generate nationally representative data about individual memory for, and response to, campaign advertisements through the National Survey of Parents and Youth (NSPY). NSPY was developed and implemented by researchers from Westat, Inc., and the University of Pennsylvania's Annenberg School for Communication (with which I was affiliated at the time). In addition, available data from the project included electronic copies of the television campaign advertisements, as well as estimates of the airtime purchased for those advertisements. In other words, three major data sources that describe either individual memory or campaign advertisements were available for analysis.

Clearly, this wealth of data offered the potential for me to study memory using a variety of theoretically compelling variables.[1] The NSPY project included measures that yielded the central data for this study's dependent variable, namely recognition-based questions that tapped encoded exposure to campaign advertisements. The NSPY effort also included a number of relevant individual-level predictors of encoded exposure. These variables included age, sex, race, the amount of television a person reported watching recently, and a variety of other demographic and psychological variables.

I decided to measure encoded exposure using a combination of closed-ended recognition measures designed to tap the simple presence of an advertisement image in a person's brain and the simple recounted frequency of past engagement of that image. During each NSPY interview, campaign television advertisements that had aired in the two months prior to a particular interview were shown to respondents on the laptop computer used for the interview. After seeing each advertisement, each respondent was asked, "Have you ever seen or heard this ad?" If they responded in the affirmative, they then were asked, "In recent months, how many times have you seen or heard this ad?" In combination, these two questions yielded a measure of encoded exposure that theoretically ranged from zero to ten or more times.

Available copies of the television campaign advertisements themselves yielded a different type of data, as they allowed me to measure formal aspects of media content that might have played a role in determining whether people remembered content from the campaign. In other words, electronic copies of the advertisements themselves were treated as data, just as we think of an individual's recorded responses to a survey question as data. In order to construct usable data from these ads, though, I needed to conduct a content analysis, which is a research method through which units of content are organized and categorized according to the existence or absence of certain specific features in each unit.

Box 9.1: Content Analysis

While survey research was invented by sociologists and political scientists, experimental methods were invented by psychologists and educators, and the ethnographic approach was invented by cultural anthropologists, content analysis was largely developed within communication research—in particular, to meet the needs and goals of mass communication researchers. While experienced communication researchers are often comfortable with several of these methodological approaches, it is content analysis that is most uniquely our own. Content analysis is a staple of media research.

Content analysis means, quite simply, the systematic description of media content. But it has many forms. Qualitative content analysis (along with its close cousins, rhetorical and discourse analysis) has much in common with other forms of humanities scholarship in that it usually does not attempt to reduce complex narrative structures to variables that can be measured numerically. Just as literary scholars write about the themes and meanings of novels and films without seeing the need to measure those themes and meanings or assess their impact on the reader, qualitative content analysts look for consistent themes and dominant meanings across a body of media content, without heavy reliance on numerical data.

These themes and meanings are often seen as having social significance—they are important evidence for gaining insight into our own and other societies. It is for this basic reason—to understand the social context—that communication researchers most often study media content, whereas works of literature are more likely to be studied for their own sake. In this sense, even though qualitative media analysis has much in common with the approaches of the humanities, it is typically used as a method for the study of society, not just the study of media, and might best be understood as social scientific in nature, even though it does not rely primarily on numerical measurements. For example, Rakow used qualitative analysis to study texts for what they could tell her about local community dynamics.

Some qualitative analysis of media content does produce numbers, however. In particular, the presence of particular themes can be counted and their relative frequency determined. This can be done by selecting particular themes and topics ahead of time, based on the nature of the research project. Or it can be done by letting what is discovered in the content determine the dominant categorizations and themes (sometimes called "grounded theory" analysis because it was first described in a classic methods book entitled *The Discovery of Grounded Theory*, Glaser and Strauss 1967). This kind of research is still considered qualitative because it is not attempting to "measure" the presence of themes but to use the researcher's own cognitive abilities to judge or assess their presence.

But much content analysis is quantitative, including that used by Southwell in this chapter to measure variables that describe the public service ads that are important to his studies. Quantitative content analysis attempts to accurately reflect, using numerical measures, the values of a variety of variables that interest the researcher. Naturally, if the researcher's goal is to measure effects or "memory traces" (as in this chapter), quantitative information about media characteristics is helpful. In these cases, content variable measurement often requires some kind of sampling scheme for media items analogous to the sampling done for opinion surveys and polls.

Even though quantitative content analysis is designed to be more reliable and less "subjective" (or interpretive) than qualitative analysis, two different researchers might define or observe the value of a specific variable differently. For example, one researcher might classify a city council member serving as a news source as a "government official," while another (noting the source also works, say, as an attorney or a teacher) might make a different classification. Large quantitative content studies often make use of multiple research assistants whose work must be consistent. Various checks of "intercoder reliability" are used to verify this, ranging from a simple percentage to a variety of more complex formulas available in methods texts. If there is only one coder, there is not really any issue of intercoder reliability, but code-recode checks might still be used to assess "*intra*coder reliability."

The most common criticism of content analysis is that it easily descends into mindless counting and measuring of variables with limited theoretical significance. Content analysis is often the method of choice for graduate students or new faculty members who have limited research funding and no access to preexisting data sets that might be "mined" for new results, or who simply do not want to bother with research involving human subjects, requiring review board approval and other permissions, recruitment, complex logistics, and sometimes payment as well. It's a bad idea to choose content analysis because it seems simpler than other methods (very often this backfires), but it can be a good and practical choice when it is used to answer a well-thought-out, theoretically driven question.

Many variables might be defined in any given selection of media messages (whether news articles, soap operas, or public service announcements). Unlike some researchers engaged in the analysis of open-ended interview data or focus group transcripts, content analysts are not trying to characterize all parts of a message. For example, a simple newspaper story is usually about an event of some kind; contains a variety of sources and themes; is a certain length and appeared in a certain section of a particular paper in a certain location on a certain date; may have been written by a reporter with a certain kind of background; was published in a specified region; uses a certain vocabulary; and might be placed in a prominent or more obscure position. It might be positive, negative, neutral, or balanced. It might have implications for how the problem it represents is to be understood (framing) or how important that problem is. Its thematic emphasis might be classifiable in any one of a dozen different ways, depending on the interests of the researcher.

Content analysis should not be designed to try to measure everything of potential interest, but variables should be chosen that will answer a specific question that will connect the analysis to some form of theoretical thinking about media or its effects.

Reference

Glaser, B., and A. Strauss. 1967. *The Discovery of Grounded Theory: Strategies for Qualitative Research*. Chicago: Aldine.

In this case, each advertisement was treated as a unit that could be coded as having one or more features within it, just as the individual survey respondent is treated as a unit in a survey project. I was particularly interested in whether an advertisement depicted many different places or time periods and if it did so in a manner that differs from the usual sequence of events you or I would see when walking down the street. Based on a large research literature regarding the impact of editing on individual processing of media content (Geiger and Reeves 1993; Lang 2000; Messaris 1997; Reeves et al. 1985), I suspected that campaign advertisements that included a high amount of time or place disjuncture (or what might be called "context instability") because of a large number of cuts between scenes would be less likely to be fully encoded and later remembered by people responding to the NSPY survey. In order to assign a value for this variable to each advertisement, I counted the number of cuts between distinct times and places in each ad.

The final type of data used was the information that was available regarding the amount of airtime obtained for campaign television advertisements. A Gross Rating Points (GRPs) estimate for each advertisement, as reported by campaign contractors based on estimates of the reach and frequency obtained for each advertisement, served as a reasonable proxy for the environmental prevalence of a particular advertisement. A GRP is a conventional unit used by advertisers to measure a population's simple physical opportunities for exposure to media content and is the product of underlying estimates of reach and frequency (Farris and Parry 1991). GRP totals essentially estimate how widely a unit of media content was available during a defined time period. GRPs should directly predict memory, as I hypothesized for this investigation.

The Units of Analysis Problem: Data Organization

Perhaps the largest frustration I faced in pursuing this investigation stemmed from the conceptual and physical tasks of arranging these different sets of data and analyzing them in a unified framework. This obstacle might appear at first glance to be a minor one. The answer to the question of how to organize data from multiple sources, however, was not initially obvious in the way that deciding how to organize data collected from a single source might have been. How should these different data sets involving people, media content, and airtime be considered together?

I also had to cope with the fact that survey responses from NSPY existed in one standard data format, whereas the GRP data was reported by campaign staff in a different format, and the ads themselves existed initially only as electronic video files. That meant that I needed to convert these varying formats into a single, compatible data set. In the case of NSPY data and GRP data, straightforward computer file conversion addressed this concern. In the case of the ads themselves, my content analysis of the video files produced data indicating advertisement structure that I could manually record in a data file and pair with gross ratings points and aggregate survey responses.

This study also required the use of different units of analysis. A unit of analysis can be conceived of as the main entity, typically an object or an event, under investigation in a study (Singleton et al. 1993). The sample (or census) used to assess a particular research question is made up of such units, whether they are people or (in this case) advertisements. The value of a measured variable, in turn, describes a unit of analysis. For example, age is a variable that can describe an individual person. While this is seemingly a simple idea, researchers sometimes ignore the importance of assigning appropriate units of analysis in organizing, analyzing, interpreting, and discussing data. The consequent ambiguity can obscure important ideas and hide potentially important explanatory variables.

In this case, I wanted to study individual-level variables, such as age, television watching, past drug use, or conversation with others, for which the appropriate unit of analysis—the person—was relatively straightforward. But what is the appropriate unit of analysis, for example, for the environmental prevalence of media content? We can think of measures such as GRPs or the number of cuts per second as usefully describing advertisements. So another relevant unit of analysis for my investigation was the single advertisement. In other words, my study involved both individual-level and advertisement-level variables.

Specific description of appropriate statistical analyses for such an array of units is somewhat beyond the scope of this discussion, but a thorough overview can be found elsewhere (Southwell 2003b). But acknowledging these two units of analysis allowed me to assess both the average degree of memory generated by a particular advertisement and the memory reported by each individual for that specific advertisement. Each approach was quite useful in addressing my research concerns. In general terms, the macro-level, or advertisement-level, variables, such as the number of cuts included in an advertisement or the number of GRPs obtained for that advertisement, were used to predict the average memory reported for that advertisement. Similarly, individual-level variables, such as age or the amount of television a person reported watching recently, were used to predict individual memory for an advertisement.

Results from Using Multiple Data Sources

Was my effort to hurdle the obstacles noted above worthwhile? What would have happened had I not pulled together multiple data sources and identified multiple units of analysis in my effort to understand memory for health campaign advertisements? Results of the study suggest that I would have missed important explanations and would have failed to identify important forces that apparently shape memory. That suggests that organization and utilization of multiple data sources can be fruitful.

At the individual level, variables such as television use mattered in predictable ways. The amount of television a person watches and the number of programs in which the campaign obtained airtime for advertisements that a person reports watching, for example, both positively predicted encoded exposure; more reported television watching generally coincided with greater encoded exposure to advertisements. Similarly, for reasons likely related to the network architecture of human cognition (see Anderson 1983 for discussion), those who reported having spoken with others about drugs in géneral also were more likely to report memory for campaign advertisements (related to drugs).

The story does not stop there, however. Individual-level variables were not the only useful predictors of memory. Analysis of advertisement-level relationships also bore important results. As predicted, the sheer environmental prevalence of an advertisement strongly predicts the average amount of encoded exposure that a campaign advertisement achieved among adolescents. Moreover, editing matters. Those advertisements that were highest in the number of cuts per second (in terms of movement from one context to another) also were among the lowest in terms of average encoded exposure achieved, even after accounting for the simple environmental prevalence of each advertisement.

Had I chosen to investigate memory for advertisements solely by relying on individual-level survey data, I would have missed an opportunity to explore and discuss aspects of memory prediction that have little to do with the individual person. By looking only at one type of data source, I would have overlooked the idea that whether media content is available in recognition memory is at least partially a function of the degree to which that content is widely available and also of the nature of the editing used to construct that content.

Conclusion

The use of multiple sources of data is not necessary for every conceivable study that is relevant to communication research. Nonetheless, many efforts to test hypotheses and to assess theory should use different types of data in order to include most relevant explanatory variables. We often fail to do so because the effort is resource demanding, inconvenient, or simply counter to research convention, but the potential reward for doing so is great.

In light of the theoretical considerations that we briefly discussed in this chapter, any attempt to thoroughly study memory for health campaign advertisements requires not only individual survey responses but also information about the advertisements themselves. If I had failed to include different types of information from different sources and had instead relied on individual survey data from the aforementioned evaluation, I would have overlooked important results. Failing to include data describing the advertisements in question, for example, would have obscured the important idea that how an advertisement is constructed and how prevalent it is in a media environment are just as important as (if not more important than) characteristics of the audience in determining whether the ideas in an advertisement become commonly shared cognitive resources or not.

Forging combinations of researcher-initiated data and other available data types, such as public domain information, can meet this common need. Arbitrary combination of data from disparate sources, however, also is risky and potentially problematic. Instead, researchers should carefully consider relevant units of analysis and then organize available data to provide description of those units and to predict relevant outcomes. Available information is only useful if it provides measurement of a theoretically pertinent variable. By collectively pursuing that arduous work when appropriate, we likely can get one step closer to constructing research that matters.

Questions for Reflection

Southwell stresses the need to study memory in order to understand the effects of messages. But he does not claim that this is the only variable that is interesting. Aside from memory, what other mental processes might be involved?

This chapter illustrates the advantages of combining the analysis of characteristics of people with the analysis of message characteristics. Are there other kinds of social or environmental conditions that you expect would be important to audience responses?

What advantages might be associated with field surveys like this one that use laptop computers to present images and record responses? Are there any major disadvantages to this approach?

Drawing from your own personal experiences, what seems to make some advertising messages more memorable than others?

Note

1. Several recent articles and papers, e.g., Southwell et al. (2002), Southwell (2003a), and Southwell (2003b), offer more in-depth discussion of measures and analyses than is possible here.

References

Ajzen, I., and M. Fishbein. 1980. *Understanding Attitudes and Predicting Social Behavior.* Englewood Cliffs, NJ: Prentice Hall.
Anderson, J. R. 1983. *The Architecture of Cognition.* Cambridge, MA: Harvard University Press.
Bower, G.H. 2000. "A Brief History of Memory Research." Pp. 1–32 in *The Oxford Handbook of Memory,* eds. E. Tulving and F. I. M. Craik. New York: Oxford University Press.
Bryk, A. S., and S. W. Raudenbush. 1992. *Hierarchical Linear Models: Applications and Data Analysis Methods.* Newbury Park, CA: Sage.
Cappella, J. N. 1996. "Why Biological Explanation?" *Journal of Communication* 46 (3): 4–7.
Cooley, C. H. 1909. *Social Organization: A Study of the Larger Mind.* New York: Charles Scribner.
Farris, P. W., and M. E. Parry. 1991. "Clarifying Some Ambiguities Regarding GRP and Average Frequency." *Journal of Advertising Research* 31 (6): 75–77.
Geiger, S., and B. Reeves. 1993. "The Effects of Scene Changes and Semantic Relatedness on Attention to Television." *Communication Research* 20 (2): 155–75.
Hornik, R. 1997. "Public Health Education and Communication as Policy Instruments for Bringing about Changes in Behavior." Pp. 45–58 in *Social Marketing: Theoretical and Practical Perspectives,* eds. M. E. Goldberg, M. Fishbein, and S. E. Middlestadt. Mahwah, NJ: Lawrence Erlbaum Associates.
Hornik, R., D. Maklan, D. Cadell, D. Judkins, S. Sayeed, P. Zador, B. Southwell, J. Appleyard, M. Hennessy, C. Morin, and D. Steele. 2000. *Evaluation of the National Youth Anti-Drug Media Campaign: Campaign Exposure and Baseline Measurement of Correlates of Illicit Drug Use from November 1999 through May 2000.* Bethesda, MD: National Institute on Drug Abuse.
Hornik, R., D. Maklan, D. Judkins, D. Cadell, I. Yanovitzky, P. Zador, B. Southwell, K. Mak, B. Das, A. Prado, C. Barmada, L. Jacobsohn, C. Morin, D. Steele, R. Baskin, and E. Zanutto. 2001. *Evaluation of the National Youth Anti-Drug Media Campaign: Second Semi-Annual Report of Findings.* Bethesda, MD: National Institute on Drug Abuse.
Jo, E., and L. Berkowitz. 1994. "A Priming Effect Analysis of Media Influences: An Update." Pp. 43–60 in *Media Effects: Advances in Theory and Research,* eds. J. Bryant and D. Zillmann. Hillsdale, NJ: Lawrence Erlbaum Associates.
Lang, A. 1995. "Defining Audio/Video Redundancy from a Limited-Capacity Information Processing Perspective. *Communication Research* 22 (1): 86–115.

Lang, A. 2000. "The Limited Capacity Model of Mediated Message Processing." *Journal of Communication* 50 (1): 46–70.

Messaris, P. 1997. *Visual Persuasion: The Role of Images in Advertising.* Thousand Oaks, CA: Sage.

Pan, Z., and J. M. McLeod. 1991. "Multilevel Analysis in Mass Communication Research." *Communication Research* 18 (2): 140–73.

Reeves, B., E. Thorson, M. L. Rothschild, D. McDonald, J. Hirsch, and R. Goldstein. 1985. "Attention to Television: Intrastimulus Effects of Movement and Scene Changes on Alpha Variation over Time." *International Journal of Neuroscience* 27: 241–55.

Shoemaker, P. J., C. Schooler, and W. A. Danielson. 1989. "Involvement with the Media: Recall versus Recognition of Election Information." *Communication Research* 16 (1): 78–103.

Singh, S. N., M. L. Rothschild, and G. A. Churchill. 1988. "Recognition versus Recall as Measures of Television Commercial Forgetting." *Journal of Marketing Research* 25: 72–80.

Singleton, R. A., B. C. Straits, and M. M. Straits. 1993. *Approaches to Social Research.* 2nd ed. New York: Oxford University Press.

Southwell, B. G. 2003a. "Modeling Micro and Macro: A Multilevel Model to Predict Memory for Television Content." Paper presented at Association for Education in Journalism and Mass Communication annual conference, Kansas City, MO., July.

Southwell, B. G. 2003b. "Information Overload? Health Advertisement Context Instability and Memory Hindrance." Paper presented at International Communication Association annual conference, San Diego, CA, May.

Southwell, B. G., C. H. Barmada, R. C. Hornik, and D. M. Maklan. 2002. "Can We Measure Encoded Exposure? Validation Evidence from a National Campaign." *Journal of Health Communication* 7 (5): 445–53.

Wright, C. R. 1986. *Mass Communication: A Sociological Perspective.* New York: McGraw-Hill.

10
Communication at the End of Life: Volunteer-Patient Relationships in Hospice

Elissa Foster

Foster's experience as recounted in this chapter comes from the opposite end of the quantitative/qualitative continuum as did Southwell's analysis in the previous one, not only because in this chapter Foster reports a study for which oral interviews are the primary "data" but also because this author is so articulate in her defense of the advantages of the researcher's subjective involvement in the research. Foster introduces the term "autoethnography" to describe her own personal narrative account of her experience as a hospice volunteer.

Rather than divorce herself (even as a qualitative researcher) from her own inclusion in the group, organization, and special circumstances she is studying, Foster eventually wrote herself and her own personal experience as a volunteer with the particular hospice patient to whom she had been assigned into her research account. But her account here suggests that this was not her original intention, and that writing about highly private details of her patient and their conversations raised ethical issues of its own. These issues were less acute when she was acting in the traditional ethnographer's role, focused on the experiences of other hospice volunteers rather than her own.

Foster describes her approach as descriptive and does not claim that her methods are explanatory in the sense that a formal experiment can test theories and produce explanations. But her project is carefully focused on communication at the end of life, as it takes place between volunteers and patients, and as it is reported by a group of volunteers. And her study makes use of substantive theoretical concepts, including not only our understanding of interpersonal communication dynamics but also the status of hospice care as a recognized movement for social change.

I'VE NEVER THOUGHT OF MYSELF AS A morbid or pessimistic person—and I don't believe I am either of those things—but I sense a slight uneasiness in the silence that tends to follow my announcement that I study "communication at the end of life." My listeners often change the subject, sometimes after a brief pronouncement like, "Wow, that must be really sad. I don't think I could do that." What drew me to this topic, however, was not a desire to dwell on trauma or sadness. Rather, I perceive the end of life as a time when the stakes are highest for our interpersonal relationships—a time when communication can render great insight and beauty from pain and incoherence. It is this potential for meaning that attracts me, because I know that there are *better* ways to communicate—better ways to *be*—particularly in those contexts we tend to avoid. My desire to improve our understanding of relationships at the end of life motivated me to undertake an ethnographic study of hospice— an organization that cares for people who are dying. What I learned about communication from this project has implications that extend beyond hospice for two important reasons. First, the difference between living and dying is influenced by our meanings and perceptions more than it is by determined physical processes. Also, many of the factors that make communication difficult at the end of life—anxiety, increasing uncertainty, and imminent change—also impact other relational contexts.

The term "hospice" has three distinct yet related meanings. Hospice refers to a type of organization (rather than a specific corporation), a philosophy of end-of-life care, and also a social movement that has been growing in the United States since 1973. As a movement, hospice was founded in response to the "medicalization" of dying in the twentieth century (Brand 1988; Connor 1998), and the subsequent stigmatization of patients who were no longer curable. Death became a cultural taboo wherein the dying person was "a medical embarrassment" and the bereaved person "a social embarrassment" (Walter 1994, 24). In contrast to a medical model focused on treatment, hospice care begins when cure is no longer possible, and it is directed toward the "whole person" (Connor 1998, 7), encompassing physical, social, emotional, and spiritual needs. Hospice services are provided for patients and their families primarily in their homes and also in residential facilities such as nursing homes (Bennahum 1996; Connor 1998). Although Lifepath Hospice—where I conducted my research—is larger than most hospice organizations, it is typical in terms of its structure and services. Each hospice patient is cared for by an interdisciplinary team that includes a nurse, a social worker, and a home health aide, and may also include other specialists such as a nutritionist, a physical therapist, or a chaplain (Seale 1998). The volunteer is considered a member of the team and is represented in team meetings by a coordinator who receives regular written and verbal reports from the volunteers.

This project began as an extension of a personal goal to learn how to communicate with people who are seriously ill or dying. In January 2001, I became a hospice volunteer by completing twenty hours of training before visiting the patient I would see every week until she died fifteen months later. As a researcher, I wanted to document what happened and share with others what I learned about communication at the end of life. Integrating my personal and research goals, I conducted and wrote a book-length narrative ethnographic project that wove together my story of visiting my patient, the stories of other volunteers, and end-of-life research from a variety of disciplines. In this chapter, I will discuss the two complementary dimensions of the fieldwork—the interviews I conducted with other volunteers and my own visits with my patient—and the challenges I faced in translating the fieldwork experience into ethnographic stories. First, it is important to outline the basic tenets of narrative ethnography and why this method was appropriate for researching hospice. These arguments were also articulated to the various "stakeholders" who supported me—the Director of Research and other members of Lifepath Hospice, and the Center for Hospice, Palliative Care, and End-of-Life Research, which funded my study. It was important that they understand the assumptions of narrative ethnography and how these assumptions differed from more common clinical and scientific methods.

Why Narrative Ethnography?

The term ethnography refers to a process of studying culture (from the Greek *ethnos*) through writing (from the Greek *graphein*). Frey et al. (2000) identify two general research questions in communication research: describing communication behavior and relating communication behavior to other variables. Ethnography is primarily descriptive in its goals, in that it seeks to represent details of the language, behavior, ritualized practices, and underlying values and assumptions of a given culture. Rather than isolating any of these elements as discrete "variables" for the purpose of measurement and analysis, ethnography is grounded in an epistemology that claims we can best understand social behaviors and meanings by directly engaging with the contexts in which they occur (Lindlof 1995). Because I knew relatively little about hospice when I began my study, ethnography enabled me to learn through active participation, in which all my experiences were potentially meaningful. I also recognized that both ethnography and the narrative form of the ethnographic research report were unfamiliar to my stakeholders, so I needed to present a sturdy rationale for how what I was doing was "research."

In ethnographic research, the term *narrative* implies more than just the practices of generating and writing stories as part of the research process. Freeman (1997) suggests that experience, language, and narrative are inextricably linked. It is narrative that ties life experiences together into a coherent pattern of connections. Just as one goal of hospice care is to find meaning at the end of life (Bradshaw 1992), the concept of narrative integrity—in life and in research—refers to our ability to "make sense" by recognizing how each aspect of our experience fits into a whole. In hospice, the everyday use of narrative as a sense-making process is most obvious in the patient's life review as he or she reminisces about the past (Dunaway 1996; Sellars and Haag 1998). However, many other communicative activities in hospice also contribute to patient care by linking a patient's experiences to a larger system of meaning (Sellars and Haag 1998). Listening, sitting in silence, exchanging looks, and touching are essential to establishing a connection between the patient and volunteer and, as communicative acts, they are most meaningful when experienced and interpreted in the context of a specific relationship. I learned that these acts were also essential for me to learn about communication at the end of life. Thus, narrative was an effective interpretive framework for understanding communication in hospice and, once it came to the writing, I could show meaningful interaction through stories—inviting readers to think *with* the narrative and not merely *about* it (Frank 1995).

I was also able to frame my project within a tradition of ethnographic studies that have contributed to the topic of aging and end of life (Adelman and Frey 1997; Diamond 1992; Lawton 2000; Myerhoff 1980). The need for qualitative and ethnographic research in these contexts is becoming widely recognized. In a review of end-of-life ethnographies, Rubenstein (2000) proposes a construct he calls "embeddedness" to describe characteristics of ethnography and processes of dying. He states, "Embeddedness refers to the quality of dying that sees its meaning in the complex panoply of person, condition, setting, culture, social structure, and other life circumstances that influence the end of life" (259). Similarly, ethnographic research is concerned with meaning as embedded in the practices, language, contexts, ideas, and events of a culture, as well as the subjective meanings of the individual within that culture. The philosophies of hospice and narrative ethnography are also similar. Earlier, I described hospice as an attractive "alternative" (McGrath 1998) to the traditional biomedical approach to dying because it is individualized, is directed by the needs of the patient and his or her family, and considers the patient's physical, emotional, and spiritual well-being. Ethnography also encompasses a perspective and a set of goals that are holistic and multidimensional (Lindlof 1995) and that emphasize understanding communication from the perspectives of the participants (Denzin 1997). As I visited my patient and spoke with other volunteers, my goal was to uncover and adequately represent practices and meanings that were specific to this unique place, at this time, and to these people. The value of ethnography, therefore, rests in its ability to provide a rich and evocative description of lived experience.

Finally, I employed a narrative approach because I wanted what I wrote to reach my readers emotionally as well as intellectually, so that I could make a positive difference to our cultural practices of communication at the end of life. A number of autobiographical narratives of illness and dying (Albom 1997; Butler and Rosenblum 1991; Ellis 1995; Frank 1991; Lorde 1980) provide insights that encompass practical, ethical, and moral concerns (Bochner 2001). End-of-life clinicians have also adopted narrative approaches; for example, some nursing journals regularly feature evocative personal stories of nurse-patient interactions in hospice (Ellner 1997; Faulkner 1997; Lafferty 1997; Pattinson 1998; Ufema 1998). In *Dying Well,* Byock (1997) presents evocative case studies of hospice care from a physician's point of view. In his book, and in Callanan and Kelley's (1992) *Final Gifts,* the power of the texts lies in their ability to take readers into the world of hospice care to *show*, rather than tell, what it means to honor and support the person who is dying. These narratives are not concerned with representing dying *as it is for everybody*, nor do they claim statistical generalizability, but rather they present dying as it *could be* for many people. As Coles (1989) suggests, powerful stories tend to work their way into our thinking life and into our "idle thoughts" (204), thus affecting our way of thinking as well as our way of being in the world. My goal at all times was to conduct a narrative study that utilized "the power of language to create and change the world, to make new and different things possible" (Bochner 1994, 29).

The narratives in the study originated from two different sources. The "volunteer stories" came from three rounds of interviews with other volunteers over a twelve-month period immediately following our training. My volunteering became a first-person episodic narrative that describes events from my first meeting with my patient through to her death. Throughout the research, methodological issues arose that were unique to the narrative ethnographic process, and I will devote the remainder of this chapter to discussing these issues in detail. Because I conducted and analyzed the interviews first, in the next section I will describe that process and how I translated the recorded stories into narrative. I will then describe how I wrote the first-person narrative and connected it to the volunteer stories, including the steps I took to protect the privacy of my patient and her family, as well as the responsibilities I accepted in conforming to the expectations of narrative truth.

Others' Voices: Narrative Ethnographic Interviewing

Interviewing—eliciting and recording information from others—is an important aspect of the ethnographic process. As a scholar and researcher, I have always enjoyed and trusted the sense making that occurs in conversation with other people, and this is how I characterize ethnographic interviewing as distinct from directive or structured survey interview procedures. During the hospice training session, my conversations with the other volunteers inspired me to make their experiences a primary focus of my study. I conducted interviews to record the other volunteers' stories and also to engage them in my investigation of how we communicate in relationships at the end of life. As I moved from a purely theoretical understanding of hospice into hands-on involvement with the organization, I had to revise some of my preconceptions about what interacting with hospice patients would entail. For example, I learned that volunteers do not always know if the patients they are assigned will be able to speak or respond to them, or if they will be with a patient long enough to establish a relationship of the kind that I had envisioned when I developed the project. By listening to the stories of several other volunteers, I was able to capture a variety of experiences and insights into what the volunteer-patient relationship could be and what it meant.

To recruit my participants, I approached twelve members of my volunteer group on the evening of our "graduation" from the training to ask if they would like to participate in a series of interviews about their hospice experiences. Of these, nine responded to my requests to set a time and date for the interview. My initial design included three rounds of interviews at four-month intervals with all nine participants—the first two rounds as one-on-one interviews and the third as a group interview. However, like any study that involves the participation of real people with real schedules, the research plan had to be flexible. Not all participants were able to take part in all three rounds of interviews; not all participants were able to meet for the single group interview, so we ended up with two groups; and the three rounds took a little over a year to complete rather than nine months. In the end, six of the original nine participants completed all three rounds of interviews, and these six provided the "volunteer stories" that were central to the final study.

In the interviews, I interacted more as a peer than as an expert researcher because I was also a newly trained volunteer who was experiencing similar thoughts and feelings about visiting my patient. The other volunteers often shared stories and asked questions that helped me to frame or reframe my own experiences as my relationship with my patient developed. The style of the interviews was interactive (Ellis et al. 1997), because we collaboratively made sense of our volunteer experiences, what they meant to us, and what we understood to be our role in relation to hospice care. In line with the expectations for this type of interview, I kept the length and progress of the interviews as open-ended as possible. With the exception of the two group discussions in the third round of interviews, which ran for over two hours, each interview lasted between sixty and ninety minutes. In total, I met with participants on twenty-one separate occasions and recorded over thirty hours of interview material.

Although I took responsibility for initiating and ensuring the continuity of the interviews, I regard these interviews as focused conversations rather than structured interviews. Before each interview in the second and third round, I listened to the previous interview recording as a way to put myself back into the story that each participant had previously shared with me. One of the interesting effects of reviewing the tapes in this way was that my sense of time was altered, and I would often greet the participants with the feeling that we were simply continuing a recent conversation rather than meeting after an absence of several months. During every interview, I asked open-ended questions to elicit storytelling (Holloway and Jefferson 2000). I often employed a two-part question format, in which I shared a story or observation and then asked a question about the participant's experience. This kind of two-part question was intended to invite the respondent into my thinking process, elicit emotional and narratively framed responses, and generate a mood of exploration and discovery rather than explanation and justification.

One of the primary methodological concerns I faced was how to treat the interviews as "data." Two goals guided my subsequent decisions. First, I wanted to sustain close attention to the voices of the participants as recorded, rather than relying primarily on a written transcript. Second, I wanted to include the participants' contributions in a manner that preserved the context of the discussions in which their words were shared. Both of these concerns were related to my understanding of the interview as a "dialogic world of unique meaning and experience" that should be treated as a whole (Denzin 1997, 38). Eventually, I would need to lift examples, expressions, and stories from their context when I wrote my analysis, but first I wanted to present the unfolding processes of discovery that took place in collaboration with my participants. My challenge was primarily one of translation, from the interviews-as-experienced to evocative stories of those interviews.

The first stage of translation involved transcribing the interview tapes. I combined detailed transcription with an oral history method advocated by Yow (1994) whereby counter numbers on the tape recorder or transcription machine are used to identify and index topics of discussion. The idea behind indexing is to permit access to participants' actual words on the tape rather than a transcript when analyzing the interviews, thus keeping the voice and the words connected. However, to distill and translate each interview into a narrative text, the interviews first needed to become text. As a compromise, I generated indexed transcripts that allowed me to access the corresponding portions of the tape recordings when necessary.

Once transcribed in this way, each transcript from the first two rounds of interviews was around twenty-two single-spaced pages in length. This presented me with the second challenge of translation: how to distill the content of the interviews and transform them into coherent and memorable narratives. Later, I compared the word counts of the raw transcripts to their corresponding stories and found that I selected less than 40 percent of each interview (and, as I write this chapter, I face the task of "distilling" these stories even further).

First, I translated the spoken word into written dialogue by "cleaning up" the repetition, unfinished thoughts, and corrections that occur in natural speech. Then, I combed through each interview to find the clearest expression of a particular idea or story, which sometimes meant rearranging the text in addition to editing and deleting. In doing this, I accepted the responsibility of interpreting what the volunteers intended to say, and the degree of intervention or editing varied greatly among the interviews. When writing the "volunteer stories," I used my primary research question about communication and the volunteer-patient relationship to help me decide what to include and what to leave out; operationally, I looked for specific descriptions of what the volunteers did, what they said, and what they felt when visiting and communicating with their patients. By continually returning to the tapes, I was able to get a sense of the volunteers' intended meanings, which were not always evident in the words as they appeared on the raw transcripts. Finally, I paid attention to the narrative framing of the interviews by describing the environment in which they took place, including vocal and physical expressions, as well as revealing my own mental and vocal responses to what the participants were saying.

Kleinman et al. (1997) point out that fieldwork and analysis are not separate processes despite the way they are traditionally presented in reports of social scientific research. In writing the interview stories, I was already initiating a process of analysis whereby I identified "themes" that recurred and resonated across and within the various interviews, as well as within my own experience of volunteering. These themes became the foundation of the formal analysis portion of the ethnography. With each subsequent interview, certain ideas or stories stood out because they resonated with earlier ideas and stories, and so I had a sense of "sedimentation" or layering as different volunteers expressed similar thoughts or ideas. For example, in the first round of interviews, many of the volunteers talked about how the training and their early interactions with patients were different from what they had expected they would be. In addition to including similar ideas or stories, I also included those that were unique or important to an individual volunteer, particularly if they related to communication and the volunteer-patient relationship. For example, in the first round of interviews, one of the volunteers discussed her interactions with her patient, who had dementia, and in the second round of interviews, another volunteer described how she became her patient's health care surrogate. Both of these were unique experiences in comparison to those of the other volunteers who participated in the study, but the stories nevertheless reveal important facets and variations of the volunteer-patient relationship.

My Voice: Autoethnography

In her detailed ethnography of an aging Jewish community, Myerhoff (1980) quickly rejected the traditional stance of a distanced observer. It was Myerhoff's subjectivity that guided her attention toward emotions and the vital moments that evoked a sense of recognition, familiarity, and identification with the people she studied, and she felt compelled to include her experiences into her ethnography. At the time, Myerhoff's decision to focus on her personal journey was unusual in anthropology. Since then, however, the methodological significance of subjectivity has been explored on several academic fronts (Ellis and Bochner 2000). As a method of social research, "autoethnography" emerged, in part, as a response to the methodological and ethical considerations Myerhoff faced in her study. Autoethnography has embraced a previously underutilized research tool—the subjectivity and humanity of the researcher.

In terms of method, autoethnography implies a process of evocative narrative writing, systematic introspection, and theoretical reflection that is grounded in the lived experience of the fieldworker. As autoethnography, the personal narrative portion of my study emerged from a combination of traditional field notes and a process that Ellis (1991) has called "systematic sociological introspection." As a "vulnerable observer" (Behar 1996) of hospice work, my subjectivity, empathy, and identification with others were central to the research process and were written into the research account. Particularly because I was writing about an emotionally and morally complex subject (Ellis 1996), an essential part of my process was to identify and reveal my own responses to the story that I was telling. This reflexivity is present throughout the ethnography in both the personal narrative and the volunteer participants' stories.

Autoethnography embraces a "communitarian moral ethic" (Denzin 1997, 274) in which the researcher is personally involved and committed to the research topic and the context being studied. The researcher establishes a relationship with study participants in which their needs and perspectives are central to each decision in the research process. Ethics are particularly important when researching a context such as hospice, in which patient and family privacy and autonomy are paramount. In fact, some researchers question whether hospice patients should ever be asked to participate in research because of the additional burden it can create (Casarett et al. 2001, 442). Methodologically, autoethnography shifts the focus of inquiry to the researcher and away from those who might traditionally be considered the "subjects" of research. This shift of focus is particularly salient in light of the criticism (Lawton 2000; Seale 1998; Walter 1994) that we tend to privilege talk as *the* way to create meaning at the end of life. Rather than interviewing the patients and asking them to explain their experiences, the autoethnographic researcher assumes that the burden of expression and sense making is on the researcher rather than on the "subjects" of the research.

Because Lifepath Hospice sponsors and uses research in a variety of ways, and because it was informed of my project, I kept notes about my initial meetings with my volunteer coordinator, the training program, and visits with my patient, Dorothy. Despite having a strong moral and ethical foundation for conducting my research using autoethnographic processes, I initially resisted writing a narrative about my relationship with my patient. Only after I had completed all the interviews and written the volunteer stories did I address the issue of writing my story, as I had originally thought I could tell my story indirectly through the conversations with the other volunteers. As powerful as the volunteer stories were, however, my own voice and my experiences were a glaring omission from the account that I was writing. My interview responses hinted at my experiences and feelings, but they appeared like enigmatic signs flashing by on a highway and were frustrating rather than revelatory. Even so, I hesitated.

Part of the power of narrative ethnography, and autoethnography in particular, lies in its ability to take the reader into a specific scene, to show sights, smells, and sounds, and to reveal the feelings associated with the experience. But *my* story is also *someone else's* story (Behar 1996), and exposing the gritty realities of a particular event or relationship implies exposing another person. The question of how to respond to the shared nature of stories presented a very real dilemma for me as an autoethnographer. In previous narrative projects, I have resolved ethical issues associated with writing about others by sharing my stories with them (Foster 2001). I've even included their writing and responses in the final manuscript (Foster 2000). In this project, however, I faced two dilemmas. First, I wanted to experience hospice volunteering as a volunteer and not as someone conducting research. Outwardly, I did not want to present myself as someone collecting information on my patient and inwardly I did not want to risk changing my interaction—or even adjusting the focus of my attention—in response to a research agenda. The second problem was related to the first because I could not employ the same strategy as I had in the past. I could not collaborate with Dorothy in writing the story because that would mean doing exactly what Seale (1998) has claimed, that I would place a burden on her to reflect upon and articulate the meaning of her own dying. Thus, although I spent the year visiting Dorothy and kept basic notes about what we did together, I focused on conducting the interviews with the other volunteers.

When it became obvious that my ethnography needed to include my own story, I felt compelled to write in a way that preserved Dorothy's privacy and that of her family. This involved not only changing the names in the story, but also creating composite characters and leaving out certain events and details that I considered to be private. Describing every fact did not seem worth the cost to my larger purpose. The patients of the other volunteers were protected by the volunteers' anonymity in the text, but my patient was not protected in the same way because I was not writing anonymously. I also decided to write this way because it protected me from feeling as though I was exposing or exploiting information that was shared with me in the context of an intimate and confidential relationship. Again, I felt my responsibilities in this regard were different from those of my participants, because the demands of writing an autoethnographic narrative meant offering intimate details of the people in the story and characterizing them in a way that invited greater scrutiny than in the volunteers' stories.

My visits with Dorothy were precious to me, so I experienced conflicting desires to protect these visits by keeping them private and also to honor them (and her) by sharing them with others. If circumstances had been different, I might have entertained the possibility of writing our story together in the context of being a volunteer. I dare say that this might even be a welcome undertaking for some patients, although the goals of such a project would certainly be different from those of autoethnography. But early on I learned that Dorothy was not interested in my life as a scholar/researcher, although she cared about me a great deal as a person. So, I followed my instincts and what I understood to be the rules of our relationship, and it never seemed right to write about my experience until I adopted the strategies I have just described.

Thankfully, narrative theorists have turned our attention away from facts and towards meanings (Bochner 2001). The objective for the narrative researcher is to create "narratives that simulate reality, applying the imaginative power of literary, dramatic, and poetic forms to create the effect of reality, a convincing likeness to life as it is sensed, felt, and lived" (Bochner et al. 1998, 42). My goal in writing the autoethnographic narrative was similarly aimed at turning away from the facts of Dorothy's life and toward the meaningful events that stuck with me as I reflected on the fifteen months that I spent with her. Ellis (1996) describes going through a similar process when writing certain parts of her book *Final Negotiations*. She writes, "I worked constantly to find a balance between honest writing and good sense, between portraying life as intimately as I could and protecting my relationships with characters in the story and with my readers" (Ellis 1996, 162). With these goals in mind, I wrote a story that reveals an emerging relationship with Dorothy, the everyday details of our weekly visits, and the negotiation between living and dying that we entered into. I understand that readers will be curious to know what aspects of my story are "true," and I am tempted to say that it is all true if one is speaking of narrative truth. By aligning myself with narrative in this way, I confine my claims regarding this part of the narrative, and ask that my story be judged in terms of its verisimilitude, its potency, and its moral consequences rather than its factuality (Bochner 1994).

Regarding the writing itself, through the writing of the volunteer stories certain moments with Dorothy emerged as particularly significant in my understanding of our relationship, and I easily identified some of these by the number of times I mentioned them during the course of the interviews. When it was time to write the personal narrative, I looked through my notes and the interview stories, fixed my mind on each specific event, and endeavored to place myself back in the context in which it occurred (Ellis 1991). I kept in mind the goals of evocative writing, remembering the feelings I experienced and the thoughts that had made the moment meaningful. When I reread the story now, I am convinced that it conveys both the truth of what volunteering was like for me and the role that Dorothy played in my life. My hope is that my readers will be drawn into the world of the narrative, trusting that it is a "good story," true in its essence and moral in its consequences.

Final Word: Writing as a Process of Inquiry

Writing is integral to all phases of ethnographic research (Goodall 2000; Lindlof 1995). For the ethnographer, writing is both a method of data collection and a process of inquiry (Richardson 1994) through which the researcher grapples with the challenges of both understanding and representing the experience of the fieldwork. As an ethnographer exploring the role of communication and relationships at the end of life, my goals were to experience the relationships, events, and emotions of hospice volunteering, to reflect actively upon the experience alone and with other volunteers, and to represent those processes evocatively. I also used the ethnographic writing process to help me articulate what I was thinking, feeling, and learning along the way, which contributed to my personal growth regarding communication at the end of life.

My challenge was to represent not only what this experience was like from my perspective, but also to reveal a sense of what it meant to other volunteers as well as in a broader context of social reality.

In the end, although my use of narrative ethnography was unusual in a hospice organization where workers and clinicians were more familiar with quantitative approaches, the novelty of the design was an advantage because it promised to bring new information and a new perspective to the current conversation about end-of-life care. My subjectivity as a researcher, the richness of the data I collected, and the aesthetic appeal of the report I wrote all became central features or "selling points" of the project.

Questions for Reflection

The author notes that asking hospice patients questions about their end-of-life experiences may force them to produce explanations of those experiences. Why is this ethically problematic? Why is it also problematic for the research project?

Foster makes a strong case for both autoethnography and the researcher's involvement in the evolving research "story." Why is this not traditionally accepted? Are there risks or disadvantages involved? Are these risks worth the benefits?

The hospice staff members with whom Foster worked were more accustomed to quantitative research projects than qualitative, narrative, or autoethnographic work. How do you imagine Foster explaining herself to them?

What kinds of data, insights, or conclusions might a project like this make possible that are not likely to be derived from formal quantitative studies? From traditional ethnography?

How would you personally respond to the claim that autoethnography is not "research"?

References

Adelman, M. B., and L. R. Frey. 1997. *The Fragile Community: Living Together with AIDS*. Mahwah, NJ: Lawrence Erlbaum.

Albom, M. 1997. *Tuesdays with Morrie: An Old Man, a Young Man, and Life's Greatest Lesson*. New York: Doubleday.

Behar, R. 1996. *The Vulnerable Observer*. Boston: Beacon.

Bennahum, D. A. 1996. "The Historical Development of Hospice and Palliative Care." Pp. 1–10 in *Hospice and Palliative Care: Concepts and Practice*, eds. D. C. Sheehan and W. B. Forman. London: Jones and Bartlett.

Bochner, A. P. 1994. "Perspectives on Inquiry II: Theories and Stories." Pp. 21–41 in *Handbook of Interpersonal Communication*, eds. M. Knapp and G. R. Miller, 2nd ed. Thousand Oaks, CA: Sage.
Bochner, A. P. 2001. "Narrative's Virtues." *Qualitative Inquiry* 7: 131–57.
Bochner, A. P., C. Ellis, and L. Tillmann-Healy. 1998. "Mucking Around Looking for Truth." Pp. 41–62 in *Dialectical Approaches to Studying Personal Relationships*, eds. B. M. Montgomery and L. A. Baxter. Mahwah, NJ: Lawrence Erlbaum.
Bradshaw, A. 1992. "The Spiritual Dimension of Hospice: The Secularization of an Ideal." *Social Science and Medicine* 43: 409–19.
Brand, D. 1988. "Dying with Dignity: Cicely Saunders Started the Modern Hospice Movement in London 21 Years Ago." *Time* 132 (10): 56–58.
Butler, S., and B. Rosenblum. 1991. *Cancer in Two Voices*. Duluth, MN: Spinsters Ink.
Byock, I. 1997. *Dying Well: Peace and Possibilities at the End of Life*. New York: Riverhead.
Callanan, M., and P. Kelley. 1992. *Final Gifts: Understanding the Special Awareness, Needs, and Communications of the Dying*. New York: Simon and Schuster.
Casarett, D., B. Ferrell, J. Kirschling, M. Levetown, M. P. Merriman, M. Ramey, and P. Silverman. 2001. "NHCPO Task Force Statement on the Ethics of Hospice Participation in Research." *Journal of Palliative Medicine* 4: 441–49.
Coles, R. 1989. *The Call of Stories: Teaching and the Moral Imagination*. Boston: Houghton Mifflin.
Connor, S. R. 1998. *Hospice: Practice, Pitfalls, and Promise*. Washington, DC: Taylor and Francis.
Denzin, N. K. 1997. *Interpretive Ethnography: Ethnographic Practices for the 21st Century*. Thousand Oaks, CA: Sage.
Diamond, T. 1992. *Making Gray Gold: Narratives of Nursing Home Care*. Chicago, IL: University of Chicago.
Dunaway, D. K. 1996. "Introduction: The Interdisciplinarity of Oral History." Pp. 7–22 in *Oral History: An Interdisciplinary Anthology*, eds. D. K. Dunaway and W. K. Baum, 2nd ed. Walnut Creek, CA: AltaMira.
Ellis, C. 1991. "Sociological Introspection and Emotional Experience." *Symbolic Interaction* 14: 23–50.
Ellis, C. 1995. *Final Negotiations: A Story of Love, Loss, and Chronic Illness*. Philadelphia: Temple University Press.
Ellis, C. 1996. "On the Demands of Truthfulness in Writing Personal Loss Narratives." *Journal of Personal and Interpersonal Loss* 1: 151–77.
Ellis, C., and A. P. Bochner. 2000. "Autoethnography, Personal Narrative, Reflexivity: Researcher as Subject." Pp. 733–68 in *Handbook of Qualitative Research*, eds. N. K. Denzin and Y. S. Lincoln, 2nd ed. Thousand Oaks, CA: Sage.
Ellis, C., C. Kiesinger, and L. Tillmann-Healy. 1997. "Interactive Interviewing: Talking about Emotional Experience." Pp. 119–49 in *Reflexivity and Voice*, ed. R. Hertz. Thousand Oaks, CA: Sage.
Ellner, L. R. 1997. "What Grandma Clara Wanted: Death with Dignity." *American Journal of Nursing* 97 (8): 51.
Faulkner, K. W. 1997. "Talking about Death with a Dying Child." *American Journal of Nursing* 97 (6): 64–67.

Foster, E. 2000. "Reaching Out, Reaching In, and Holding On: Friendship, Attempted Suicide, and Recovery." *American Communication Association Journal* 2 (2). Available from http://hcjournal.org/holdings/vol2/Iss1/essays/foster.htm.

Foster, E. 2001. "Hurricanes: A Narrative of Conflict Cycles in a Distressed Marriage." *Studies in Symbolic Interaction* 24: 171–94.

Frank, A. W. 1991. *At the Will of the Body: Reflections on Illness.* New York: Houghton Mifflin.

Frank, A. W. 1995. *The Wounded Storyteller: Body, Illness, and Ethics.* Chicago: University of Chicago Press.

Freeman, M. 1997. "Death, Narrative Integrity, and the Radical Challenge of Self-Understanding: A Reading of Tolstoy's 'The Death of Ivan Illich.'" *Aging and Society* 17: 373–97.

Frey, L. R., C. H. Botan, and G. L. Kreps. 2000. *Investigating Communication: An Introduction to Research Methods.* 2nd ed. Boston: Allyn and Bacon.

Goodall, H. L., Jr. 2000. *Writing the New Ethnography.* Walnut Creek, CA: AltaMira.

Holloway, W., and T. Jefferson. 2000. *Doing Qualitative Research Differently: Free Association, Narrative, and the Interview Method.* London: Sage.

Kleinman, S., M. A. Copp, and K. A. Henderson. 1997. "Qualitatively Different: Teaching Fieldwork to Graduate Students." *Journal of Contemporary Ethnography* 25: 469–99.

Lafferty, C. L. 1997. "A Parting Gift: A Simple Bed Bath Would Mean So Much?" *Nursing* 27 (8): 80.

Lawton, J. 2000. *The Dying Process: Patients' Experiences of Palliative Care.* London: Routledge.

Lindlof, T. R. 1995. *Qualitative Communication Research Methods.* Thousand Oaks, CA: Sage.

Lorde, A. 1980. *The Cancer Journals.* San Francisco: Aunt Lute Books.

McGrath, P. 1998. "A Spiritual Response to the Challenge of Routinization: A Dialogue of Discourses in a Buddhist Initiated Hospice." *Qualitative Health Research* 8: 801–12.

Myerhoff, B. 1980. *Number Our Days.* New York: Touchstone.

Pattinson, S. 1998. "Learning to Fly: How a Hospice Patient and a Nurse Taught Each Other about Living." *Nursing* 28 (6): 104.

Richardson, L. 1994. "Writing as a Method of Inquiry." Pp. 516–29 in *Handbook of Qualitative Inquiry*, eds. N. Denzin and Y. Lincoln. Thousand Oaks, CA: Sage.

Rubenstein, R. L. 2000. "The Ethnography of the End of Life: The Nursing Home and Other Residential Settings." *Annual Review of Gerontology and Geriatrics* 20: 259–72.

Seale, C. 1998. *Constructing Death: The Sociology of Dying and Bereavement.* Cambridge, UK: Cambridge University Press.

Sellers, C. S., and B. A. Haag. 1998. "Spiritual Nursing Interventions." *Journal of Holistic Nursing* 16: 338–54.

Ufema, J. 1998. "Insights on Death and Dying." *Nursing* 28 (10): 66–67.

Walter, T. 1994. *The Revival of Death.* London: Routledge.

Yow, V. 1994. *Recording Oral History: A Practical Guide for Social Scientists.* Thousand Oaks, CA: Sage.

11
Scientific Knowledge and Personal Experience: Mutually Exclusive?

Loreen N. Olson

In the final piece in this section, Loreen Olson reflects on her private struggle as a researcher who has a personal history that is directly relevant to the subject of her scholarship, violent relationships. Must she set aside the personal knowledge she has obtained as a victim of such a relationship in order to study this topic "objectively"? Would doing so be entirely fair to the other victims who have (by serving as research subjects) contributed to her studies? At the same time, would revealing herself as a member of the group she is studying tend to undermine her own credibility as a researcher?

Like Foster, Olson uses the term "autoethnography" to refer to the inclusion of her personal history in her scholarship about a wider problem. These two authors' experiences with this technique were somewhat different. Foster knew at an early stage of her association with a hospice volunteer group that one of her goals in joining them was to complete a research project about their parallel experiences. Olson, on the other hand, describes a process of learning to reinterpret her own earlier lived experience in the light of insights from her evolving scholarship. Yet both authors seem to recognize that in deviating from the traditional role of the researcher by (in a way) studying themselves, they are raising subtle issues about the relationship between their private lives and personal observations and relationships, on the one hand, and their public identities as scholars and openly published research work, on the other.

Olson's comments call into question the traditional distinction between subject and object, researcher and researched. What is the role within the social science enterprise of knowledge that is based on personal experience? Can the interpretive study of one's own direct life experiences offer a valid contribution to the collective understanding of a social problem? Both Foster and Olson recount their deliberation, even ambivalence, about this point, but in the end both decide that the answer is certainly "yes."

As a communication scholar, I received all of the *traditional* methodological training. My graduate studies included the usual statistics courses, where I learned how to do correlations, chi-squares, t-tests, ANOVAs (analysis of variance), MANOVAs (multvariate analysis of variance), multiple regression, and path analyses. In these classes, I was also exposed primarily to the positivist way of thinking about the research process: a social scientist should remain as objective as possible and prevent, or at least control for, personal biases. I was taught that one's personal thoughts, feelings, and perspectives could only get in the way of doing science. While I still agree that objectivity has its place in scientific inquiry, I also have come to appreciate the role that personal experience can play in our search for knowledge—that all research is intersubjective and researcher, participant, and process are all interrelated, each informing the other. Thus, contrary to conventional thought, personal experience and scientific knowledge are not mutually exclusive. Let me explain.

Students in methods courses often hear the saying, "The question should drive the method." This means that your choice of method should be determined by the type of question you are seeking to answer. For example, if you are hoping to explain what effect verbal aggression has on a person's use of physical aggression, then you would want to ground your design in the positivist tradition of inquiry and choose the appropriate statistical method in analyzing your data (which often is in the form of a survey or experiment). In contrast, if your goal is to understand how abused women leave their abusers, then you would use a more interpretive approach and choose a qualitative method such as grounded theory (via interviewing) in hopes of gaining a deeper insight into their experiences. My primary research focus happens to be on violent romantic relationships, and I have had several occasions where I needed to make similar methodological choices based upon the type of question driving my project.

However, what happens when your question involves your own personal insight and experiences? Do you ignore these, believing that to do science one must assume an objective stance? If you say "yes" to that question, you are not alone. Many would agree with you. However, there is a growing group of scholars, especially feminist researchers (Foss and Foss 1994), who believe that personal knowledge and scientific expertise are naturally intertwined—they each inform and are affected by the other. Thus, a person's individual perspective can be a basis for knowledge production.

I recently completed a project (Olson 2004) where I was confronted with such a dilemma. Do I ignore my own personal experience because it is not considered a legitimate form of scholarship? Or, do I openly disclose what happened to me personally because it is a valid form of knowledge production? I chose to share my story for several reasons—both personal and professional. First, the purpose of the project was to look at how an abuser communicatively persuades his victim to alter her sense of self. Understanding this early relational process helps explain why it is so difficult for abused women to leave. The abuser's rhetoric is effective in changing the victim's identity; the victim loses her autonomous sense of self, which in turn is replaced by an enmeshed, subjugated selfhood that is told repeatedly it is "no good" and "not worthy." No research had examined the very early beginnings of relationships that become abusive to see what communication strategies abusers employ in order to reconstruct their lovers' (victims') identity into one of subjugation.

As you can imagine, it can be challenging, albeit not impossible, to find individuals who are willing to share their experiences and reflect upon them in such a way as to give necessary insight into the processes. Here is where my experience, both personally and professionally, became key. I am both a researcher of violent romantic relationships and a survivor of a violent marriage. I had been driven professionally to understand what happened to me personally—and, hopefully, to help others avoid the same situation. While conducting my research for approximately six years, I had simultaneously been reflecting upon my personal experiences. Why me? How did I end up in a violent marriage? Didn't I see the signs? Were there any signs? If so, what were they? I had begun to piece together some answers to these questions—to those early beginnings of the relationship, long before the physical abuse started—to the point in time when my abuser's rhetoric became controlling. Thus, I felt my own introspection, informed by the scholarly dialogue, could make a contribution to the academic community because I had a keen sense of what had transpired in these early days.

A second reason I chose to tell my story and share my personal experience was because of the questions guiding the project: How is a subjugated identity constructed during the entrapment process? And how does an autonomous, confident self reemerge (Olson 2004)? The personal nature of these questions propelled me toward a methodology that combines personal experience and scientific expertise. This method is known as "autoethnography." The autoethnographic method combines two methods, autobiography and ethnography. It is both a self-narrative (Gergen and Gergen 1997) and a cultural analysis (Ellis 1997). According to Denzin (1997), autoethnography affords the researcher an opportunity to look at one's self (auto) within the larger context (ethnography) in which the self is experienced. In other words, this project was a story of my personal experiences with abuse informed by my social network, our society at large, and the academic community of violence researchers. I have described the perspective this way:

> In many respects, my identity is unique. I am a survivor of an abusive marriage, and now I study violent relationships. The dualistic role of personal survivor and academic is a reflexive one, each informing the other, never separate from one another. Further, being both researcher and subject of study simultaneously offers a unique combination of "experiential expertise" and "presentational expertise" (Foss and Foss 1994), whereby my first person accounts as survivor and scholar hopefully offer fresh insight into the personal, scholarly, and political conversations on domestic violence. (Olson 2004, 7)

Autoethnography became the method of choice because of its ability to combine the personal with the professional and to shed light on a new and understudied aspect of violent relationships into which I felt I had particular insight.

Finally, I must admit that this decision was not without its complications. After all, I was deviating far away from my traditional social science training. My alternative methodology has not been embraced by the dominant research community. As an untenured professor, was I taking a risk by spending time on something that was not publishable? Fortunately for me, some of our communication journals are beginning to embrace new methodological formats. Therefore, my fear was never realized. I submitted my article to a journal with such a reputation, and it accepted the article for publication.

Ironically, as I sit here reflecting on the entire process, the article is in the midst of being published. It should appear in the next several months, which is both exciting and frightening all at the same time. It's not hard to imagine how an author would feel joy in seeing her article in press, knowing all of the labor and stress involved in getting it to that point. But why would seeing your work in print prompt fear and apprehension? I must admit that this emotional response took me by surprise—it was an unanticipated reaction to the receipt of my scholarship that I had never before experienced with my other, more traditional formats. Unlike the fear of spending time on scholarship that would not find its way to press, this fear feels more dangerous. It involves the risk of disclosing my story, thereby jeopardizing my image and ultimately my career. I wonder, how will my reputation fare? Because I will be exposing myself to the larger academic community, I worry about how others will view me. How will they react knowing that I had been a victim of abuse? Will they shun me, be embarrassed for me, or pity me? How will they react to my future work, knowing that I am a member of the group I often study? Will they question my objectivity or ability to interpret without excessive bias?

To be honest, I have struggled with these questions for many months. There were times when I was tempted to "pull the plug," so to speak, and stop the publication process. However, I kept hearing the voices of other victims ringing in my ears. How could I, as an educated, independent, financially stable woman, possibly ask them to share their stories for my research, especially when many of them are financially and emotionally dependent upon their partners and families, if I was too afraid to tell mine? The answer to this question gave me the necessary strength to do what I considered the right thing—to stand with them and share my story too. In so doing, I am resolved to assume any and all risk that may come my way, for I believe that power and social change come about through voice and expression rather than silence and fear.

Lest we forget, research *can* speak of human life—real life, real experience. In my opinion, the research process is enhanced by acknowledging its humanness—by recognizing that we are all part of the process and cannot remove our own feelings and biases from it. For one project, I chose a particular methodology to tell my story to a particular audience. I think it is a prime example of how personal experience can advance scientific knowledge. Hopefully, this story also adds to your knowledge about the research experience. If it does, then the circle of knowledge and experience continues.

Questions for Reflection

Is Olson's experiment in autoethnographic reflection different from the way everyday people reflect on their ordinary experiences? How?

How exactly is this approach different from other qualitative techniques for doing social scientific research?

References

Denzin, N. K. 1997. *Interpretive Ethnography: Ethnographic Practices for the 21st Century*. Thousand Oaks, CA: Sage.
Ellis, C. 1997. "Evocative Autoethnography: Writing Emotionally about Our Lives." Pp. 115–39, in *Representation and the Text: Reframing the Narrative Voice*, eds. W. G. Tierney and Y. S. Lincoln. Albany, NY: State University of New York Press.
Foss, K. A., and S. K. Foss. 1994. "Personal Experience as Evidence in Feminist Scholarship." *Western Journal of Communication* 58: 39–43.
Gergen, K. J., and M. M. Gergen. 1997. "Narratives of the Self." Pp. 125–42 in *Memory, Identity, Community*, eds. L. P. Hinchman and S. K. Hinchman. Albany, NY: State University of New York Press.
Olson, L. N. 2004. "The Role of Voice in the (Re)construction of a Battered Woman's Identity: An Autoethnography of One Woman's Experiences of Abuse." *Women's Studies in Communication* 27: 1–33.

Part IV
RESEARCH ACROSS CULTURES

THE CHAPTERS IN THIS SECTION STRESS the challenges of doing research with cross-cultural dimensions. The projects involved technology's impact on a non-Western Australian culture, the experiences of women parliamentarians in South Africa, health-related knowledge and beliefs in Belize, and how cultural values affect television choices for teenage African-American girls. The settings are on three continents (Africa, Central America, Australia) and among girls from a cultural minority in the United States.

In the first three cases, the researchers are working in cultures that are not their own. In the fourth case, Edwards's study of African-American girls, the researcher has a similar ethnic identity to her research subjects, but nevertheless faces problems parallel to those of the other researchers in trying to capture subtle dimensions of cultural difference within the constraints of a formal research design. Even though in this case the research was not done in a "foreign" place but involved a minority subculture, and even though the researcher is a member of that minority, her project is at least as much about cultural identity as are the other three selections included here.

While we have met both descriptive (or ethnographic) methods and research with cross-cultural dimensions in several previous chapters, these particular projects are more explicitly concerned with studying cultural variations, and taken as a whole they help round out the idea of cross-cultural research more completely. Despite the diversity of topics and settings, common threads are apparent. Research outside familiar locales means conditions may be unpredictable; logistical challenges are almost inevitable; the research is unlikely to unfold exactly as foreseen. And even within one's own culture, capturing the essence of cultural similarity and difference is difficult.

Further, the carefully planned use of formal quantitative designs—often pursued in order to establish cause-and-effect relationships—is especially difficult when dealing with cultural variation as part of the research question. It is hard to predict how well these methods will work or whether they will capture important aspects of cultural perspective. Of the four studies presented here, two were planned as qualitative studies; one was planned as a quantitative study but became largely qualitative by necessity; and the last was intended to be a qualitative study, but a quantitative substitute was adopted for practical reasons, with mixed results. All help illustrate why qualitative methods are a more common choice for exploring questions related to culture.

Having been involved in a major comparative study of cultural values and receptivity to gene technologies that was carried out quantitatively, involving data from over a dozen countries (Gaskel and Bauer 2002), I would hesitate to assert that quantitative methods can never be effective in comparative work. I believe that sometimes they can, provided there is a cross-cultural research team that has the understanding needed to interpret the data and also resources sufficient to overcome unexpected design problems. We had both, along with focus group data to help set the survey work in cultural context. We were also working within the so-called developed world, where the idea of filling out questionnaires was not entirely alien.

However, instances of truly successful cross-national studies using quantitative methods such as surveys are rare because these conditions are rare. Significant resource needs and formidable language barriers must be overcome, let alone coping with the subtle nuances of cultural difference and the emergence of a variety of unanticipated conditions. To ask a substantial number of people the same questions at the same time across national boundaries is difficult enough. And is a question translated into a different language even the same question? Since my own first degree was in cultural anthropology, I am a champion of qualitative approaches to studying culture, even though I believe that good quantitative studies are only difficult—not entirely impossible.

Reference

Gaskell, G., and M. Bauer, eds. 2002. *Biotechnology 1996–2000: The Years of Controversy.* London: Science Museum.

12
Stories in the Sand: Field Research with Pitjantjatjara Yankunytjatjara Media in Central Australia

David I. Tafler

David Tafler's contribution might also, in a way, have been included under Part V as a technology-oriented study, or even in Part III as a problem-focused study. He is specifically concerned with the way new communication technologies may be associated with cultural and social change among a remote group of indigenous Australians. But his research has called on him to grasp the culture of those he is studying as a whole rather than concentrate only on the technology itself— to think about how traditional spatial and celestial markers, used for navigation in a thinly populated landscape, might structure interactions with cyberspace; to understand the historical impact of missionary-led resettlement projects on traditional socioeconomic relations among a recently nomadic people; to appreciate the way that values and traditions once vital to the group's survival persist despite domination by an outside, alien culture. For this reason, Tafler's experience serves as the ideal study to introduce this section on cross-cultural research.

A very valuable feature of Tafler's work is his recognition that the cultural traditions he describes—despite their being under assault from a variety of external forces—will help shape the adoption, understanding, and use of new technologies, just as the technologies may help reshape the culture. So he does not write exclusively of media "impact" or "effects" (even though he seems to believe media are one of the external forces pressing the culture to change). Rather, he gives us a vision of a culture and a set of technologies interacting to produce a new fusion not attributable to either element alone.

This chapter also introduces the idea that researchers—especially Western researchers building careers working within indigenous, non-Western people— have an obligation to provide "payback" to those they study. This "payback" need not take the form of monetary pay, but if the relationship between the researcher and the group he or she is studying results in benefit only to the researcher, then the activity is simply a new form of colonialism. Information about the culture is the commodity that the researcher extracts for his or her own benefit, at a cost (in terms of disruption, time, and trouble, at a minimum) to the group being studied. While not all researchers will agree, and some valuable projects can be imagined that may afford few "payback" opportunities, this is an argument all researchers headed for "foreign lands" should consider.

IN 1997, I BEGAN WORKING WITH a Central Desert Australian Aboriginal media organization on the Pitjantjatjara Lands in South Australia. Pitjantjatjara Yankunytjatjara Media, or PY Media as people know it, is in a remote environment sprinkled with a small number of somewhat arbitrarily formed communities spread across a large expanse of land. In the 1930s, missionaries founded these communities in an effort to concentrate and reorganize a 50,000-year-old seminomadic population. The six major communities harbor transient populations of 250–300 individuals each. A number of smaller communities, the smallest called "homelands," house clusters of people that range in size from one to a half a dozen families. Some few groups of individuals reportedly live outside the homelands and communities. The low population density across the land reflects the challenges of living in a rough environment with limited water, considerable summer heat, lots of dust and flies, and few resources. Ironically, the formidable obstacles to making this land habitable helped maintain the relative isolation that enabled indigenous culture and social and economic life to survive.

Since 1981, the Pitjantjatjara Lands (the "Lands") have had freehold status. Freehold legal status permits the indigenous governing council to restrict access. Only indigenous residents and "white fellas" affiliated with supporting organizations have permission to visit or reside on the Lands. Even nonlocal indigenous people have to hold valid permits. Trespassers assume the risk of a substantial fine. The ubiquitous tourist does not surface in this zone. Access by the outside press, not to mention researchers, remains limited and controlled. Pitjantjatjara survives as the principal language. But as a long-term white fella resident of the Pitjantjatjara Lands describes the situation, "This land cannot endure as a game preserve cut off from the world. White fellas, even now, can drive through the Lands without a permit if they do not stop or camp. Limited access is a myth, though the myth keeps out the riff-raff."[1]

In 1991, the local governing council established an on-site regional administrative center called Umuwa, situated halfway between two of the principal communities. Umuwa has a resident population of roughly fifty, no store, no school, and no clinic or other community amenity—only an automotive garage. The other communities have more, though little beyond the aforementioned list, sometimes including an old persons' center, an arts and crafts environment, or an education center for adult continuing training. In Umuwa, the white fella population matches that of the black fellas when meetings do not bring extra people into the community.

Based in Umuwa for part of each year, I live in a country of people whose culture has gone through a dramatic revolution in a very short period of time. As recently as fifty years ago, the culture embodied a traditional economic and social system that guided everyday life. Their traditional culture differed sharply from the codes and structures of our own signifying systems. While much of Anangu (Pitjantjatjara, Yankunytjatjara) culture remains intact, especially its language, the outside world—and in particular the media mainstream—has succeeded in eroding a lifestyle fundamental to the culture's survival. That includes so-called "walkabout"—where young fellas learn the stories and codes inscribed in the land—and "men's and women's business," which formalizes that process. A way of life predicated on knowing where to gather food and find water has yielded to the convenience of patronizing a store and turning on the tap. An economy built on the labor expended for basic survival finds its working population listless and bored. The people face the challenge of making the obligatory adjustments to an outside capitalist economy and alien social system.

As part of my work, I have spent considerable time speculating on the insights and codes that may transfer across the cultural divides. Some seem clear. As a marketable commodity, indigenous arts offer exchange value. Indigenous painting presents one of those points of exchange. Other cultural practices, however, may provide even greater value by offering insights and models. More specifically, indigenous people have forged an extraordinary relationship with the land, reconstructing it indexically as a text for recording their law and history. Many other scholars have produced thorough documentation of these systems.

My interest, however, goes beyond the documentation of this remote culture and the tremors caused by its contact with the outside. Indigenous cultures' spatial and temporal processing might inform those emerging systems on the outside that seek to negotiate the relationships that individuals and groups develop with fabricated cyberspace environments. Indigenous orientation systems build on narrative constructions tied to spatial and celestial signifiers passed from generation to generation. Each generation adds a new dimension, reinforcing family codes woven into a tighter net. Those systems serve as a useful alternative model.

Different means of measuring time and space on the Pitjantjatjara Lands offer insights into those systems operative in industrial urban societies. On the

Box 12.1: What Is Culture?

While the concept of "culture" is not likely to be entirely new to most readers of this book, its appearance as a theme for the studies in this part of the book calls for more explicit discussion of this concept. Culture might best be defined as the knowledge needed to navigate everyday life within a given group of people. This definition encompasses the technological knowledge needed by peoples of the far North or those in desert areas to cope with extreme climates; the ecological knowledge that hunting-and-gathering peoples must have to locate food; and the values, beliefs, rituals, practices, norms, customs, and preferences characteristic of any culture, including our own. Some cultural practices, like coming-of-age and marriage ceremonies, seem nearly universal, but take different forms in different societies. Others, like preferred dress and body decoration, seem much more variable.

This sense of the word "culture" should not be confused with the concept of "high culture" like opera and oil painting in comparison with the "low culture" of soap operas and graffiti, which is essentially a class distinction within a broader culture in which the idea of class is deeply embedded. The fact that something is "cultural" in the sense of "high culture" is a statement about the perceived worthiness of the activity, usually higher if that activity is associated with people who have power, wealth, and prestige. This is not what social scientists mean by culture, of course—though it is amusing in this context to recall that Shakespearean plays were written as "low culture" and only later discovered by "highbrow" audiences.

Because every member of a culture has access to essentially the same stock of knowledge, any member can serve as an "informant" (sometimes called a "guide") who shares this knowledge with the researcher. Everyone living in Western culture knows you buy food in a grocery store and drive cars on only one side of the street, for example. Ask any reasonable person about these things and you will get essentially the same answer. The likely name of the store and exactly which side you drive on is more variable. Specialized knowledge held by healers, priests, shamans—or our own scientists, doctors, attorneys—is yet another matter. But most knowledge essential to understand and participate in everyday life is available from any "insider."

Despite the fact that cultural knowledge is broadly shared within a given culture, ethnographers still need to choose informants (sometimes referred to as "guides") with care. Sometimes those who are marginalized in their own cultures are said to be especially anxious to attach themselves to outsiders, especially outsiders who seem to have resources. While we may sympathize with their marginalized (excluded or pushed-to-the-margins) status, they may not have a "typical" perspective. Notwithstanding this caveat, ethnographers (whether cultural anthropologists or media scholars) are not generally concerned with developing a random sample of survey respondents or experimental subjects for research purposes. The whole concept of the research enterprise is different.

Cultures are best studied and understood holistically, meaning as a whole. Elements of cultural practice may make no sense taken out of context, especially when examined through the lens of another culture's values. Practices, values, and beliefs are slow to change and are best understood as embedded in a culture's history, necessities, and traditional way of life. We may not "get" the jokes in a film or sitcom made in another country. Respect for other cultures means recognizing that cultural elements that make no sense to us today, out of context, viewed through our own cultural lens, may have made perfect sense from the point of view of members of the group from which they came. Even ethical standards can be viewed in this way. Though some basic principles of human rights seem universal and it is not always appropriate to endorse all practices of all cultures equally, the right action to be taken in one culture may not be the same as the right action in similar circumstances in another (an idea sometimes referred to as cultural relativism).

Media are a significant reflection of culture, as the field of cultural studies (which is largely focused on media products of Western culture) demonstrates. In modern, media-saturated societies, media products can be appropriately analyzed as important artifacts of cultural processes in which values and conflicts are inscribed, just as the pottery and art of earlier cultures are studied for the insights they can yield into the societies that produced them.

In cross-cultural contexts, media and media technologies may have a different cultural significance. Not all cultures and societies are equally powerful. Media are one instrument through which one society (often Western) can run roughshod over the culture of another society (often non-Western). Alternatively, non-Western cultures, ethnic minorities, and other less powerful groups can and do create their own media products reflecting their own values and priorities. And members of different subcultures may "read" or interpret the same media material quite differently.

Lands, the continuum of time cycles backwards and forwards from an awareness of that very tentative center, the present.

My research here surveys the technomedia land grab: the growth of satellite reception, the use of video camcorders, the potential loss of language, the evolution of radio, the new vocabularies of the Internet, the opportunities of wireless communication as witnessed in this very unusual context. The evolution of electronic media and the fabrication of virtual environments warp the temporal and spatial horizon and therefore threaten the indigenous culture.

I have written a number of articles addressing a range of the corollary issues in anticipation of my current book project. My methodology favors a qualitative approach. For me, quantitative systems tend to misrepresent the complexity of the differences that mark individual and group cultural perspectives here. While the population has considerable regional stability, many individuals and families move about from community to community, homeland to homeland. Complex family relationships impact on the more immediate processes of both social and media interaction. The political, economic, and social platform remains volatile, a situation fueled by federal and state intervention. Traditional assessment tools do not work in this environment. Many of the insights that I have gained in my ongoing relationship and growing understanding have preempted my earlier research objectives and methodological approaches.

In this chapter, I will discuss the genesis of my relationship with PY Media and the nature and value of the fieldwork and research I am doing here. I will explain the challenge of doing research on the Lands and discuss the concept of "payback," a responsibility that the researcher has to make a contribution not only to the academic community but also to the indigenous community providing the field environment.

The Challenges

Unlike most research projects, targeting a remote indigenous culture sometimes necessitates placing the cart before the horse. Hypotheses formulated when entering an alien world undergo revision when circumstances provide the appropriate insight. Aimee Glass captures that transformation of insight when she writes in her book *Into Another World*, "Coming here is like being transported into another world. It couldn't be more different if I had gone across the sea" (Glass 1990). As the researcher builds his or her text of knowledge acquired, the frame motivating and organizing that information shifts during the process in a very dramatic way.

Anangu values differ markedly from those cultivated within "Western" culture. Relationships, even family interaction, conform to rigid parameters. Family relationships prevail and shape behavior in the public sphere well beyond loyalties manifest in Western family structure. Not only does this determine who has the appropriate "skin" to marry whom, it dictates who speaks to whom.

For an outsider, not having a "skin name" places the individual outside the social order. Not having the status of an initiated man renders the individual a child without adult responsibility. Acquiring a skin name or undergoing the initiation process (assuming that the individual earns that privilege) compromises the researcher's ability to move with impartiality through the community. Integrating within the community both provides and denies access, depending on the social order. The communities' priorities take precedence over the research objectives. Community ethics prevail over research ethics, particularly when it comes to distributing money. In a world of limited resources, accumulating and saving capital have no meaning. Saving becomes the equivalent of hoarding and will incur severe penalties. The family or family elder determines relative need and distributes resources accordingly.

In Anangu society, even family structure has a different meaning. For example, conjugal bonds operate outside of a Western structure of legally binding marriage. The responsibility of looking after a lover even when both parties have moved on to other relationships endures throughout each of their respective lives. Extended families accommodate to the accompanying social taboos.

All postulates and presumptions must operate within this universe, which colors the interpretation of data. To attempt to situate outside hypotheses within such an "alien" culture risks oversimplifying a complex situation—or worse, generating "New Age" assessments that pick and choose information to build a superior model. That pitfall characterizes quite a number of short-term research projects where the researcher, a brief interloper, makes a quick tour of the Lands, conducts a handful of interviews, assembles the data, and arrives at broad sweeping conclusions.

Another challenge lies in the insufficiency of prior research. While there have been anthropological studies focusing on the "other," little intensive theoretical work focuses on the long-range implications of minute events in these remote indigenous societies. Position papers may address the immediate difficulties and challenges, but few take a broadly theoretical perspective.

A number of reasons contribute to this lack. Native indigenous contact with outside Western society began in earnest a little over fifty years ago. Fifty years ago, the missionaries introduced a regimented lifestyle that provided food, running water, power, modern mechanized transportation, shelter, clothing, and entertainment. The missionaries brought indigenous people together in artificial settlements, producing artificial communities with a much greater concentration of family groupings than normally might characterize life on the Lands. Activities, such as obligatory work, regimented the time. Indigenous people helped with construction, managed cattle and sheep, attended school, and participated in religious indoctrination classes. Many indigenous people look back at this phase of protective guardianship with fond nostalgia. They had ample food and water, followed a regimented lifestyle that voided boredom, and acquired skills that allowed them to build homes and service motor vehicles. Eventually, they had film and later television. Communities also had access to HF (two-way wireless) radio.

In the 1960s, times changed. Indigenous people gained legislative rights that provided citizenship and more adequate protection from white fellas. Encouraged to assume responsibility for their own welfare, indigenous communities parted company with the missionaries. Unfortunately, during the parting neither the missionaries nor the government provided adequate transitional guidance and support. When the economic situation deteriorated, the government reluctantly assumed the overseer role formerly held by the missionaries, but without the nurturing presence. That situation continues. Now, through a process of gradual maturation, a new generation of Anangu attempts to do a better job of self-management. Nevertheless, the monetary stream continues to come directly from government subsidization.

Meanwhile, the situation changes yearly. With each new administration, new guidelines shift the prevailing trends. With advances in technology, the most isolated parts of the Lands become accessible. Solar cells power the homes. Satellite television and now satellite telephony have transformed the most remote homelands into consumers of prevailing media representations. Ten-year-old articles and books about telecommunications on the Lands seem obsolete, no longer characterizing contemporary conditions.

Some relevant and well-developed writing already exists. The work of Eric Michaels, an American visual anthropologist who worked in the 1980s with the Warlpiri people to establish Warlpiri Media, had groundbreaking impact. His work has greatly influenced my own. Michaels, however, did not have the opportunity to follow up for any great length of time. His untimely death from AIDS left a vacuum. Other writers, including Philip Batty, cofounder of the Central Australia Aboriginal Media Association (CAAMA), have made a significant contribution to an understanding of indigenous media. Batty has mentored me through much of my own experience.

But Michaels' work with the Warlpiri people did not cross tribal lines, and Batty focused on his own experience with CAAMA and with the Pintupi people. A comparable movement in the community of Ernabella on the Pitjantjatjara Lands received little or no attention. When I discovered Ernabella Video Television (EVTV), the lack of information and publication surrounding its existence aroused my own curiosity and eventually brought me to the Lands.

In the 1990s, other documents have emerged to describe a broader array of activities by indigenous communities, including those of the Ernabella group. Several flaws exist. Subsidized by government agencies (such as the Aboriginal and Torres Straits Islander Commission or ATSIC), the urban academic writers reflect the vested interest of the government in advocating for the policies supporting its own political initiatives.

First Contact

Beyond the research issues, other practical challenges come to the fore when trying to negotiate a means of "going out bush." Negotiating access becomes the foremost problem. An invitation poses the first challenge. In order to receive an invitation, a researcher must establish a relationship with a representative of the community. The most viable method comes from taking advantage of opportunities to meet people at academic conferences, and at various local institutions (such as the Land Council offices in Alice Springs).[2] My own ability to gain access came about after several trips to Australia starting in 1991, each of which included numerous engagements, meeting people at conferences, in their offices, on their campuses, and even abroad. One such individual offered to help on my fourth visit to Australia. I had met this individual on one of my previous visits and crossed paths with her again at a conference in Europe. On a return visit to Adelaide, I called her and made a lunch appointment. At that meeting, she asked my reasons for returning. I explained my interest in visiting EVTV. Having lived in Ernabella, my contact offered to help. She invited me to stop by her office the following day.

The next morning, when I arrived in her office, she secured the telephone number for the EVTV studio. When the telephone rang, she handed me the receiver. A man answered and I proceeded to explain my intent. Quickly, I realized that this man had little inkling of my presentation, for he spoke a different language, both literally and figuratively. As I began to adapt my presentation over the telephone, my friend asked for the handset. To my great surprise, she spoke the language. She proceeded to explain to this man in fluent Pitjantjatjara my mission.

From that conversation, we learned that the new coordinator of the organization, now called PY Media, would arrive in the studio the following morning. His availability gave me a platform for presenting my credentials and interests, which I did on the following day by sending a detailed fax. I tried to follow up by phone to no avail, and so I moved on to Perth. A week later, the coordinator of PY Media contacted me to extend an invitation and to make the appropriate travel arrangements.

Reaching the Lands poses its own challenges. No commercial transportation services the region. A small private air service carries the mail and supplies. Its planes land on designated dirt strips. Unsealed roads in and out of the region have inadequate signage and no roadside services. Cell phones do not work, though much more expensive satellite telephones may provide contact for government workers and teachers. Then, once on the Lands, little or no accommodation exists. Most visitors must share accommodation with a resident or they must camp. Camping poses a number of difficulties. Aside from the rigors of bringing the necessary gear, the appropriate family or community leaders must authorize the location of the campsite in advance.

To establish the necessary relationships and in order to build trust, the researcher must make a number of trips. Each stay must take account of the schedule fluctuations endemic to the Lands as a consequence of unpredictable events ranging from political crisis, to sorry business, to men's or women's cultural events. One visit often provides only limited perspective. A multiple-year commitment yields significantly stronger content. Trust builds, more information becomes available, and insight grows.

I had a very brief tenure during my first visit to the Lands. That short stay did, however, provide me with the opportunity to have a firsthand overview of the community, of the state of communication, of the challenges of building relationships. My second visit and subsequent ongoing contact came about as a matter of chance. When I first visited Ernabella in 1996, the operation of PY Media had more or less come to a halt. The previous administrator had resigned and the situation demanded both remedial attention and new initiatives to catch up with the times. While some video recording continued, the organization of the operation had dissipated.

The new coordinator had a number of ideas, not only for reviving PY Media but for updating and enriching its contribution. He invited me to spearhead one of those initiatives, the development of Internet and online resources. This responsibility allowed me an entry into the operation. It gave me the rationale and legal permit to continue returning to the Lands over a multiple-year period, as it turns out every year from 1997 to the present. I became a player, and that raised other challenges.

Over the course of those repetitive visits, my status changed. Initially, individuals might display some curiosity as to my background, my work, my site of origin, my family status. Otherwise, I met indifference. Many, perhaps too many, anthropologists and other researchers have moved through the Lands. The people have grown suspicious of intent and reticent to build relationships with outsiders.

My second year back (my third, including my very first visitation) drew marked attention. Most notably, some of the elders expressed their surprise and strong appreciation at my demonstrated sense of commitment and dedication to my work with them. This feeling grew even stronger once they realized that in the interim time between visits I had flown to the far side of the planet, resumed my life there, and then took the time and the initiative to return, assuming the related expense. On numerous occasions during explanations of my return, an elder would pick up a circular object in order to illustrate to his peers my return passage around the planet. The appreciation for this feat intensified even more with each subsequent visit. After five or six years, the fascination wore off, but the appreciation continues.

At this stage, I have received reassurance that I have a lifetime invitation to return. People recognize me. Those who do not recognize me respond when they learn the story of my return. Nevertheless, the situation remains volatile and I never take my time on the Lands for granted.

Looking more closely at that ongoing relationship, other factors might play a role in my evolving relationship with Anangu. As a foreigner, I represent a different sort of outsider. As an American in Australia, my historical lineage immunizes me somewhat from the challenges indigenous people confront with European and other settlers on the Australian continent. I exist outside their immediate history. That might allow me some additional access. On the other hand, indigenous people do acknowledge the struggles of indigenous people elsewhere. I entertained many questions seeking some understanding of how Native Americans contend with "white fellas."

Whereas black fellas demand some accountability from Australian white fellas, my position seems to elicit greater tolerance. Again, within indigenous culture, noninitiated men have not reached adulthood. As one indigenous elder remarked when speaking to a group of white workers at a PY Media meeting, "While in your culture they regard you as men, in our culture we consider you boys. Therefore, we must guide you and protect you."[3] For someone coming from another country, that custodial relationship is inflated.

Coming and going in cycles means negotiating the presence and absence of being there and then not being there. Here, timing plays a role. My cycle of presence coincides with the North American summer, a period of academic leave, and the Australian winter, when activity, particularly in the Central Desert, reaches its optimum levels. In Australia, activity begins to heat up in May as the temperature cools. I arrive in June and normally depart in August. By December, people in the Central Desert regions wrap up their affairs at year's end in anticipation of an extended break for the New Year. Therefore, I feel I have experienced the heart of what goes on during my series of interim presences.

Conversely, my absence from the Lands, which coincides with the period of greatest activity in North America, overlaps the period of least activity in Australia when many people travel away from the center. According to some Australian colleagues, some indigenous people might not even suspect that I return to my overseas home every year, instead believing that I have retreated to the shore.

Payback

> They appear, these splendid men hold our gaze—and walk on, out of history. They embody our European fantasy of autonomous freedom. To see them as they were then is to glimpse what we have taken from them, and what both they and we have lost. (Clendinnen 1999, 50)

Research on the Lands must exist as some sort of equivalent exchange for both ethical and economic reasons. Naturally, this raises some concerns. Indigenous people must exist within a Western capitalist economy. Within that environment, operating as a separate contiguous estate means that they must have exchangeable commodities or services. In the Central Desert, the limited resources mean negotiating what few marketable resources exist. Cultural information arguably provides the most promising and least damaging commodity. Therefore, the researcher must realize that the information that he or she acquires on the Lands bears a price. This in turn challenges academic ethics. The solution lies in "payback," the notion that the researcher must contribute something to the community that has comparable value to the information that he or she uses as part of his or her professional development.

Notions of beginning, ending, and closure arise when thinking about this long-preserved culture. The text remains open-ended. Will the loss of culture signify closure? Are we heading toward a climax? In my second year of developing the Web environment for PY Media, I spent considerable time explaining the concept of an Internet-based Web environment to the people working alongside me. One worker in particular displayed unusual interest. With him, I reviewed the evolution of each page and explained and demonstrated how it became a part of the overall site environment. I even demonstrated and explained the process of uploading the page and its component parts to a server in Adelaide. When it became apparent that my time on the Lands had nearly expired, that same individual came up to me and asked if the website would depart with me. Surprised, I could not fathom how he missed the basic understanding of a networked computer environment. I realized the years of precedent, the numbers of researchers who came on the Lands, compiled their information, departed with that information, and published their books for an outside world.

Too many researchers come to the Lands for a short, one-shot visit. They interview a handful of white fellas, extrapolate enough information to compile a report, and publish a short article. Some of those writings do capture some essence of the situation in the field. Unfortunately, they miss the subtleties and therefore misrepresent as much as they inform. Negotiating the fine line between representation and misrepresentation means validating one story against another. This process means stepping outside one flow of information in order to find another. That takes time and trust.

Even when researchers carefully negotiate their access to the Lands, other obstacles might impede their research activity. Several years into my ongoing relationship with PY Media, an anthropologist working for the Pitjantjatjara Council in Alice Springs discovered that my research activities had never crossed her desk. Feeling marginalized, she decided to confront me. She announced over the telephone that I could expect her visit.

The day of her visit began shortly after I arrived in the office. The senior anthropologist stepped into the room, recognized my voice, and demanded that I accompany her to see the AP Executive (the governing council). Confident of my community validation, I resisted going anywhere until she clarified her concerns, though I did agree to step outside so that she might smoke. Outside, she asked a number of aggressive questions accompanied by threats. Surprisingly, she bullied me by making light of every contact that I had formed with traditional owners. The situation reconciled itself when the manager of PY Media arrived and negotiated a settlement whereby we established a council website for her office directed at individuals or groups requesting permission to do research on the Lands.

Turf issues do arise from time to time. People invest considerable effort building archives and compiling research. Insofar as the property actually belongs to the indigenous people, the value that these researchers have acquired seems tentative. They become very wary of others engaged in parallel projects.

Relationships

On the Lands, white fellas speak English. Black fellas understand English but speak Pitjantjatjara. When a Pitjantjatjara man speaks English, he abbreviates the complexities of thought into a system of metaphors and other suggested references. For this reason, most itinerant researchers will rely on white fellas.

To work with the Pitjantjatjara people directly, it obviously helps to speak the language. Shortcuts exist, however, for those who do not have the requisite time or skill. Without using an interpreter, a researcher can learn enough language—a list of key words—to understand the intent of the communication and to respond in kind. With the important use of gesture and with drawing in the sand, the limited vocabulary expands proportionately. The use of key words facilitates relationship building, an essential prerequisite to communication.

This relationship building is especially important in this particular field situation. The region's remoteness and the people's relative isolation have limited the number of secondary texts that may exist for fortifying observations made while visiting the Lands. Therefore, primary sources become crucial. The strongest method for building the most fruitful type of relationship is becoming involved in those issues that generate the most attention in the community. This involvement provides access to the critical forums. Here, one runs the risk of mishandling confidential information. Self-policing becomes essential when the researcher has earned the trust of the community.

On the Lands, all writing requires the approval of the appropriate elder before the researcher can submit the material for publication. This helps protect against unwarranted disclosure. The clearance process might raise its own ethical dilemma but it reduces the researcher's self-policing pressures. Nevertheless, the researcher must have the insight to recognize how outside groups might contextualize information in such a way that it damages the public perception of the people on the Lands. That perception remains crucial for Anangu when it comes to lobbying for support.[4]

Other aspects of disclosure revolve around the taboos associated with acquiring and disseminating sacred knowledge. While chronicling the evolution of new media technology may not require crossing these boundaries, the investigation of it might impact on traditional culture. Shooting any photographs on the Lands requires permission. Should the researcher compile a catalogue of imagery, copyright issues would arise. Not only do indigenous people depend on their traditional imagery for much-needed income, cultural integrity necessitates that circulation conform to their intent for the imagery. Moreover, the overcirculation of prevailing images may make those images meaningless.

Working with primary sources incurs other problems. When interviewing individuals, the researcher must recognize the interviewee's agenda. During the course of an interview, one indigenous elder dictated his story from his pre-prepared written transcript. I made editorial adjustments. He challenged every one. Issues arose regarding the use of first versus third person. He had begun his first paragraph in the first person and then switched to third person, referring to "the people." The elder wanted his wage situation spelled out in order to demonstrate his volunteer status so he could maintain eligibility for certain programs. Meanwhile, I had reservations about building a portrait of EVTV as less than a competent, professional operation in these days of intense scrutiny.[5] In an effort to reconcile the stories, the objective was to keep the Native Australian speech intact without diminishing the quality of the language for an outside listener.

Other Factors

Conditions on the Lands tend to evolve over a long period of time. On the other hand, from one year to the next dramatic differences can take place. Without a sense of perspective, the researcher might misinterpret those dramatic short-term aberrations as indicative of long-term trends.

The cycles of funding account most for the disparity between the short term and the long term. For political, social, historical, economic, and moral reasons, governments feel inclined to develop programs to increase resources for the original occupants of the Lands. Indigenous people contribute to the identity of Australia. They operate as a tourism resource. The government will often assure the indigenous people of this area their survival as a means of promotion. They will also offer barely enough subsistence to keep the people on the Lands, masking the dire circumstances of their survival. Several years ago, after the departure of the missionaries, many central Australian indigenous people had to beg for subsistence. Beggars would greet tourists alighting from trains. The government now avoids this embarrassment through a system requiring that indigenous people collect their subsidy from their local community office.

Other factors affect the waxing and waning of financial resources. Most recently, the federal government elected to privatize the national telephone company to the extent that parliament would permit. In order to guarantee passage, the governing coalition, made up of two key parties, had to reach agreement. One of those partners, the National Party, represents pastoral regions. It worried that the privatization of the telecommunication company would impact on the quality of service rendered to regions that do not have the concentration of population to provide adequate corporate profits. In order to placate its junior partner, the Liberal Party set up a program called the Rural Telecommunication Infrastructure Fund to distribute some percentage of the profits from the sale to pastoral regions to assure a self-sustaining margin of service.

When this money became available through a competitive grant process called Networking the Nation (NTN), other groups besides farmers became eligible. PY Media took advantage of this opportunity to upgrade telecommunication resources. PY Media filed for and successfully received funding support.[6] Since the turn of the century, that money has increased until this year's final rollout of several million dollars. The influx of funding has meant an explosion of activity in this arena, which of course promises dramatic changes in a very short period of time. For a communication researcher, the transition provides a dramatic laboratory for exploring the effects of new telecommunication systems ranging from wireless communication to Internet access. When the cycle plays itself out and the funding declines, will those changes endure, or will the equipment age, the population lose interest, and the situation revert? For the long-term researcher, funding initiatives become critical junctures for measuring cause and effect. The effect takes time to calculate fully.

Separation and Protection

When the researcher returns from the field, the distillation of information demands adherence to a framework that recognizes the complex interrelationships that exist on the Lands. The researcher must identify the anecdotal and determine its validity for the stated objectives of the text. Some of the anecdotal accounts provide the type of insight that enables the resultant writing to transcend the limitations of an academic resource. On the other hand, the researcher cannot lose sight of his or her objectives.

On the Lands, indigenous people vocalize their differences. In an open forum, each party has his or her say. Each individual can return to the microphone to refute, repeat, or challenge an idea. Inevitably, the families arrive at a consensus, though the process may last for an excruciating period of time. Returning from the Lands, that dynamic informs my research. My hypotheses, observations, and conclusions must coexist in two worlds. The work must adhere to a system of "payback." It belongs to the people and has some impact on their lives. The work must also conform to the standards of the "academy," adhering to deadlines and demonstrating a certain detached objectivity. Operating within those invisible lines, achieving both goals elevates the research to the highest moral and ethical plane. The articulation of that struggle in this chapter represents one small part of that greater effort.

Questions for Reflection

What kinds of "payback" do Tafler's research subjects receive for providing him with information about their way of life?

How is Tafler's idea of the researcher's role subtly different from that of Foster and Olson in the previous section? In this context, think about what it means to be "objective."

Tafler uses the example of former lovers' continuing obligation to look after one another's welfare as an example of how the Pitjantjatjara concept of family relationships is different from our own. Is this really so different, or are there also some similarities?

Exactly what sort of cultural change do you suppose these indigenous Australian people will eventually experience as a result of widespread Internet access?

Notes

1. David Peacock, 2000.
2. Other local organizations in Alice Springs for establishing contacts might include Batchelor College and the Institute for Aboriginal Development (IAD).
3. Donald Fraser, words spoken at a meeting of PY Media staff in Umuwa, 2002.

4. Support might mean the difference between adequate and inadequate medical, economic, educational, and other services. Statistically, far fewer Australian dollars support each indigenous individual living in the Central Desert region than support white fellas living in the big cities.
5. Kinyin MacKenzie. July 29, 1998. Umuwa.
6. I played a key role in the early formulation of the NTN grant and an active consultative role in its genesis.

References

Clendinnen, I. 1999. *1999 Boyer Lectures: True Stories.* Sydney: ABC Books.
Glass, A. 1990. *Into Another World: A Glimpse of the Culture of the Ngaanyatjarra People of Central Australia.* Alice Springs: IAB.

13

Adventures in a Foreign Field: Complexity, Crisis, and Creativity in Cross-Cultural Research

Karen Ross

In this chapter, author Karen Ross describes her experiences interviewing women parliamentarians in South Africa as part of a larger cross-cultural project concerned with the intersection of gender, culture, politics, and media. Here, Ross introduces the complex logistics of navigating a somewhat unfamiliar culture (though one with elements borrowed from the North, including both parliamentary government and the use of the English language) on a continent in which the concept of time seems fluid and the bureaucratic organization of official institutions can be a formidable barrier to an outsider. Technology itself—cell phones, recording tapes—further hinders the whole enterprise if (as described in this account) it does not work quite as expected.

The logistical issues of work in a somewhat unfamiliar culture are daunting. It may be that Ross's chapter makes it look too easy, as her persistence meant she was able to complete a significant number of interviews even though things did not always go as planned. However, anyone who has ever traveled outside his or her own country is aware that getting even ordinary things done (doing grocery shopping, mailing a package, finding an address) can sometimes loom as substantial challenges. Ross is to be congratulated on her accomplishment, despite the inevitable difficulties she encountered. Yes, Internet cafes are on every corner in major cities around the world (as Ross's account attests), but this does not mean that culture has become completely homogenized, nor that finding one's way around a foreign landscape has stopped being easier said than done.

Ross finds that on some occasions she does not agree with the political positions of the women she is studying. While ethnographers often talk about the development of "rapport" or a sense of personal connectedness between the interviewer

— 185 —

and the person being interviewed, achieving this may require researchers to compartmentalize their personal opinions to varying degrees. Traditionally, ethnographers working outside their own culture have been admonished to avoid value judgments that might spring from their cultural backgrounds and biases. In practice, this may be difficult, highlighting the whole constellation of issues surrounding the notion of disinterested or "objective" research.

IN TEACHING RESEARCH METHODS and particularly when discussing interviews, I always stress the importance of being prepared, doing homework, checking equipment, and so on. But in a world that has become increasingly bureaucratized and rule-bound and where statistics multiply alongside ever more restrictive lifestyles, part of the appeal of qualitative research to me, as a communication scholar interested as much with the users and producers of media as with media texts themselves, is the unpredictability of field research, especially when the fields in question are foreign. It is precisely the methodological messiness of research with human beings, where both the researcher and the researched are irrevocably fallible, which can nonetheless create unexpected paths of enquiry, where questions slip off the rails and bounce along altogether different tracks, throwing up the seeds of new ideas. When those tracks are in strange and different territories, there are ever more layers of complexity to explore.

About halfway through the research methods module I teach to our postgraduate students, we get to talking about their dissertations and about the importance of research design and of finding methods appropriate to their research questions. And we talk about doing fieldwork and the need to be aware of differences in cultural mores when researching in contexts with which we are unfamiliar. Most of the students in the class are international students, and although some of them go home to undertake their research projects, most stay in England and choose to research people close to or in the university. Nearly all these students regularly experience culture shock in their everyday lives while they study in England, shock at the way the "locals" talk, at what they eat, at how they dress. So cross-cultural research works both ways, depending on who we are and whose culture is being "crossed."

What research methods textbooks don't and perhaps cannot tell you is how to be a good researcher, because research is more than simply the collection, analysis, and interpretation of data, more than the possession of certain kinds of technical skills and training. To be a good researcher is to learn through experience and, importantly, to learn that no project, despite its suggestion of logical coherence and linear regularity, ever travels the path expected at its beginning. For qualitative research in particular, the twists and turns of a creative and often rather fluid methodology are rarely detrimental to the final outcome and mostly enhance our understanding of the complexity of the human condition.

Of course, methods textbooks are incredibly useful in identifying paradigms and exemplar methodologies, but what I want to do in this short piece is to offer some thoughts on the *process* of doing cross-cultural research and, moreover, of doing research with "elite" subjects (in this case, women politicians). Through this essay, I want to expose some of the issues with which researchers routinely grapple during fieldwork, as a way to share and learn from experience, and, importantly, to make entirely explicit that good research is reflexive and reflective, able to accommodate unexpected complications in the research process such as accessing elusive research subjects, getting lost on the subway, or finding that you need a visitor's pass for which there's a three-week waiting time. Coping with such vicissitudes helps us grow and develop.

The Bigger Picture

As part of an ongoing research interest in the inter-relationship between women, politics, and media (see also Ross 1995, 2002), I have interviewed women parliamentarians from four legislative assemblies (the U.K.'s Westminster—1996, 2000; Australia—1998; South Africa—1999; Northern Ireland—2002). While *all* the interviews I have undertaken have been fascinating and revealing in many different ways, the rest of this chapter will focus on some of the issues that have arisen when researching far away from home, in an unfamiliar cultural context, where the assumption of a shared common language both complicates and eases a novel research journey.

What I want to argue is that undertaking cross-cultural research is rewarding and frustrating in almost equal measure, not only because we have no recourse to the familiar patterns and norms of our routinized daily life, but also because we actually become different people when we're working across cultures. We are emboldened by our sense of intrepid enterprise and adventure, but also disempowered by our lack of local knowledge and fear of the unknown.

The Cape Town Experience: Cultural Mechanics in the Rainbow Nation

In March 1999, I visited South Africa to interview women parliamentarians just before the second democratically held elections were to take place in May. I had already spent much of the latter months of 1998 setting up the interviews upon which I was now to embark, having sent a personalized letter to all 117 women who were then members of both houses of Parliament in October that year. By December, only six women had agreed to be interviewed, so I sent out a follow-up letter in January. By the time I left for Cape Town, fifteen women had agreed to interviews, most insisting that I make a firm arrangement with them once I had arrived in Cape Town, as their diaries were in a constant state of flux. I could do nothing but agree to this highly unsatisfactory beginning to the fieldwork, although (thankfully) five women had given me a firm date and time for an interview before I left, around which I then attempted to build my interview itinerary. Discussing this frustrating situation with a new colleague at the University of Cape Town on my first evening, he said, rather phlegmatically, "Welcome to Africa."

Within twenty-four hours of arriving, I do my first interview, having been faxed the previous Thursday to be told that I had an audience with Minister Shandu (Inkatha Freedom Party or IFP) at 10:00 A.M. sharp at the Good Hope Building at Parliament. While Mrs. Shandu had been on my circulation list, as she was Deputy Minister for Public Works, she had since moved on to become Education Minister in the Province of Kwa-Zulu Natal. She was not, therefore, a national politician but a regional one. However, it seemed ridiculous *not* to interview her. Eventually, having negotiated the maze of buildings which comprise the parliamentary complex, I find the one in which she has her office and, upon entering, tell the armed guard that I have an appointment to see her. Security is very, very tight and I am kept in the very small lobby area while the security police try to understand my accent and the name of the person I wish to see. No, there is no Shandu listed, I am told; I must have made a mistake. I explain that she had recently moved to the Provincial Government in Kwa-Zulu Natal but had arranged to meet me here in this building. I suggest they ring the IFP offices for confirmation.

Eventually, I am allowed through the security cordon and directed to the IFP offices. I explain my story once more to the woman staffing the desk and when I finish, she looks pityingly at me and reports that Mrs. Shandu is in Kwa-Zulu Natal right now but will be flying down to Cape Town later in the day. Could I come back at 1:30 P.M.? I say "Of course" and walk back through the security gate and hand my pass in at reception. The two guards look at me with raised eyebrows, as if I had tried to perpetrate some kind of con and it had backfired. I say I will be returning later and they give me a "yeah, yeah" kind of look. I leave the building, walking into a warm, sultry day.

At 1:00 P.M., I arrive back at the Good Hope Building only to find that the security guards have changed shift and I have to go through the whole story again. Once more, I am directed through security and on to the IFP offices with which, at least this time, I am now familiar. But still no sign of Mrs. Shandu. Or anyone, in fact. After a couple of minutes, a man appears in the corridor and he seems familiar—I realize that he is Chief Buthelezi, the leader of the IFP! I tell my story for a fourth time and he takes pity on me, explaining that Mrs. Shandu *will* soon be arriving and perhaps I would like to wait in the library and he will arrange tea. Forty-five minutes later Mrs. Shandu rushes in, saying that her office had tried to contact me two days before to change the plan, by which time I was already on my way to Cape Town. Anyway, she tells me, she can't do the interview now because she must go immediately to the Chamber to listen to the debate on education. Could I come back at, say, 3:30 P.M.? Of course I can. I tell myself that I have no other plans and this is why I'm here after all, but I'm still immensely irritated. During that frustrating first day and subsequently, I get to know all the cafes and bars in the immediate vicinity; having conducted interviews with parliamentarians in other parts of the world, I realize being jerked around by people whose diaries are much more important than yours simply goes with the territory.

I make contact with most of the women on my list (or their assistants) that first Monday, but by the end of the day, no one has rung me back. Strange. I ring one MP[1] on the home number she gave me and she is nice and friendly and says that she has in fact tried to ring me back on the cell phone number I gave her several times but all she got was the engaged tone. From my end, the phone has remained sullenly silent all day. I discuss this conundrum with my guesthouse host and he says, "Ah, I think you need to tell people to include the international code for the UK at the start of the number, as the call has to go first to the UK and then on to South Africa." Well, that explains it.

Back again at the Good Hope Building at 3:30 P.M.—same frustration with the security guards since one is a new guy and the other had not, apparently, witnessed my meeting with Mrs. Shandu, although we had been speaking together in front of his desk scarcely an hour before. I get directed back to the IFP library. At 4:00 P.M., Mrs. Shandu arrives, a little breathless. She tells me she can give me twenty minutes and shall we take tea in the Members' Tea Room? Yes, please! She sits herself in front of the TV, which is broadcasting the debate in the Chamber. It is important that she follow the debate as she will be returning to the Chamber after our interview, but I want to tape record the interview and wonder how the microphone will be able to compete with the television. She compromises by sitting two tables away, and in between sips of tea and mouthfuls of cake, she answers my questions. She is still in full flow when the tape clicks off and she realizes that she has been talking for sixty minutes. She asks me if I would like to accompany her to the Chamber to listen to the rest of the debate. I don't need asking twice.

We hurry down the cobbled pathway to the Chamber, she dispatches an aide to get me a pass while I'm loitering in yet another lobby, and she goes up to the Gallery. The aide eventually arrives back with the pass and I'm checked through security. The aide takes me to the Strangers' Gallery and sits me next to Mrs. Shandu, who takes my hand and squeezes it in acknowledgment before turning back to observe the proceedings below. She proceeds to maintain a running commentary of gossip and invective in equal measure as successive parliamentarians stand to speak. The Chamber is even emptier than an ordinary sitting in the House of Commons in Britain, which comes as a surprise so near to the election and given the nature of the debate, where education for nonwhites is an extremely hot issue. I am also surprised by the number of parliamentarians talking on their cell phones without any concern for either privacy or decorum. Oh well, when in Africa. . . . When the debate concludes, Mrs. Shandu collects her various papers, bags, phone, and other accoutrements and we leave together. She bids me farewell at the door and wishes me well for my work. It's been a curate's egg kind of day but one that brought its own unexpected rewards: it also set the tone, inevitably, for the rest of my time in Cape Town with its mix of strangeness, frustration, and joy.

And on the Second Day . . .

My second day is more of the same, again trying to make contact with the women on my list to arrange appointments. Conscious of the high cost of all these telephone calls, on one of my walks down Parliament Lane I realize that I have passed the British High Commission. I go in and ask if I can use the phone to make some calls to Parliament. The staff members there are very obliging and usher me into the front office, giving me a chair, a cup of tea, and a telephone. I begin again. This time the process is about three-quarters successful. In any case, I have three interviews today, starting with Melanie Verwoerd. She immediately dispels my preconceptions about what a member of the ANC[2] might be like: she is young, lively, and white. She is candid and charming and makes a number of suggestions about other women I should contact, including the head of the South African Broadcasting Corporation team at Parliament and the head of the parliamentary team at Independent Newspapers. Dropping Melanie's name with both these women the following day when I ring them opens the door to an interview with the latter but a "Sorry, but I'm out of town" from the former. Thank you, Melanie!

Throughout my interview with her (and in subsequent ones), the brief history of democratic South Africa in the post-1994 period of transformation is brought alive for me in a way that is otherwise impossible to know because nearly all the information we receive about South Africa in the West is refracted through the lenses of other people. Issues of race, class, and gender continuously crosscut and inform Verwoerd's narrative, making complex what is more usually seen as the "simple" process of Mandela's release, the dismantling of apartheid, and the dawn of a new South Africa. It *is* all that, of course, but also so much more, and the gender dimension, which is the aspect in which I am especially interested, insinuates itself throughout the agenda.

At lunchtime, I interview Koko Mokgalong, a backbench ANC MP who has much to say about cultural politics and the role of women in the democratic process. I notice that my tape recorder clicks off a lot sooner than forty-five minutes, but turn the tape over anyway and continue with the interview. On leaving her office, I check the tape and find that the second side is blank and the first side stops peremptorily midway along. Damn. That means most of the interview has not been recorded. I curse the tape and the street vendor who sold it to me. I have barely ten minutes to find somewhere else that sells tapes as I have now lost confidence in the viability of the rest of the batch I bought at the same time. Walking quickly to a major street, I find a computer store and buy one ninety-minute tape. This one will be okay; it's wrapped in cellophane. I unwrap it as I walk along and shove it in the machine. I press record and start and nothing happens. I fast forward it a little and try again. It won't budge. I take the tape out and examine it. It looks all right. Then I notice that the tabs on the top are missing. This is getting very slightly ridiculous. There's nothing for it: I approach another street vendor selling perfect-looking, wrapped TDK90s. They are 40p each. I buy one and stand at the stall, unwrapping it and putting it in the machine. It records perfectly. I have five minutes to get to my third and last appointment. There is a god and she is smiling on me!

Another New Dawn

A new day arrives and I have four interviews set up for the day, with another six in the bag for next week and only four outstanding appointments yet to make. Having now been backwards and forwards to Parliament a number of times over the past few days, it continues to surprise me that the guards do not know the names of their own parliamentarians, even ministers. Each time I arrive for an appointment, I have to show them my now dog-eared matrix of names and contact numbers and even then, they seem reluctant to look up names in their internal phone directory and prefer that I tell them the appropriate extension, which I rarely know. Even when I show them the correct spelling of a parliamentarian's name, they read it as if for the first time, blankly and with incredulity.

At first I decide it is simply a problem of pronunciation and my inability to get my tongue around the unfamiliar Xhosa names, but the same thing happens when I ask for a parliamentarian with an "easy" name like Gill Marcus—well, easy for *me* at least! Each time I try and access a parliamentarian (and this feeling never left me) I am made to feel like I'm trying to con my way into the hallowed space, and it's always a huge effort to be taken seriously. Bizarrely, though, once I have been verified and checked through security, I am then free to wander wherever I please, with no one accompanying me and nowhere apparently off limits. Throughout the two weeks I spend in the various parliamentary buildings, once I've been checked through, I am never challenged, and I am never asked for identification, even when I use the Members' Tea Room on my own. It feels both daring and dangerous and quite unlike any other parliamentary context I have experienced.

Nearly the End of Week One

Towards the end of the first week, I interview Mrs. Botha (Democratic Party), who collects me in person, takes me up to her room, and asks if I'd like the air conditioning switched on and some tea. I say "Yes" to both. It is only 9:00 A.M., but already I am soggy and tired. We are constantly interrupted while she orders tea, answers her phones (desk and cell), and entertains visitors. She apologizes profusely for each interruption, throwing up her hands in horror at the "lot of the politician," and eventually takes a few minutes to work out how to turn the ringer off on her cell. We have a few minutes' clear interview time before I realize that it is now 10:00 A.M. and I have to leave for another interview. She also needs to go on to a meeting and, as we are saying our goodbyes, her secretary arrives with the long-awaited tea. She gives me an accusatory look when I say that I must leave, and Mrs. Botha gives her a mean "eye" back.

My next interviewee is Tersia King, someone I had seen in full flow on Monday during the education debate. As I am waiting to be checked by security—all the opposition MPs are housed together in a building on the opposite side to the Chamber—I spot her rushing through the security arch. As she goes through, she mutters something about a meeting and I call out to her that it is probably with me. She turns and asks, "Dr. Ross?" and I say, "Yes." The security guard quickly takes my bag off the conveyor without it being camera-checked and whisks me through. I run to keep up with her and am practically panting as we get to her door. She unlocks it and flops down inside, having been summoned by her secretary at 8:00 A.M. that morning to attend a meeting about which she had had no prior knowledge. I ask if she would like me to wait a few minutes before starting but she brushes my concern aside and seems eager to talk.

She is the first National Party MP I have interviewed and as soon as I ask the preliminary question about being a woman in Parliament, she launches into a potted history of her career (parliamentary and otherwise), including her divorce and the difficulties of running two households and having to remember to buy the toilet paper for *all* the bathrooms as she doesn't have a servant in Cape Town. She is, unsurprisingly, scathing about the government and displays the same kind of sullen disrespect that I witnessed in the Chamber earlier. She doesn't believe in quotas—the ANC has a quota of 30 percent women throughout the party structure, including for elected members—and feels that many (women) parliamentarians are there as "voting fodder." She talks fondly about the "good old days" (apartheid) and insists that she is proud to be a woman. She is wearing a shocking pink Chanel-style two-piece with gold jewelry and is pleased when her male colleagues tell her that she's looking especially nice. As I listen to her talk, I am already mentally arranging her remarks under suitable subheadings. Although I hate her politics, I know this is a very good interview.

I have a lunchtime appointment next with Dr. Tshabala-Msimang, Deputy Minister for Justice, and when I arrive her assistant is looking apologetic. She explains that the afternoon debate has been brought forward and the minister is no longer able to keep the appointment. However, the minister would like to tell me this sad news herself and I am ushered into her office. She greets me warmly and wastes no time telling me that her husband was, until recently, the High Commissioner in London and that she knows Britain well. However, the meeting is now impossible and perhaps I could kindly try to rearrange with her secretary. I go back to her assistant, Zethu, and we check our diaries. The minister's one is impossibly full but she could probably fit me in next Tuesday at 11:30 A.M. I check mine and see that I'm down for an interview at 12:00 noon. Zethu suggests that I simply rearrange my noon appointment, but I am loath to do so as it is with Jenny Malan, the only other National Party MP who I am due to interview. We nonetheless agree to the 11:30 time, and I say that it will simply be a short interview. Although this new appointment is in both our diaries, Zethu cautions that things might change again, so I decide not to try and change the 12:00 noon meeting after all—a good decision, as it turns out, as I never do get to interview the deputy minister.

As I now have several hours to spare before the next interview, I go off in search of an Internet cafe where I can check my e-mail, drink mango juice, and "chat" with colleagues back home. I find the cafe recommended by the Lonely Planet guide, and it's the perfect blend of high technology, psychedelic wallpaper, and laid-back "waitrons." My last interview of the day is with Gill Marcus, Deputy Minister of Finance, who turns up bang on time and invites me into her office. Despite us wearing matching "hers'n'hers" AIDS ribbons, I immediately sense a restrained hostility, and she takes a rather combative stance in response to my questioning. This is not the first time I have experienced this response, but each time I am taken aback.

When I write to prospective interviewees, I make it very clear that I am working on a project focused on women parliamentarians' experiences of politics as women, of their experiences of the media as women politicians. When they then agree to be interviewed, I foolishly assume that they are interested in talking to me about their experiences. But occasionally, as with Gill Marcus, they simply refuse to be drawn into anything to do with their sex, insisting that being women is entirely irrelevant to their politics and/or experiences. Oh, well! However, in the end we speak for forty-five minutes until the tape clicks off and by then, I think she's warmed to me a bit. She gives me an excellent closing quote about the media's portrayal of her colleague, Nkokosama Zuma, which instantly redeems her in my eyes.

Friday

I had arranged a lunchtime interview with "Sarah" (ANC; not her real name). When I speak to her from the lobby phone, she expresses surprise that I am there, saying that she had me down in her diary but as I hadn't confirmed, she had gone ahead and made another appointment. I know that I *did* confirm but am not about to argue. She suggests we meet for lunch anyway as her other visitors have not yet arrived. We meet in the parliamentary restaurant and I begin to conduct an impromptu interview although she is a little anxious about being taped. Eventually she agrees. Ten minutes into the lunch interview, her visitors arrive. They are from a women's project and she has commissioned them to do some research on women political prisoners. As she talks it becomes clear that her interest is not purely academic as she talks about her own life as an exile and prisoner. We have an interesting lunch and she then takes me back to her office to do the interview proper.

As we talk, the reason for her caution about being taped becomes apparent: she is rather critical of the ANC's commitment to follow through on its pledge to empower women within the political structure. I reassure her that I will let her have a copy of the interview transcript and that she can identify which of her comments should be anonymized. The interview goes well. As I'm leaving, she suddenly remembers that the Commission on Gender Equality is launching its annual report the following week and rushes off to photocopy the program for me. I check my diary and see that I can attend. But the invitation is for MPs only and I'm not sure how "public" it is. She assures me that I simply need to wave the invitation at the security guards, say that I'm there by her personal invitation, and I'll be let in. All my previous dealings with the parliamentary guards would suggest this might not be as straightforward as she seems to think, but I'm going to try my luck anyway.

I discover another Internet cafe round the corner from Parliament and check my e-mail. I find that two more MPs have agreed to be interviewed, and

I e-mail them back straightaway with promises to contact them on Monday. I might yet achieve my goal of twenty interviews after all. At the end of my first week, I'm happy with the way in which the research is going and looking forward to spending the weekend eating and shopping and not feeling guilty because I haven't made a start on all the work I've brought with me in case I got bored. I have seven confirmed appointments next week with the possibility of a further four. The itinerant researcher's life is not so bad. The second week is more of the same, and the final tally of interviews is seventeen—not as many as I had hoped for, but certainly enough to have made the trip worthwhile.

Post-Hoc Reflection: Theory, Practice, and the Gaps Between

The work that I have undertaken with women politicians has been fascinating, amazing, insightful, and (mostly) sisterly. I am privileged to have had the opportunity to talk to so many good women, and their experiences have informed my thinking and writing about the gendered nature of formal politics and the expectations (reasonable or otherwise) we might have, as feminists, of women in decision-making positions. While I recognize something of the power play that other critics speak of in the context of the sometimes tetchy dynamic between researcher and elite subject (see Moyser and Wagstaffe 1987), I actually experienced very few overt attempts to dominate the interview.

While there is a small literature that discusses some of the problematics in researching elite subjects (see Williams 1980; Ball 1994; Neal 1998), there are very few authors who talk specifically about working with elite women such as politicians (but see Puwar 1997), so I hope that this short piece and the other works that have emerged from this particular, extended study (see Ross 2002) make thoughtful and provocative reading. I didn't always like what women said to me in the same way that some women politicians were vehemently opposed to other women's policies while at the same time being in sympathy about the way in which they were being treated by the media. To a large extent, this was also my position. I mostly liked the women but sometimes I hated their politics. That's part of the conundrum of exploratory research, but also part of what makes it worth doing.

Questions for Reflection

Technologies like telephones and tape recorders seem to get in the way in this project, but most researchers find them convenient. How would similar interview information have been gathered by earlier generations of researchers?

Ross's informants seem impolite, some of them rearranging appointments at the last minute. To what extent do you suppose this springs from her pursuit of busy and important people? To what extent might it also be the result of cultural differences?

How should researchers deal with situations in which they do not personally agree with the opinions of their research subjects? Should they disguise their opinions, if asked?

Notes

1. Member of Parliament.
2. African National Congress.

References

Ball, S. J. 1994. "Political Interviews and the Politics of Interviewing." Pp. 96–115 in *Researching the Powerful in Education*, ed. Geoffrey Walford. London: UCL Press.
Moyser, G., and M. Wagstaffe. 1987. "Studying Elites: Theoretical and Methodological Issues." Pp. 1–24 in *Research Methods for Elite Studies*, eds. G. Moyser and M. Wagstaffe. London: Allen & Unwin.
Neal, S. 1998. *The Making of Equal Opportunities Policies in Universities*. Buckingham: Open University Press.
Puwar, N. 1997. "Reflections on Interviewing Women MPs." *Sociological Research Online* 2 (1) http://www.socresonline.org.uk/socresonline/2/1/4.html (accessed 2 Feb. 2004).
Ross, K. 1995. "Gender and Party Politics: How the Press Reported the Labour Leadership Campaign 1994." *Media, Culture & Society* 17 (3): 499–509.
Ross, K. 2002. *Women, Politics, Media: Uneasy Relations in Comparative Perspective*. Cresskill, NJ: Hampton Press.
Williams, P. M. 1980. "Interviewing Politicians: The Life of Hugh Gaitskell." *Political Quarterly* 51 (3): 303–16.

14

On Our Way, On the Ground, On Cloud Nine: Research Planning and Adaptation in Belize

Joy L. Hart and Kandi L. Walker

Joy Hart and Kandi Walker (and their students) joined a health services project in Belize as communication researchers. Like all cross-cultural researchers, they found that their methods had to be adapted to the cultural setting in ways their careful research did not anticipate. Language and questionnaire problems arose that were not anticipated, but cultural norms relevant to condom distribution turned out to be less restrictive than they had thought. An unexpected U.S. military presence at a time of international tension added to the complexity of the situation, as well as upset some of the logistical planning.

Prepared to use the type of scaled attitude questionnaires so familiar in the developed world, these researchers did not initially realize that having people complete these would be a difficult challenge, even to literate Belizeans. Our own culture takes answering multiple-choice questions and filling out attitude scales for granted; others do not. Culturally inappropriate questions also can be created through asking a question in the wrong vernacular, asking a question that simply makes no sense to someone in the culture being studied, or asking a question that is offensive according to local norms and expectations. It seems that sometimes, no amount of advance planning can eliminate this risk entirely.

This contribution reinforces messages learned in the chapters just preceding it. To "outsiders," a culture may appear unpredictable, even though conditions and practices there make perfect sense to "insiders"; successful researchers in such contexts are those who are flexible enough to adapt their approaches to the conditions they find and to the constraints imposed on them, as each of our previous contributors to this section has pointed out.

*Perhaps one of the most important "lessons learned" from this experience—
beyond the observation that the best-laid plans can go somewhat awry—was noting how much the time spent informally getting to know the community (not actually a formal part of the research design at all) enhanced the project. These authors' students also report that the project changed their own lives at least as
much as it changed the lives of the Belizeans it was designed to help.*

On Our Way: Project Background

Now that I'm back home the whole trip seems like a dream. I could never have believed that so much could go so wrong and still turn out so right. I learned more from this project than I ever imagined, and I think I learned much of it because we got to talk through the planning stages and yet we had to improvise on the spot.

—(Student Journal Entry, March 26, 2003)

GALES POINT IS A REMOTE COASTAL VILLAGE in Belize, Central America, and the opportunity to work there was appealing. As professors, we would have a chance to work closely with some of our best students—developing their research skills and making a difference in the world—and spending spring break in the tropics seemed a fine idea, too. Thus, we were on our way to Belize and a new project was underway.

As part of the University of Louisville's International Service Learning Program (ISLP), we agreed to form a communication team and work collaboratively with students and faculty from the medical, nursing, and dental programs. Thus, the international health team was born, and we began our project of providing health education and health care (free medical and dental clinics) in Gales Point.

The primary goal of the medical, nursing, and dental program students and faculty was to run the free clinics. Our own goal (the goal of the communication team) was threefold: (1) to promote the clinics to residents, (2) to provide information and health education materials on common illnesses, and (3) to gather data on health beliefs and practices to lay the groundwork for future health communication campaigns in Gales Point. Although all three goals were important, the third one, discovering health beliefs and practices, was critical to our future work in the village. That is, if we could understand how residents viewed health and illness and the behaviors in which they engaged, then we could better target health information, education efforts, and health care campaigns in the future.

Much coordination was required to prepare for the project, and we spent eleven months getting ready for the trip. Crucial facets of this phase of the project involved coordination across the full interdisciplinary team, research on Gales Point (on such things as literacy levels, languages, and general health), advance publicity in Belize, and designing data collection instruments for health beliefs and practices. In this chapter, we focus our attention on the last two of these, preparation for data collection and advance publicity in Belize.

The Village of Gales Point

Although the exact population of Gales Point (also called Gales Point Manatee) is not known, based on current records in Belize, estimates suggest that about 380 adults and children live in or near the village. More than 98 percent of the residents are of Creole descent, and 56 percent are female (Bent 2000). More than 80 percent of the villagers completed elementary school, with an additional 12 percent having completed high school. At present, more than 50 percent of the villagers are unemployed, and the most common way villagers describe their occupation is subsistence fishing (Bent 2000). Although Belize is located in Central America, most Belizeans speak English, which is the national language, with a few speaking Spanish or Creole; thus, language differences were not anticipated to be an obstacle in this work.

Gales Point is located on a peninsula and is accessible by a dirt road from outside Dangriga, the nearest town. The drive is generally a bumpy and dusty thirty- to forty-five-minute one. Living conditions in the village are basic. Some people have running water; others do not. Some people have indoor plumbing; others do not. Until quite recently, most residents used outhouses, which emptied directly into the surrounding waters. Diseases and medical problems not often seen in the United States are not uncommon in Belize (such as malaria and rabies).

Routine medical and dental care is limited in Gales Point. Recent research suggests that at least half of the Belizean population in remote areas has limited access to health services (Barry and Vernon 1995; Chanecka 1998). Most villagers in Gales Point do not own automobiles, with 92 percent relying on public buses for transportation (Bent 2000). By bus, the nearest medical services are approximately two hours away. However, a rural health care nurse is assigned to the village and lives in the village clinic, which is housed inside the community center and consists of one exam room and a few supplies. Essentially, the level of care available parallels basic first aid. Basic medical screenings (e.g., blood sugar, blood pressure) are not commonly done, even though hypertension and diabetes are common medical conditions across Belize. Without detection, such conditions usually worsen. In Gales Point, few people retain all of their permanent teeth, and few have had access to dental care. Following practices across Belize, it is common for Gales Point citizens to use herbal remedies and "bush medicine."

Project Planning

In order to prepare for the spring break project in March 2003, we began meeting with students in summer of 2002. From then until the trip, we met at least weekly and sometimes much more often. Several key decisions had to be made and much information needed to be prepared. One of the first questions we confronted was, "How do we publicize medical and dental clinics in a small village where people don't know us?"

The answer that emerged from our research team was a multimethod approach. First, we decided to prepare press releases and send them to newspapers, radio stations, and television stations in Belize. Despite considerable research, we were never able to determine how many people subscribed to newspapers or had televisions or radios or access to these media, but we hoped that some coverage of the story might encourage participation in the clinics. We did learn that although there was electricity in the village, it did not always work twenty-four hours a day.

Second, we decided that some type of more direct contact with villagers was necessary. Although some of the villagers had met a few people associated with the project, we needed to develop a way to introduce the health team and explain the clinics. Advance notice seemed important, as did establishing trust. We decided to draw on contacts of the assistant director of the university's ISLP, who is Belizean. Through him, we began coordinating efforts with the mayor of Gales Point. We learned of village meetings held in the community center, where the clinic was set to take place. Our students designed flyers that were mailed to the mayor for distribution at these meetings and to post in key spots at the community center building and in the village. We also sent informational announcements for these meetings. Because we discovered that the mayor was an admired and respected official who been elected for several terms, we believed that having his support for the project was crucial. Throughout the months prior to our visit, we sent press releases to the media and information to the mayor of Gales Point several times.

Beyond activities such as arranging for the inoculations and medications (such as those for malaria, typhoid, and hepatitis) recommended by the Centers for Disease Control in the United States for travel to Belize and determining proper clothing for work in the tropical climate, we spent considerable time developing measures for uncovering health beliefs and practices. We created two types of measures—an interview guide for the in-depth interviews and four survey instruments, with Likert-type rating scales (that is, the answer responses were in scales, in this case ranging from 1 to 5). Care was taken to avoid culturally biased wording (such as U.S. slang) and to ensure readability. The fact that our initial research revealed elementary school completion for most adults, combined with the data we had found on literacy rates in Belize, suggested that most people would be able to complete these instruments. Thus, we finalized the measures, secured Human Subjects Committee approval for the project, and packed our bags to leave for Belize.

On the Ground: A Time for Change

There's a saying about "the best-laid plans" and it certainly applied to us! Despite our months of intense preparation, once we were on the ground in Gales Point, we needed to start adapting quickly. Despite how thoroughly our instruments and research plan had been conceived, several measures needed an immediate revamping. We met with our students and drew parallels with what we tell them in public speaking classes—you need to prepare thoroughly for a speech or presentation, but you must also adapt to the audience and situation. So, now was the phase of adaptation—and, in some ways, radical change.

A Change of Venue

The morning of our arrival we were scheduled to canvass the neighborhood, which consisted of houses along the main dirt road, encouraging people to come to the clinics, and to begin data collection on health beliefs and practices in the clinics. However, what we didn't know in advance was that the U.S. military would be in Gales Point for two days on a humanitarian assignment, which included medical, dental, vision, and veterinary care. The military group also included a communication team, but with a different focus than ours (on photography and writing for military publications).

The overlap in several of the major goals prompted some integration of teams—our medical, nursing, and dental staffs joined efforts with the military. However, because of extremely limited space, there was no longer room for our "station" in the clinic for data gathering on health beliefs and practices. We should also note that this was mid-March, 2003. Although the U.S. war with Iraq had not yet begun, it would before the week's end, tensions were already high, and views of the U.S. action were mixed. In addition, the military presence in this small town created quite a visual effect, with guns, sections of space cordoned off, and lots of camouflage vehicles and uniforms. We immediately wondered about the numerous ramifications for our project.

We had planned initially to do some face-to-face recruiting for the clinics once we were in Gales Point. Now that there was no space for our planned in-clinic activities, we decided to focus on meeting villagers, talking with them, and encouraging them to come to the clinics. The original plan to use the community center also had been abandoned for the first two days. With the military, the team would work in the school, located farther up the dirt road, and then for the remaining days, we would move to the community center, located closer to the center of town and closer to the lodge where we stayed. This location was important, in part because we had no transportation and thus walked the mile to and from the clinic. Generally, a mile each way may not be much, but in 105-degree temperatures in a tropical climate one is not acclimated to, often carrying supplies, with ten-hour work days, it is a factor to consider.

With the community center now unused, we selected it as our base of operations. From there, the communication team went out in dyads, stopping along the road to talk to anyone who might have time for a chat—and that was essentially everyone! It is commonplace for people in Gales Point to sit on their porches and under trees during the day. Their "laid-back" approach helped us a great deal. Very quickly, we were all engaged in various conversations, standing along the roadway, sitting on steps to people's homes, sitting on the community center porch, or sitting in the grass with people along the road. Nearly everyone assured us that they would be coming to the clinics, though several stated that they wanted to wait until the military left as the guns made them nervous.

We also learned that most people had heard about the free medical and dental clinics from the mayor, a flyer, or a radio announcement; thus, we received some confirmation that our initial publicity efforts had worked. We answered a few questions about the clinics and engaged in lots of "small talk," which actually was "big talk" for us because we were learning a great deal about the village and villagers. Several children gathered around the community center, and some of our students took out Frisbees and began playing with them. This "play time" allowed our students to learn the children's perspectives as well. We believe that the play time helped ease the children's minds, as well as assure their parents that we were not a group coming in to "fix" their village. Rather, we were there to help and learn from them.

Although we hadn't planned to begin this way, the time was well spent in learning people's names and learning about the village. In addition, without realizing it at the time, these informal interactions let people get to know us as well and come to trust us. Though it wasn't intentional, these initial hours on the first day were perhaps the best PR that our program could have received.

A Shift in Measures

Given that people knew about the clinics and did not seem to have many questions or concerns, we decided to begin our data collection on health beliefs and practices outside the clinics—along the dirt road with whomever was willing to talk with us. We found that virtually everyone was willing to be interviewed and to share their views on health, but we quickly learned that all of the instruments needed to be completed orally. The scaled surveys were too challenging for people to complete independently. The difficulty was in part based on literacy, but it also had to do with the "unusual" (for them) nature of the task. In the United States, most people are exposed early to selecting answers from a list (starting with multiple-choice test items in elementary school) and to rating items (using scales to assign preferences), but in Gales Point such tasks were not common and thus were very difficult. We had not anticipated this difficulty, but we quickly restructured so that all data collection would take place orally and in an open-ended fashion.

Unanticipated Language Barriers

A second unanticipated difficulty centered on language differences. English was spoken by virtually all residents in and around Gales Point; we had a few Spanish speakers, but a student fluent in Spanish translated. But Belizean English had evolved from British English. Thus, spelling, pronunciation, and some vocabulary are different than in U.S. English. In addition, several Creole and some Spanish words are commonly employed amid the spoken English. These factors, combined with the quick rate of speech, made it difficult for us to understand interviewees, as well as people in passing conversations on occasion. But the longer we were there, the easier understanding others became. Thankfully, we also discovered that the Gales Point residents were very comfortable repeating information if we needed them to do so.

Our initial research suggested that due to cultural norms, Belizeans would be hesitant to discuss certain health topics. So, we had planned subtle questions and methods of probing to uncover some information. Also, beyond the provision of free health care and medications, part of our service work included distribution of other free health-related materials and items. Because HIV/AIDS is a serious health problem in Belize and we were doing health education, our students had secured donations of more than one thousand condoms. Preparing to transport these condoms to Belize led to a number of jokes among our team—mainly centering on how a customs search would reveal hundreds of condoms in the suitcases, suggesting someone anticipated quite a spring break! However, initial research on religious customs indicated that distributing the condoms might be an issue and general norms suggested that people might be hesitant to ask for them. To ensure cultural appropriateness, we talked with the mayor after arriving, and he saw no problems with the condoms being freely distributed. And though our initial research on norms might apply to other places in Belize, the residents of Gales Point were not at all reserved in asking for condoms. In fact, several days as we left the clinic to walk back to our lodge, we were approached on the road by residents asking for condoms or invited into homes by children so that their relatives could ask us for condoms. One member of our team who carried the condoms in her backpack quickly became labeled the "condom lady" and was quite popular with the residents.

With the many adjustments we made once we were in Gales Point, our data collection went very well. The time passed quickly, and soon it was time to return home.

On Cloud Nine: A Time for Reflection

As our bus pulled out from the lodge and headed down the bumpy dirt road taking us away from Gales Point and back to the United States, we were both saddened and exhilarated. We were saddened to be leaving people who had become our friends in only a week and exhilarated by what we had learned and the experience overall. Our students were both excited to be returning home and sorry to be leaving as well. One echoed the views of many by stating, "I know that I'll always remember these people. I'll remember them and treasure this experience all of my life," and then asking, "Do you think that they'll remember us?" Another remarked, "When I first got here I thought that they were so poor and that I'd never want to live like that. Now I think that they are so much happier and more generous than the people in the U.S. They taught me so much—this has changed my life." And still another stressed, "I wanted to be involved in this project because I wanted to make a difference someplace in the world where help was needed. And I think that we did do good work in Gales Point and we helped some people, but I know this project helped me far more than I ever dreamed and in so many different ways."

Along with the students, we were touched with the parting gifts that several people brought to us at the clinic or the lodge, how many of them turned out to wave good-bye, and the number who expressed that they hoped that we'd return next year. Though exhausted from days that started well before sunrise and ended very late, we soared on cloud nine—our students had benefited so much and we had all learned a great deal.

As we prepare for travel again this year, we ask ourselves what we can do to improve the project. And we are again excited by the prospects ahead of us!

Questions for Reflection

Hart and Walker report that they did extensive background research on Belize before embarking on this project. Is there anything else that they might have tried to anticipate problems?

What would be the most difficult challenge to you personally in visiting a culture where items like indoor plumbing and clean drinking water cannot be taken for granted?

Have you experienced any "culture shock" in your own past travels that might help you relate to the experiences described here?

What is the best way to prepare for an unfamiliar cultural experience? If you were helping plan the orientation for Hart and Walker's students, what would you include?

References

Barry, T., and D. Vernon. 1995. *Inside Belize*. Albuquerque, NM: Interhemispheric Resource Center Press.

Bent, A. 2000. *Community Profile Survey in Belize Rural Central*. Belize City, Belize: Government of Belize.

Chanecka, E. J. 1998. "Traditional Medicine in Belize: The Original Primary Health Care." *Nursing and Health Care Perspectives* 19 (4): 178–85.

15

Choices and Voices: Assessing Television Preferences of Teenage African-American Girls

Lynne Edwards

This chapter by Lynne Edwards approaches culture from another vantage point, that of a minority subculture within a dominant or "mainstream" culture. Edwards postulates that African-American adolescent girls have distinctive cultural values and identities. Uses and gratifications theory suggests how a variety of needs are met by media consumption. Would the emerging values and identities of these girls create identifiable patterns of television preferences?

It would seem that the unique struggles and concerns of African-American girls (at an age when their sense of self is emerging) should result in specific patterns of TV use that might help illuminate this question. Using identity formation theory from psychology, Edwards explores how emerging adolescent identities may be associated with consistent TV choices among the girls she studied. Her results provide some evidence that as they become committed to particular identities, their choices might be more consistently related to their values.

But this chapter also reflects several intense struggles—between Edwards's original desire to use qualitative methods and the logistical realities that prevented this; between her original goal of studying African-American girls on their own terms and her supervisors' interest in seeing comparative data from Whites; between a rich personal vision of what it means to have an identity as an African-American girl and the dry reality of scales and test scores.

Culture is not easily reduced to numbers. Yet Edwards rightly considers her project at least a limited success. Her results do suggest she might be on the right track, and her study can help guide future research in the right direction.

My mother's two favorite stories about my childhood provide an amusing omen for my future dissertation research. According to my mother, every day I came home from nursery school, took off my bib-alls, tied them around my neck and ran around our house with my arms in standard "flying" position, claiming to be Underdog, my favorite action hero. I'd leap from stairs and off the dining room table in my desperate need to fly and to save Sweet Polly Purebred, Underdog's damsel in distress. What I find amusing about this story, aside from my fanatical identification with a cartoon male canine hero, was that at the age of four, I knew that Underdog was my secret identity. Like the "real" Underdog, I kept my secret by day and flew at night.

When I graduated from nursery school to kindergarten, I graduated to a whole new identity crisis. I no longer thought I was a cartoon dog; I just thought I was White. This wouldn't have been a problem (or a source of amusement) for my mother if we weren't African-American. One day, as we talked over dinner, I told my mother about "those bad Black kids" who got in trouble at school that day. My mother was briefly confused by my reference to my classmates as "those" Black kids since I, too, was Black. When my mother questioned me closely, she discovered that despite the fact that I *knew* she and my dad were both "very Black," I apparently believed I was "White" and just happened to have two very nice, loving Black parents. After spending *many* days clearing up that mess, my mother eventually discovered the basis for my confusion: there weren't any kids in my class who were fair-skinned like me—and there weren't any people who looked like me in the television programs I watched, either.

The point of these stories was that television filled my need for escape, while also providing a continuing source of confusion *for* me *about* me. There weren't a lot of girls in my school who looked like me, and there certainly weren't any girls who seemed to share my interest in being a superhero, so I turned to television as a child and haven't turned away since. Given my early, and ongoing, fascination with action heroes and my early (and not ongoing) racial identity confusion, it is no wonder that I grew up to pursue a doctorate in communications. As an African-American doctoral candidate, I was interested in research that would not only satisfy my inner child but also benefit my community. Were there girls out there like me who lost themselves, literally, in television? Where did their sense of identity come from, and was it related to their television viewing?

Ultimately, my dissertation explored the relationship between television viewing preferences for African-American girls and their values, asking the following two questions: Is there a relationship between the viewer's values and her television program preferences? And does the viewer's identity status influence the relationship between values and program preferences? I hypothesized that the relationship between values and program choices would be stronger for girls who were committed to their values than for girls who were not.

My interest in this topic was met with sincere interest and one major question by my dissertation committee: Why not study White girls, too? It was just this sort of comparison, however, that I hoped to avoid. I wanted to demonstrate that African-American girls are unique, with culturally different value and preference norms that didn't require a White sample for comparison. I was able to successfully defend my decision to study this particular population by agreeing to collect data from both White and African-American girls, while only analyzing the data that I wanted for this project. The committee was also persuaded by the limited research about this population's media habits and values. The literature on mass media use by minority children revealed few studies about girls, few studies that included interviews with these children, and many studies that involved problematic comparisons to White children, three areas that my study would address.

Literature Review

In a review of the literature, I found that uses and gratifications research often focused on individuals' motivations for and expectations of the television viewing experience in order to predict their program choices. To this end, several uses and gratifications researchers posited models of viewer program choice, including models that examined leisure, social, and psychological factors as possible predictors of choice behavior (Frank and Greenberg 1980; Rosengren 1974; Rubin 1977; Katz et al. 1974; McQuail et al. 1972; Perse 1990; Dominick and Greenberg 1970; Lee and Browne 1981).

Implicit in most of this research were several assumptions concerning the relationship between viewers' program choices and program content. First, the uses and gratifications perspective assumed that the viewer's program choices consistently demonstrated some preference for those content types that best gratify certain needs. The second assumption was that viewers have program preferences that are systematically related to types of content. A third assumption was that viewers demonstrate their preferences through their program choices (Webster and Wakshlag 1983). Also implicit in most of this research was the knowledge that the uses and gratifications perspective lacked a single, unifying theoretical base that adequately explained program choice.

Researchers who focused on Black subjects argued that being a member of a minority race in America carries with it certain psychological burdens that may impact on behavior (Clark 1989; Gibbs 1989; Jones 1989; Taylor 1989).

Other research linked motivations for television viewing with negative psychological states in Black viewers such as low self-esteem (Tan and Tan 1979) and depression and alienation from self (Kubey 1986). Stroman (1986), however, found that viewing habits of Black children were not related to low self-concepts. Other research, however, suggested that Blacks watch television primarily for learning and entertainment purposes (Carey 1966; Albarran and Umphrey 1993; Lee and Browne 1981; Greenberg and Dominick 1969; Frank and Greenberg 1980; Comstock and Cobbey 1979). This research demonstrated that girls were rarely studied as a target audience and that most studies at that time were interested in the relationship between media use and problem behaviors for African-American youth. But none of these studies explained what was going on in teens' lives at the time of the research, nor did these researchers interview the teens they were studying. Because these studies primarily looked *at* teens, I wanted my research to talk *to* them.

In an effort to better understand the teens I wanted to study, I reviewed literature about adolescent development and identity. Human development theorists suggest that individuals seriously begin to reconsider their previously learned values and to explore value alternatives during adolescence. Erik Erikson (1959) suggests that the formation and adoption of a personal value system is one of the critical elements of adolescent development. The internal conflict that adolescents experience as they struggle to determine which values to adopt as their own is the crux of what Erikson terms the "identity crisis."

Determining which values to commit to and to adopt is a crucial element of the process of identity development. Those who are able to commit to a set of values after seriously exploring the alternatives are considered successful in the development process; those who cannot commit are considered unsuccessful. Erikson (1959) suggests that the exploration and adoption of a personal value system is a critical task in resolving the identity crisis faced by adolescents during the process of maturation. Those who are able to commit to a value system are considered successful in the maturation process, or identity-achieved. Those who cannot commit are considered unsuccessful, or identity-diffused. Marcia (1964) operationalized Erikson's "task" construct using the adolescent's experiences with "crisis" and "commitment." According to Marcia, "crisis" refers to the period during which the adolescent moves away from previously held values and expectations about occupation and ideology; she becomes actively involved in choosing among meaningful alternatives. Marcia also determined that there are two additional statuses, "moratorium" and "foreclosed," which exhibit differing degrees of value exploration in addition to differing degrees of value commitment.

Not only did Erikson's theories provide insight into the developmental issues and obstacles faced by teens, they also provided a potential measure for the "value commitment" component of my study. The extent to which the adolescent is successful in achieving an identity is reflected by her ability to consider the occupational and ideological alternatives available and to choose among them. "Commitment" refers to the strength of the adolescent's personal investment in her occupational and ideological choices, the strength of her values, and her willingness to act upon them (Marcia 1964; Trigg 1973; Bratman 1987).

Very few studies had explored identity status for African-American teens; the two I found both reported a high level of identity achievement among their female participants (Watson and Protinsky 1991; Aries and Moorehead 1989). The identity-development research was crucial to my research since it provided a construct for "value commitment," although the particular values that Erikson examined were ideological values related to careers, politics, and religion. For my study, I wanted to use those core values that could arguably be said to reside in all of us; therefore, I turned to Rokeach (1973). Rokeach defines a value as an "enduring belief that a specific mode of conduct or end-state of existence is personally or socially preferable to an opposite or converse mode of conduct or end-state of existence" (5). He estimates that there are approximately thirty-six values that represent the full spectrum of human goals and beliefs. He divides these values into two groups, terminal and instrumental values.

Terminal values[1] are the ideal "end-states of existence," or where and how the individual sees herself in the future. Instrumental values[2] refer to the ideal actions necessary for functioning successfully in society and for achieving desired end-states of existence. Rokeach and others (Kluckhohn and Strodtbeck 1961; Pugh 1977) claim that we only hold a limited number of values to facilitate our decision making. We are faced with an unlimited number of values-related choices throughout our lives; such choices would be impossible to make if we had to "sift through" an infinite number of values in order to make a decision.

Communications researchers who have explored the relationship between values and mass media preferences have found that values are reliable predictors of program preferences, when studied in the context of other demographic variables (McCarty and Shrum 1993; Gandy 1984). These findings suggested to me that race, gender, and identity development, in concert, could influence the relationship between values and television program preferences for African-American adolescent girls. Deciding to study this topic was easy; however, developing a project through which the girls' voices could be heard was not.

Method

The interview-based, qualitative method that I wanted to employ would allow me to explore in-depth questions about values, commitment, and television viewing choices with a small number of girls who could tell their stories in their own voices. I planned to use three open-ended interview instruments to collect data: Marcia's (1964) open-ended Ego-Identity Status Instrument, Rokeach's (1973) Terminal and Instrumental Values Survey, and a television program preference instrument. As I began to search for participants, however, I quickly hit several obstacles that forced me to reconsider using this qualitative method. The first obstacle was gaining access to adolescent girls for the interviews. Initially, I approached the parents of students in my community dance classes; however, I was only able to secure permission for three of the girls. The other parents were not fully convinced that a dance instructor was really conducting legitimate research with their daughters. The second obstacle was the length of the study instruments. Lasting over two hours, the one-on-one interview was a hard sell for those school-age girls whose parents would have allowed them to participate in the study. The third obstacle was money. As a graduate student, I was on a twelve-month fellowship and couldn't afford to extend my research beyond that period; I'd already lost two months trying to line up girls from my dance classes. I needed to find participants quickly or I wasn't going to be able to conduct this study at all.

At this point, I decided to switch to the quantitative method, which required survey instruments and a new approach for securing a sample. I immediately contacted the Philadelphia School Board and several New Jersey school districts for permission to survey their female students. The switch from qualitative to quantitative methods was also relatively easy; the three qualitative instruments were also available as quantitative measures. The biggest difficulty that I faced was getting over the feeling that I was letting these girls down by not giving them a more active voice in my research. However, as I embarked on this new study, I found that the quantitative method had greater benefits than I could have imagined. First, the shorter instrument was readily approved by both school boards because it could be administered during a standard class period (forty-five minutes) and students were guaranteed anonymity. Second, I was able to collect data on non-African-American females, too, since they were in the classroom when the survey was administered. Finally, I reached far more girls during the data collection process than I would have with the qualitative method.

Sample

The sample for this study, 218 Black adolescent girls, was obtained from three test sites: a senior high school (grades 10 through 12) and a junior high school (grades 7 through 9) in Atco, New Jersey, and an all-girl high school (grades 9 through 12) in Philadelphia, Pennsylvania. The only distinction between the Philadelphia area school and the New Jersey schools, other than the presence of boys, is that the Philadelphia school is considered a "magnet" school with a curriculum designed for girls who are academically exceptional in comparison to their peers of the same age. The identity status literature, however, does not report any difference in identity development between academically exceptional teens and their non–academically exceptional peers.

Program Preference Measures

Barwise and Ehrenberg (1988) suggest there is a strong relationship between audience liking and frequency of viewing of a program; therefore, program preference was measured both in terms of "frequency" of viewing and in terms of program "liking." Subjects were provided with a list of thirty-three programs[3] and were instructed to indicate how frequently they viewed each television program during the past year (from 0 = "never" to 5 = "every day") and how much they liked each program (from 0 = "never heard of it" to 5 = "I like it a lot"). The list of television programs was originally derived from the Arbitron Television Ethnic Report for November 1993. This report provides audience estimates for Black households in the Philadelphia metro rating area for the period November 3, 1993, to November 30, 1993. The thirty highest-rated programs for Black teens, ages twelve through seventeen, were selected for analysis. The list was refined based on responses from subjects participating in pretests that indicated preferences for programs other than those identified by Arbitron ratings, particularly those programs that were no longer on air.

Values Measure

Value preferences were measured using Rokeach's Instrumental and Terminal Value Survey (1973), which presents the participant with eighteen terminal values and eighteen instrumental values and asks respondents to indicate how important each value was to her independently of the other values. Respondents were asked to circle the number (from 0 to 10) that "indicates how important the value is to you." They were told that a score of "0" meant the value was "not important at all" and that a score of "10" meant the value was "extremely important."

Value Commitment Measure

Identity status was measured using the Objective Measure of Ego Identity Status (OMEIS) (Adams et al. 1979). The OMEIS is a twenty-four-item Likert-type scale questionnaire with six items forming a subscale for each of the four identity statuses (diffused, moratorium, foreclosed, and achieved). Of these six items, two items deal with each of the three value domains: occupation and political and religious ideologies. Subjects were asked to indicate the degree to which they agreed or disagreed with each of the items and their responses were scored according to the manual developed by Adams et al. (1979). This particular measure has been used in several studies that have provided strong evidence for the measure's validity and reliability (Abraham 1984; Adams 1985; Adams and Jones 1983; Adams and Montemayor 1983; Adams et al. 1979). Marcia (1993) also suggests that the instrument can be substituted for his open-ended interview instrument when surveying large groups.

Procedures

At the junior high school in Atco, female students of all races were separated from male students during eight gym classes throughout the school day. Students were informed of the survey prior to the test day. On the test day, students were informed that the study was anonymous and they were not to put their names on the surveys. They were told that there were no wrong answers and that it was important for them to answer all items on the survey. Survey administration time was approximately thirty-five minutes, with instructions read aloud by a graduate student. Parental permission for participation was obtained prior to survey administration. A total of 457 surveys were collected; 317 subjects were non-Black and 140 were Black (136 of these were usable). The data collected from non-Black students were not included in this analysis.

At the senior high school in Atco, male and female students of all races were administered the survey during seven health classes throughout the school day. Once again, they were instructed not to put their names on the surveys, they were told that there were no wrong answers, and they were also told that it was important for them to answer all items on the survey; survey length and permission procedures were as before. Data collected from non-Black students and male students were dropped from analysis. Thirteen cases were Black females; 125 were non-Black students and/or males.

At the all-girls high school in Philadelphia, surveys were administered to students during two class periods of psychology and in one after-school session with members of the Black Student League. The researcher visited the psychology classes two weeks prior to survey administration to present a program about basic theories of psychology and communications and how they are related. The program ended with an invitation to the students to participate in this research. No program was presented to the Black Student League;

their advisor scheduled the survey during a regular group meeting. Group members who participated in the study with the psychology classes were excused from participation with the Black Students League.

As before, students in the psychology class were instructed not to put their names on the surveys, were told that there were no wrong answers, and were told that it was important for them to answer all items on the survey. Survey administration time was again approximately thirty-five minutes, with instructions read aloud by a graduate student. Parental permission for participation was obtained prior to survey administration. Data collected from thirty non-Black students were dropped from analysis. This site generated a total of sixty-nine usable surveys.

Statistical Analyses

Subjects were categorized by identity status using the guidelines set forth in the Adams et al. (1979) *Objective Measure of Ego Identity Status Reference Manual*. The amount of hours spent viewing television and the perceived importance of television were also analyzed using these procedures. To examine the first research question of whether there was a relationship between the viewer's values and her television program preferences, values and program preferences were measured for association using Spearman's rank order coefficient or Spearman's rho. Spearman's rho is a statistic that indicates the degree of monotonic relationship (correlation) between two ordinal variables[4] that are arranged in rank order (Vogt 1993). To examine the second research question of whether the viewer's identity status influences the relationship between values and program preferences, value-program preference correlations were examined for both committed and uncommitted viewers to determine if the relationship between the variables was different in terms of magnitude or direction.

The study's hypothesis, that viewers in the committed identity status group will exhibit higher correlations between their values and program preferences than the viewers in the noncommitted identity status group, was tested in two ways. First, value-program preference correlations for just those values that empirically demonstrated strong predictive abilities were compared for the committed and noncommitted groups. Values were identified as demonstrating strong predictive abilities if they were significantly correlated with preferences for at least eight television programs, approximately 25 percent of the program sample. If the average value-preference correlations of the committed status group were higher than those of the uncommitted group, then the hypothesis was supported. Individual value correlations for each group were

Box 15.1: Correlation Coefficients

The research in this chapter uses two different kinds of "correlation coefficients." The term refers to a statistic that represents the degree of association between two variables. By convention, various kinds of correlation coefficients almost always take values between zero and one, with zero indicating no relationship and one indicating a perfect relationship. A negative coefficient indicates an opposite relationship: instead of more of variable x being associated with more of variable y, the opposite is true. The term "correlation" is part of many people's everyday vocabulary, but the concept can sometimes be tricky.

A simple example of a problem that a correlation coefficient might be used to examine would be the relationship between the number of hours spent studying and the student's score on an exam. We would expect that this would be a positive correlation but not a perfect one. Other factors, such as the student's background and abilities and the quality of the test, might affect performance. We would hope that in most cases, if the test has been well designed, the correlation would be positive. That is, a good test would reward students who spent extra time studying; they should achieve higher scores. However, some tests are intended to measure conceptual understanding, and here the reflective student (rather than the one who spent extra time memorizing everything in the textbook) would be rewarded with a higher score. In this case, because of different study styles and abilities, it is possible we might see a lower correlation, but we would still expect a positive one.

While it is difficult to imagine a negative correlation in this example, it is not impossible. If some of the students who studied lots of extra hours got too little sleep, for example, it might be possible (though unlikely) for a negative correlation to result. A more natural example, however, would be the correlation between hours spent in other activities in the period immediately prior to the test (such as working, goofing off, watching TV, or studying for other classes) and test score, which we would expect to be negative. On average, the students who spent so much time on other things that they could not study for the test probably would have lower scores. It would still be possible for this correlation to be positive—we can imagine that perhaps these extra activities could make students more relaxed—but it seems less likely.

Just as for statistical tests, correlation coefficients are of many different types, and choosing the correct correlation calculation often depends on the level of measurement, as illustrated in this chapter in which data are used in two different types of correlation analysis—one using Spearman's rho to look at the relationship between values and categorical (ordinal) preference data, and one using Pearson's r to relate values to a "factor score"[1] based on the same basic type of preference information converted to a form that could be treated as measurement data. In both cases, the researcher is searching for a relationship between values and program preferences, but the evidence is not very strong on this point.

But a zero correlation can also be deceptive if the relationship is complex. For example, Pearson's correlation coefficient (the correlation most commonly used for data obtained at higher levels of measurement) assesses the strength of the linear association between two measured variables. This means that for every unit of change in one variable, a relatively consistent average change in a second variable is observable. But the calculation will miss relationships in which the nature of the relationship is "nonlinear" (that is, if it is graphed, it does not resemble a straight line).

Let's say that in our example (the correlation between study time and test scores), calculating the correlation coefficient yields a zero (or perhaps a very low) correlation. It may be that for many students, more studying yielded a better score, as we would expect. Yet for some especially anxious students who put in the most time studying, the extra study time actually resulted in reduced scores because they didn't get enough sleep and were too stressed to perform well. When these are averaged together, it might look like study time doesn't matter, but in fact there is a positive correlation among those studying up to a certain number of hours combined with a negative correlation among those studying the most hours. This is an example of a "nonlinear" relationship. Examining an actual graph of the two variables is often the easiest way to identify and grasp these.

Statistical tests of correlations evaluate the likelihood that an observed correlation has been obtained by chance. A high correlation can have a low statistical significance and a low correlation can have a high statistical significance, depending on sample size and other factors. If sample size is very large, even small correlations will be statistically significant. This does not always assure that they are meaningful. Very low correlations, even if statistically significant, are not evidence of a strong relationship between two variables.

For Pearson's r, the square of the correlation coefficient indicates the percentage of variance (or variation) that can be predicted in variable y by patterns in variable x. If the r is (say) .10, the result means that only 1% ($.10 \times .10 = .01$) of the variance is accounted for by the relationship.

Note

1. Factor analysis is a technique for reducing complex data sets, in this case program preferences, to a smaller number of factors.

---

also examined to determine if each correlation was stronger for the committed group than for the uncommitted group. If the proportion of instances in which individual value-preference correlations for committed subjects are higher than correlations for uncommitted subjects is greater than 50 percent, then the hypothesis would also be supported.

For the second analysis to test the study's hypothesis, the value and program preference variables were factor analyzed and were correlated using Pearson's product-moment correlation coefficient (Pearson's r), a correlation coefficient for measurement data. Once again, average correlations for each identity status group were compared, in addition to individual correlations for each group. If the correlations for subjects in the "committed" statuses were observed to be higher than the correlations for the "noncommitted" status groups, then the hypothesis was supported.

Findings

Overall, the findings from my research, unfortunately, did not offer strong support for my hypothesis. To answer the first question, I examined the correlations between thirty-six values and thirty-three programs measured by frequency of viewing and liking. Although several of the values were associated with some programs, the correlations were rather weak, suggesting that, in response to the first research question, there is a meaningful but weak overall relationship between Rokeach's values and the sample of programs used in this study.

To answer the second research question, subjects were categorized into one of the four identity statuses—diffused, moratorium, foreclosed, or achieved. I was surprised by the breakdown of the status groups. There was nothing in the literature to explain why over 50 percent of the sample fell into the "moratorium" status. Previous research examining Black adolescents found that the majority of subjects tend to fall into one of the two committed statuses, foreclosed or achieved. However, none of these studies had used this particular version of Adams's survey.

The scores showed that the groups differed. For example, the diffused group viewed cartoons, *Living Single*, *Martin*, and *South Central* more frequently than the other three status groups. The foreclosed group viewed *Family Matters*, *Full House*, *Sinbad*, and *Sister/Sister* more than the other status groups, on average.

The average correlations for the liking and frequency measures were slightly higher for the committed group than for the uncommitted group, therefore offering limited support for the hypothesis. For the frequency measure, the value-preference correlations were higher for 61.3 percent of the correlations; however, value-preference correlations were higher in only 48 percent of the correlations for the liking measure. For the frequency measure, these findings lend only weak support for the hypothesis; these findings do not support the hypothesis for the liking measure. Additionally, a test for significance revealed no significant difference between correlations for the committed and uncommitted status groups.

Using the Pearson's r correlation for the factor analysis results for committed and uncommitted status groups, committed group correlations for both the liking and frequency measures were noticeably higher than those for the uncommitted group, offering further support for the study's hypothesis; however, the differences between the correlations were not statistically significant.

Conclusion

Like the little girl who wanted to be Underdog, I dreamed of saving "damsels in distress"; my ideal research project would have "freed" African-American girls to speak from the pages of scholarly research to tell us what they really thought, felt, and believed about themselves. Like that little girl, I let go of the dream and embraced a better reality. Through the choices I made in response to time and financial constraints, I may not have given a few girls the "voice" that I imagined; however, fully 200 girls were eventually included in my study.

My findings were recently published in a sociology text about minority and ethnic audiences, and the additional data I collected about White and other non-African-American girls is currently being analyzed by undergraduate research students in psychology. Like the little girl who looked around her world and found no one who looked like her, I found that African-American girls generally look for characters like themselves in their television program viewing. While my statistical results were mixed and this study was not exactly what I'd hoped for, I am extremely pleased with the outcome, not only for myself, but also for the girls in the study, and for the readers who will (I hope) benefit from my experience.

Questions for Reflection

Why did Edwards want to use only data from African-American girls (excluding male and White respondents)? Do you agree?

Had Edwards used qualitative interviews as she had originally planned, would her results likely have been different? In what ways?

In your opinion, what are some of the reasons this study did not produce clearer conclusions? Are there competing explanations of this?

Think about your own personal values, both today and during your adolescence. How well do Rokeach's terminal values capture some of the things in life that you feel are most important?

Notes

1. Rokeach's 18 terminal values are: Accomplishment, Comfortable life, Equality, Exciting life, Family security, Freedom, Happiness, Inner harmony, Mature love, National security, Pleasure, Salvation, Self-respect, Social recognition, True friendship, Wisdom, World of beauty, and World at peace.

2. Rokeach's 18 instrumental values are: Ambitious, Broadminded, Capable, Cheerful, Clean, Courageous, Forgiving, Helpful, Honest, Imaginative, Independent, Intellectual, Logical, Loving, Obedient, Polite, Responsible, and Self-control.

3. The 33 programs were: *Amen, Beverly Hills 90210, Blossom,* cartoons, *The Commish, Cops, The Cosby Show, Entertainment Tonight, Family Matters, Fresh Prince/Bel Air, Full House, Home Improvement, The Jeffersons, Living Single,* local news, *Married with Children, Martin, Matlock, Melrose Place,* music videos, *Oprah, Real World* (MTV), *Roc, Roseanne, The Simpsons, Sinbad, Sister/Sister, Soul Train, South Central, Star Trek Next Gen., Step by Step, Wheel of Fortune,* and *X-Files.*

4. Ordinal variables are categorical variables that can be ranked, like high school versus college graduates or small, medium, and large.

References

Abraham, K. G. "Ethnic Differences in Identity Development." Paper presented at annual meeting, National Council on Family Relations, San Francisco, CA.

Adams, G. R., et al. 1985. "Ego Identity Status, Conformity Behavior, and Personality in Late Adolescence." *Journal of Personality and Social Psychology* 47 (5): 1091–1104.

Adams, G. R., and R. M. Jones 1983. "Female Adolescents' Identity Development: Age Comparisons and Perceived Child-Rearing Experience." *Developmental Psychology* 19 (2): 249–56.

Adams, G. R., and R. Montemayor. 1983. "Identity Formation during Early Adolescence." *Journal of Early Adolescence* 3: 193–202.

Adams, G. R., J. Shea, and S. A. Fitch. 1979. "Toward the Development of an Objective Assessment of Ego-Identity Status." *Journal of Youth and Adolescence* 8 (2): 223–37.

Albarran, A. B., and D. Umphrey. 1993. "An Examination of Television Motivations and Program Preferences by Hispanics, Blacks, and Whites." *Journal of Broadcasting and Electronic Media* (Winter): 95–103.

Aries, E., and K. Moorehead.1989. "The Importance of Ethnicity in the Development of Identity in Black Adolescents." *Psychological Reports* 65: 75–82.

Barwise, P., and A. Ehrenberg. 1988. *Television and Its Audience.* London: Sage.

Baumeister, R. 1986. *Identity: Cultural Change and the Struggle for Self.* New York: Oxford University Press.

Bratman, M. 1987. *Intention, Plans, and Practical Reason.* Cambridge, MA: Harvard University Press.

Carey, J. W. 1966. "Variations in Negro/White Television Preferences." *Journal of Broadcasting* 10: 199–212.

Clark, M. L. 1989. "Friendship and Peer Relations." Pp. 175–204 in *Black Adolescents,* ed. R. Jones. Berkeley, CA: Cobbs and Henry.

Comstock, G., and R. E. Cobbey. 1979. "Television and the Children of Ethnic Minorities." *Journal of Communication* (Winter): 104–15.

Dominick, J. R., and B. S. Greenberg. 1970. "Three Seasons of Blacks on Television." *Journal of Advertising Research* 10 (2): 21–27.

Erikson, E. 1959. "Identity and the Life Cycle: Selected Papers by Erik Erikson." *Psychological Issues* 1 (1): 1–171.

Frank, R., and Greenberg, M. 1980. *The Public's Use of Television*. Beverly Hills: Sage.
Gandy, O. 1984. "Is That All There Is to Love?: Value and Program Preference." Pp. 207–19 in *Studies in Communication*, vol. 1., Studies in Mass Communication and Technology, ed. S. Thomas., 207–19. Norwood, NJ: Ablex Publishing.
Gibbs, J. T. 1989. "Black American Adolescents." Pp. 179–223 in *Children of Color: Psychological Interventions with Minority Youth*, ed. J. T. Gibbs et al. San Francisco: Jossey-Bass Publishers.
Greenberg, B., and Dominick, J. (1969). "Racial and Social Class Differences in Teenagers' Use of Television." *Journal of Broadcasting* 13: 331–44.
Jones, R., ed. 1989. *Black Adolescents*. Berkeley, CA: Cobbs and Henry.
Katz, E., J. G. Blumler, and M. Gurevitch. 1974. "Utilization of Mass Communication by the Individual." Pp. 19–32 in *The Uses of Mass Communications: Current Perspectives on Gratifications Research*, eds. J. G. Blumler and E. Katz. Beverly Hills, CA: Sage.
Kluckhohn, F., and F. L. Strodtbeck. 1961. *Variations in Value Orientations*. Westport, CT: Greenwood Press.
Kubey, R. W. 1986. "Television Use In Everyday Life: Coping with Unstructured Time." *Journal of Communication* 36: 109–23.
Lee, E. B., and L. A. Browne. 1981. "Television Uses and Gratifications among Black Children, Teenagers, and Adults." *Journal of Broadcasting* 25: 203–8.
Marcia, J. 1964. "Determination and Construct Validity of Ego Identity Status." Unpublished dissertation, Ohio State University, Columbus.
Marcia, J. 1966. "Development and Validation of Ego-Identity Status." *Journal of Personality and Social Psychology* 3 (5): 551–58.
Marcia, J. 1967. "Ego Identity Status: Relationship to Change in Self-Esteem, 'General Maladjustment,' and Authoritarianism." *Journal of Personality* 35: 118–33.
Marcia, J., and M. Friedman. 1970. "Ego Identity Status in College Women." *Journal of Personality* 2: 249–63.
Marcia, J. E. 1993. "The Status of the Statuses: Research Review." Pp. 22–41 in J. E. Marcia, A. S. Waterman, D. R. Matteson, S. L. Archer, and J. L. Orlofsky, eds. *Ego Identity: A Handbook for Psychosocial Research*. New York: Springer Verlag.
McCarty, J., and L. Shrum. 1993. "The Role of Personal Values and Demographics in Predicting Television Viewing Behavior: Implications for Theory and Application." *Journal of Advertising Research* 12 (4): 77–93.
McQuail, D., J. Blumler, and R. Brown. 1972. "The Television Audience: A Revised Perspective." Pp. 135–65 in D. McQuail, ed. *Sociology of Mass Communication*. London: Penguin.
Perse, E. M. "Audience Selectivity and Involvement in the Newer Media Environment." *Communication Research* 17: 675–97.
Rokeach, M. 1973. *The Nature of Human Values*. New York: Free Press.
Rosengren, K. E. 1974. "Uses and Gratifications: A Paradigm Outlined." Pp. 269–86 in J. G. Blumler and E. Katz, eds. *The Uses of Mass Communications: Current Perspecitves on Gratifications Research*. Beverly Hills, CA: Sage.
Rubin, A. M. 1977. "Television Usage, Attitudes and Viewing Behavior of Children and Adolescents." *Journal of Broadcasting* 21 (3): 355–69.
Stroman, C. A. 1986. "Television Viewing and Self-Concept among Black Children." *Journal of Broadcasting and Electronic Media* 30 (1): 87–93.

Tan, A. S., and G. Tan. 1979. "Television Use and Self-Esteem of Blacks." *Journal of Communication* 29 (1): 129–35.
Taylor, R. L. 1989. "Black Youth, Role Models and the Social Construction of Identity." Pp. 155–74 in R. Jones, ed. *Black Adolescents*. Berkeley, CA: Cobbs and Henry.
Trigg, R. 1973. *Reason and Commitment*. London: Cambridge University Press.
Vogt, W. P. 1993. *Dictionary of Statistics and Methodology*. London: Sage.
Watson, M. F., and H. Protinsky. 1991. "Identity Status of Black Adolescents: An Empirical Investigation." *Adolescence* 26 (104): 963–66.
Webster, J., and J. J. Wakshlag. 1983. "A Theory of Television Program Choice." *Communication Research* 10 (4): 430–46.

Part V
NEW TECHNOLOGIES AND RESEARCH

NEW COMMUNICATION TECHNOLOGIES—especially the Internet, the personal computer, and the Web—have turned a good deal of communication research upside down. Old theories of mediated or "mass" communication, especially those that had envisioned audiences as the passive targets at which media "effects" were aimed, had to be rewritten to accommodate these new channels. The interactivity of the new system demanded a renewed research focus on the user or consumer of information—the choices that the user makes, the way that user might interpret and evaluate information, the array of user needs the information can fulfill.

Organizations have seemingly been transformed by these new technologies, largely freed from many of the traditional confines of time and space. Political activism and social movements are taking powerful new forms that seem at least partially technology driven; education itself is being transformed by these technologies, as are libraries and archives. And interpersonal communication has taken on new dimensions as well, with professional collaborations, friendships, and even romances developing between individuals who have never met in person. All of these phenomena began to present both exciting new opportunities and new challenges for communication researchers.

Patricia Radin, who was on the faculty at California State University, Hayward when she died unexpectedly in June of 2003, had planned to complete a chapter for this section of this book on her research about an Internet support group for breast cancer victims. Unfortunately the chapter was never finished, but in her proposal for it she captured the excitement characteristic of many scholars who became enthralled by the Internet's potential as a research site:

> In 1998, WebMD was just an entrepreneur's dream. Dr.Koop.com had not yet gone public—much less bankrupt, as it eventually did. And only a few nonprofit Web-based online communities had cropped up to serve the informational and emotional needs of people with breast cancer. . . . Looking for a paper topic for a graduate class, I decided to run a content analysis of the messages [from one such site] to sort out the supportive from the technical, the hope-filled from the hopeless; the messages that referred to mass media versus those referring to medical journals; messages referring to alternative remedies versus conventional; and so on. . . .
> I began reading the messages with greater and greater emotional attachment, and with more and more questions. I went to the psychosocial research to define the parameters of support groups, in an effort to categorize this burgeoning mutual-assistance community. Of course, I also went to medical literature to find out more about breast cancer. . . . Before I knew it, I had spent months as a regular lurker—laughing, crying, wanting the very best for these gallant people.

Without planning to, Radin (not a breast cancer victim herself) had become a true participant observer in the group she'd chosen to study, which she had originally planned to research through a content analysis of the postings. Of course, among the problems she had to confront were very serious ones about the ethics of online research involving a very private issue. While public postings on a publicly accessible site might appear to many investigators to be "fair game" for research use, Radin felt the issues were more subtle. She consulted a medical ethicist and the site's own Webmistress for guidance, and eventually (with the support of the Webmistress and other opinion leaders associated with the site) announced her presence to the group. She also gradually became something of an activist herself, organizing a conference presentation, hosting a gathering of group members in her home, establishing personal relationships with a number of the participants, and in the end posting a pdf version of her dissertation on the website itself—to "a flurry of virtual toasts and applause," as she put it!

Internet phenomena challenge our notions of community and society, friendship and family, mass and interpersonal communication, public and private spheres. It is this latter distinction, especially that between public and private communication, that creates many of the ethical dilemmas with which we are still struggling. Published work—that is, work that has formally been made available to the public—can always be used as data for a study, with appropriate attention to citation and copyright issues, but private behavior may not be. What about private words intended for a particular individual or an identified group, but which the Internet makes available to everyone? Are they public, or private, communication?

Our first chapter in this section, written by Jennifer Gregg and Pamela Whitten, is essentially a needs assessment for a telemedicine project that would support hospice workers in rural locations. But the main struggles—logistical and ethical—that Gregg and Whitten confront are not about the new technology proposed for the support services project but the much more familiar technology of telephones and the challenges of conducting research involving health issues (a type of research that often collects sensitive information about individuals, even though their particular effort was directed at caregivers rather than patients).

The chapter by Tara Crowell and Traci Anderson tackles the unique ethical challenges of actually collecting data online. Internet data gathering offers the advantages of greater anonymity and quite possibly comfort (not to mention the ability to reach members of small, dispersed populations with particular characteristics). In a period of decreasing public responsiveness to requests they participate in phone surveys, some are even beginning to argue that the Internet is the best way to reach the more general population, despite a lingering bias toward those who can afford (and are comfortable using) Internet-linked computers. But their Institutional Review Board was not sure how to apply the standards developed for more traditional research approaches to their online approaches.

Our final chapter, by James Tankard and Cindy Royal, takes a different tack. Not persuaded by the cliché assertion that everything is available on the Web—or if not, that this is certainly just around the corner—Tankard and Royal make a systematic study of what is available on the Internet and what is *not*. Their contribution helps bring our thinking full circle by reminding us that issues of balance, bias, and reasonable representation that have concerned scholars regarding the more familiar mass media (such as television, newspapers, and so on) have certainly not disappeared in the brave new world of cyberspace.

16
Health Communication Research on Hard-to-Reach Populations Using Telephone Interviews

Jennifer L. Gregg and Pamela Whitten

In this chapter, investigators Jennifer Gregg and Pamela Whitten use a relatively familiar communication technology (ordinary telephones) to study the potential of a relatively unfamiliar concept ("telemedicine," or the delivery of medical services at a distance using various telecommunications technologies) to assist a unique and hard-to-reach population (hospice caregivers in isolated rural areas). Their subject harkens back to Foster's chapter on hospice care in the section on problem-focused studies. However, the subject of discussion here is a very different kind of hospice care because much of the caregiving takes place in individual patients' homes. Instead of being a member of a group of volunteers who attend training together, the caregivers are scattered.

Because these hospice workers—generally friends or family of the hospice patient—are relatively isolated, compared to the volunteer groups with which Foster interacted, Gregg and Whitten wanted to address the issue of how telemedical services might provide a support network to help avoid the stress and "burnout" that would otherwise ensue. Their article lists a number of services they felt could be delivered electronically and that they hope would alleviate the situation these individuals face.

After considering a variety of options (ranging from mail-out surveys to focus groups to face-to-face interviews in a variety of settings), the research team settled on telephone interviews, using a mix of open- and closed-ended questions, as their primary method for this project. The choice was primarily a reflection of logistical considerations, including the extra time and travel that would have been needed to interview members of this far-flung group in person.

CHOOSING THE MOST SUITABLE research strategy should be based on the type of research question being asked; the extent of control an investigator has over actual behavioral events; and the degree of focus on contemporary as opposed to historical events (Yin 1989, 1994). The research design, in effect, is a plan for getting from *here* to *there*, where *here* is the set of questions to be answered, and *there* is some set of conclusions (Yin 1994). This chapter describes how we used telephone interviews in health communication research to contact a hard-to-reach population.

This was our challenge: How do we talk with a hard-to-reach population about a hard-to-talk-about subject? We were interested in talking with caregivers of hospice patients in rural areas. Meeting the health care needs of people in rural areas is critical because 56 million Americans live in nonmetropolitan areas. They make up one-fifth of the U.S. population but are spread out across four-fifths of the land area (Ers 2002). There is a shortage of health providers in rural areas, and even though rural America has 33 percent of the population, only 12 percent of physicians and 18 percent of nurses choose to practice in rural areas (Buckingham 1996). While the physician-to-population ratio has more than doubled since 1960, it has risen by less than 15 percent in the smallest rural communities, those of less than 10,000 population (Greene 1999).

For people living in rural areas, getting access to the services they need may prove to be a significant challenge (Buehler and Lee 1992; Buckingham 1996). In addition, the United States is facing a widespread critical nursing shortage. Projections estimate that by the year 2020 the number of registered nurses working in America will be 20 percent below the estimated need (Brownback 2002). According to the American Hospital Association, hospitals around the country today have 126,000 nursing vacancies, or 12 percent of capacity (Janofsky 2002). Increased cost, difficulty accessing services, and the shortage of nurses and other providers mean that families and neighbors are taking on more of the responsibility for providing care to patients near the end of life. While the role of caregiver has many benefits for both the patient and the care provider, it places considerable stress on the relationship and on the individual lives.

Becoming a caregiver places individuals in a unique position on two spectra of social support. On the one hand, they are acting primarily as the *donors* of support to the persons for whom they are caring; on the other, they are the *recipients* of support from members of their own social network. The caregivers may be providing extensive personal care such as bathing and feeding the patient, or less personal care such as cleaning the patient's home, paying bills, or cooking meals. As care recipients, they may be receiving financial assistance from other family members, receiving respite care from volunteers and friends, or receiving spiritual or emotional counseling from professionals. Persons' ability to provide support may depend on the support they receive from their network, and (vice versa) the support they receive from their network may depend on the care demanded by the patients (Pearlin et al. 1996). Our belief was that caregivers could benefit from services provided by the hospice organization via telemedicine technologies. Telemedicine is the use of telecommunication technologies to deliver health services over a distance.

Hospice is care designed to provide comfort and support to patients and their families at the end of life, when a life-limiting illness no longer responds to cure-oriented treatments (HFA 2002). It represents a supportive philosophy of providing care to those whose life expectancy is measured in weeks or months. Hospice recognizes death as the final stage of a life journey, and enables patients and families to live their final days to the fullest in the comfort of home, surrounded by loved ones. Hospice care is primarily provided in the home by a team of specially trained professionals, volunteers, and family members, who address all symptoms of a disease. A family member typically serves as the primary caregiver and helps make decisions for the terminally ill patient (NHF 2002), though the primary caregiver could be a life partner, a friend, or another relative.

The goal of hospice care is to improve the quality of a patient's last days by offering comfort and dignity (HFA 2002); hospice neither prolongs life nor hastens death. The core interdisciplinary team of professionals and volunteers provides medical, psychological, and spiritual support to the terminally ill and their families (HAA 2002), with a special emphasis on controlling a patient's pain and discomfort. The team—which typically includes the patient's personal physician, hospice physician, nurses, home health aides, social workers, clergy, volunteers and speech, physical and occupational therapists as needed—coordinates an individualized plan of care for each patient and his or her family (Hospice 2002). Hospice staff is on call twenty-four hours a day, seven days a week, and there is no age limit for hospice care. Though approximately two-thirds of hospice patients are over the age of sixty-five (HFA 2002), both children and adults can receive the support of hospice during the final stages of life.

Services available through hospice include medical and nursing care, personal care, homemaker services, social work services, grief and counseling services, volunteer assistance, spiritual care, case management, and family training in patient care (HospiceWeb 2002). Because the nature of dying is unique for each person, the goal of the hospice team is to be sensitive and responsive to the patient's needs. A typical plan of care includes intermittent nursing care (often one visit each week) with twenty-four-hour on-call nursing available for emergencies. Bereavement services and counseling are available to the patient's family for approximately one year after the patient's death (HospiceNet 2002).

While caregivers are encouraged to take advantage of services provided by the care team, much of the research on hospice caregivers shows that they are isolated and depressed, and they may have physical ailments as a result of their caregiving duties. Most of the research documenting the stress on caregivers, however, has not focused on rural caregivers. We believed that rural caregivers faced additional challenges to those of their urban counterparts. The goal of this research, then, was to evaluate the feasibility of using technology to provide support and meet the emotional needs of rural hospice caregivers in their homes.

Because of limited research on rural hospice caregivers, we worked with the regional offices of a statewide hospice provider to set up focus groups with rural caregivers. We needed to talk with caregivers to determine what the real issues were for people in rural areas. Prior to arranging focus groups, the hospice provider suggested that some caregivers would be unwilling or unable to leave their loved one, the hospice patient. In an effort to facilitate participation in the focus group, we offered respite care providers and transportation to the focus group at no cost to the participant. Despite these services, recruiting participants proved to be difficult. While we were able to complete a number of focus groups, we wanted more detailed information from rural caregivers as to their needs. We needed another means for gathering information.

Data-gathering Strategies

We considered four different strategies for gathering additional information. For example, we considered sending out a standard "paper-and-pencil" survey. While self-administered mail surveys are easy and inexpensive, response rates are typically low, with very slow returns. We were concerned that participants would either not return the survey, or would not answer the open-ended questions. The caregiving role can be difficult to express for some caregivers, and we were hoping for rich descriptive information about their roles as caregivers. We determined that a mail survey would not be the best solution.

As an alternative, we also considered face-to-face interviews in the home. However, by the very fact that the caregivers were living in rural areas, they were difficult to reach in person. Some of the caregivers lived hundreds of miles from the researchers. We determined it would have been very time-intensive to travel to each caregiver's home. Furthermore, the hospice experience is very personal, and we believed that many of the caregivers and their loved ones would not want a stranger coming into their homes. While interviews in the homes would have allowed us to gain rich descriptive information and flexibility in clarifying caregivers' answers, distance and privacy were prohibitive for this strategy.

Face-to-face interviews at a neutral location were another alternative. Because of the privacy concerns involved with doing an interview in the caregiver's home, we considered the option of a face-to-face interview in another neutral setting such as the regional hospice office or a local coffee shop. This would also alleviate some of the distance concerns, as participants and researchers could meet at one location. While researchers would have to travel to rural towns, they would not have to travel on unfamiliar country roads to caregivers' homes. However, based on our experience with the focus group, we determined that caregivers would not want to take time away from their caregiving duties, even if we were able to arrange respite care for them. Furthermore, caregivers may not feel comfortable talking about a sensitive, personal topic in a location where they could be overheard by others.

Given all the challenges described above, we ultimately decided to use telephone interviews as a means of talking with caregivers about the challenges they face in their caregiving role. Previous research has shown that there are few consistent differences in data quality between in-person and telephone interviews (Lavrakas 1998). There are several advantages to using telephone interviewing. For example, the equipment is readily available and relatively inexpensive; there are no travel costs associated with the method, and the minimal long-distance charges are much less expensive than travel costs. Also, we were able to conduct the interviews at the convenience of the caregivers. Scheduling a telephone interview in the evening is easier than scheduling a face-to-face interview in the evening.

Conducting telephone interviews does present risks that must be addressed. Telephones may strengthen confidentiality but limit the interviewer's knowledge about the participants' emotional response or "affect." There can be interruptions or even unexplained disconnections. Finally, the length of the interview is necessarily shorter than for face-to-face interviews because most people do not want to spend long periods of time on the telephone. But we had used telephone interviews successfully in other projects and believed this to be a reasonable strategy for gathering information. Despite the lack of indications of affect, the telephone interviews did communicate the personal and sensitive aspects of the caregivers' perspectives more clearly than using only numerical data from standardized instruments. For example, one caregiver offered this comment: "I have a friend who lives out of town, but she's very busy. Often she's not available. But she's been there forever. I can talk to her about my fears, my hurt, my anger, my sadness." This caregiver provided an important example of an aspect of support that we felt could be enhanced through technology, information that was very relevant to goals in this project. We would not have had this rich example from a survey.

Respondents

After determining the strategy for gathering information, one of the first things we had to decide was who to interview. We limited the participants to those who were in an active caregiving role, who were living in rural areas, and who were English speakers. Furthermore, because cancer is the dominant diagnosis in the hospice population, we decided to focus on these cases and limited the sample to caregivers of cancer patients. These restrictions left us with a potential sample of one hundred caregivers.

This investigation centered on each participant's experiences as a hospice caregiver. The purpose was to get at the main significance of the experience to these individuals as they discuss their social support network and the effect that being a caregiver has had on their quality of life. This would in turn help us address the overall goal of determining the efficacy of using technology to provide additional support services via telemedicine. Caregivers were asked to describe what they perceived to be their sources of support through a series of open- and closed-ended questions. The open-ended questions allowed the caregiver to volunteer information he or she thought appropriate and was not led or biased by the interviewer. One problematic area with open-ended questions is getting the respondent to give fully detailed responses (Seidman 1998). To address this concern, probes were developed to encourage caregivers to continue, amplify, or clarify an answer.

Working with the regional and state hospice offices, we designed a workable questionnaire guide that would allow us to gather a topic-centered narrative. This in turn allowed us to identify major themes, concerns, and experiences that related directly to the individual's adjustment to becoming a caregiver. The open-ended questions were intended to facilitate the participants' describing their individual experiences in a coherent manner (Agar 1980; Agar and Hobbs 1985). This strategy is known as a "key informants" approach for collecting data (Pelto and Pelto 1979). Key informants are selected because they are knowledgeable about the topics being researched. They are also able and willing to communicate their knowledge (Kumar et al. 1993). This approach has many advantages. Key informants can "provide insights that no amount of observation would reveal. They can also provide insights into processes, sensitize the researcher to value dilemmas, and help the researcher see the implications of specific findings" (Borg and Gall 1989, 399). We also used closed-ended questions so that our responses could be compared to those of earlier hospice caregiver research.

IRB Concerns

The questionnaire guide was submitted to the university's Institutional Review Board (IRB). We did not anticipate serious problems with the IRB, as this effort was part of an ongoing project using similar techniques. However, the Health Insurance Portability and Accountability Act (HIPAA) of 1996 was on the horizon for U.S. citizens. HIPAA, in addition to protecting health insurance coverage for workers and their families in case of job loss, establishes national standards for the security and privacy of individually identifiable health information. In 1999, Congress directed the Department of Health and Human Services (DHHS) to further develop privacy and security requirements in accordance with HIPAA's national standards for electronic health care transactions. President Bush approved the regulations on April 12, 2001, and the official effective date of the regulations was April 14, 2001. The university's IRB was very concerned that this research should fall within the guidelines established by HIPAA, even though the research was to take place before these were effective.

The IRB determined that in order to conduct telephone interviews we needed to send a consent form in the mail to the potential participants. Furthermore, we could not telephone the participants until the form was returned. We discussed with the board the difficulties of this situation. As with mail surveys, the return rate for a mail consent form would be very low. Furthermore, time was a critical factor in this research. Not only do caregivers have stressful situations to cope with, but hospice patients by definition are at the end of life. We did not want to further burden caregivers at a difficult time.

The IRB agreed that requiring a returned consent form in advance would be unreasonable. We were able to compromise with it by sending out letters two weeks in advance of the calls, then confirming by telephone that the person had received the letter. At the start of each interview the caregiver gave verbal consent to continue the interview. Furthermore, caregivers were reminded of their right to refuse to participate at any time during the interview. No names or identifiers that could single out a caregiver were used during data collection, and caregivers were assured confidentiality. Another compromise we made with the university's IRB was that the calls could not be recorded. While recorded interviews add to the trustworthiness of qualitative data by allowing the researcher to go back and closely analyze the information, the IRB would not permit the interviews to be recorded under any circumstances. In this case, we took notes that were as copious as possible, had the questionnaire guide available for each interview to aid in taking detailed notes, and considered each interview immediately after it happened.

Box 16.1: Human Subjects Issues and the IRB

Several of the chapters in this book have mentioned authors' interactions with Institutional Review Boards (IRBs) charged with assuring the ethical use of human subjects. In the case of the project reported in this particular chapter, the authors report a fairly lengthy negotiation process with their IRB authorities. IRBs take their work seriously; to do otherwise would not only open the institution to charges of misusing human research subjects, but would also jeopardize the institution's eligibility for government funding. On the other hand, getting an envisioned project off the ground is the leading objective of every research team. By the time IRB approval is requested, plans for the project have to be in place and the team is usually about ready to go. Sometimes this creates frustration on both sides.

Every university and most research-oriented medical facilities in the United States have such boards, created to prevent abuses of privacy and to protect people who act as the subjects of research projects from unnecessary harm. The existence of such a board is mandated for all organizations that get any part of their funding from the federal government. The requirement applies to the entire institution, however, not just the individual project. University-based research done without funding, that done with private donations, and sometimes even class projects done as part of a research methods class must be approved by the IRB. This surprises many beginning university researchers.

Subjects' involuntary exposure to physical harm is one of the original and more obvious problems IRBs guard against. But there are many other serious but much less obvious problems that arise on a routine basis. Confidentiality, especially for sensitive information such as disease status, psychiatric treatment, or illegal drug use, is an extremely important area for IRBs. It was once common practice to keep track of survey respondents by name so that follow-ups could be sent; now procedures must be implemented to separate the data from anyone's personal identity, either by making the data collection anonymous (no one knows who is responding) or confidential (the identity is available to at least some members of the research team but the information is kept secure).

Psychological harm is another important area; such harm might possibly result to some participants from the simple act of asking questions about the very most sensitive topics, such as (for example) personal sexual experience or emotions at the loss of a family member. If the topic of research is especially sensitive, the IRB may request that information on counseling and support services be made available. If research participants must be deceived in any way in an experiment, there has to be a good reason, and they must be "debriefed" afterwards. Subjects must also be actual volunteers; prisoners, hospital patients, welfare recipients, even university students cannot ever be forced (or in any way coerced) into being research subjects.[1]

Typically, if collaborators from different universities or from a university and (say) a teaching hospital join forces on a project, IRB approval must be obtained from *both* institutions. As different IRBs may have slightly different policies as well as different procedures and forms, this type of situation can be a real challenge—as can studies in which some collaborators are working within the United States and others are in countries without equivalent institutions or whose IRB-type institutions follow different rules.

No one likes filling out IRB forms, which are designed to probe a project's potential for creating any of these problems and many more. Sometimes, like any bureaucracy, IRBs can seem to be unreasonable; this became a special problem for Internet-based research projects at first, as we will see in the next chapter. However, cooperating with IRB requirements is an essential part of being a responsible and ethical social scientist. Many universities are placing IRB information and forms online in an attempt to streamline the process; others have distributed the job of reviewing some proposals among various individuals so that the person who is reviewing each one understands something about the researcher's (or "principal investigator's") discipline.

Notes

1. These are only examples, *not* an exhaustive list, of IRB considerations. Also, university students can generally be required to participate in research for course credit, but they cannot usually be required to participate in *any particular project.*

Once the research was approved by the IRB office (on a one-year, nonrenewable basis), the potential participants were selected with the aid of the hospice office. Due to the participant criteria for the project, one hundred letters were sent directly from the hospice office on its letterhead, so as to lend credibility to the project. We then waited two weeks before making any calls. At this time, we met with hospice organization representatives and determined that in the two weeks since the introductory letters had been mailed, approximately one-fourth of the caregivers' patients in the original sample had died. We began making calls immediately. After three weeks, more than one-third of the patients had died. We had determined that caregivers would not be called if their loved one had died. At the end of data collection, due to death and nonparticipation, fifty-one interviews, or half of the original sample, had been completed. Most of this research relied on rich descriptions of caregiving. However, some of the research included quantitative questionnaires on quality of life, for which this small number of respondents allows for only limited analysis.

Challenges

One challenge we encountered while making calls was that the research office of the hospice organization required us to make the initial calls from its office.

This meant we had to drive nearly two hours to make the initial calls. While this was an inconvenience, it was also a benefit in cases where the caregiver had questions for the hospice organization. We could easily talk with one of the hospice staff and forward the information to the caregiver, or immediately reroute the call to hospice staff.

Another challenge we encountered while making calls was that some of the caregivers worked full time outside the home and then came home in the evening to caregiving duties. In some cases the patient could be left alone during the day. More commonly, another relative or paid caregiver came in during the day so that the primary caregiver could go to work. This meant many of the calls had to be made in the evening and during weekends. While this was not a significant concern, it did extend the scope of the research process. University researchers, and more importantly their families, need to create flexibility in their personal lives to accommodate their professional lives.

Finally, this project dealt with a topic completely unfamiliar to many of the respondents. Most of the caregivers had never heard of telemedicine technologies and had no understanding of how they might be used in conjunction with their caregiver responsibilities. We found it difficult to describe the proposed telemedicine technology to the hospice caregivers without the use of pictures. While we were able to describe possible uses they might have for the technology, we were not able to give them a detailed, understandable description of the technology itself.

Conclusion

In hindsight, despite the difficulties in obtaining IRB approval, telephone interviews were the best option we had for contacting rural hospice caregivers. While many of the concerns and subsequent compromises with the university IRB would have been alleviated by conducting in-person interviews, this would have turned our project into a different kind of study. In-person interviews could have been taped, allowing for more in-depth analysis, but we would not have been able to interview fifty-one caregivers. We may have been more successful in gathering in-depth information, but researchers must live within the pragmatics of the real world. In the current case, both researchers also had families with small children. Arranging evening and weekend interviews for caregivers who work would have taken even more of a toll on the researchers' families. Furthermore, research occurs within a limited budget. We could not have afforded to make numerous trips to rural counties to interview caregivers. Health care research that is taken out of the traditional college setting and moved into the "real world" is difficult, and our emphasis on hard-to-reach populations was a particular challenge.

Questions for Reflection

Do you agree with these authors that telephone surveys were the best choice, given the practical constraints that they faced in designing this project? What were some of the trade-offs?

If charged with designing this survey, what questions would you ask? Are there areas you would find especially difficult to probe? What would you do about the fact that some of your respondents might have a hard time imagining the concept of "telemedicine"?

Of the variety of services that hospice organizations might provide to isolated caregivers, as described here, which do you think could actually be delivered at a distance using communication technologies such as the telephone, the Web, interactive video, and so on?

What challenges do you think would be especially likely to arise in providing these "telemedicine" services to hospice caregivers in isolated rural areas? What questions might you have included on a telephone survey like this to probe some of these?

References

Agar, M. 1980. "Stories, Background Knowledge and Themes: Problems in the Analysis of Life History Narrative." *American Ethnologist* 7: 223–39.

Agar, M., and Hobbs. 1985. "How to Group Schemata out of Interviews." Pp. 413–31 in *Directions in Cognitive Anthropology*, ed. J. W. D. Dougherty. Urbana: University of Illinois Press.

Brownback, S. 2002. "Nursing Shortage." United States Senate. Accessed March 24, 2004 from http://www.senate.gov/~brownback/LINursingShortage.htm.

Buckingham, R. W. 1996. *The Handbook of Hospice Care*. Amherst: Prometheus Books.

Buehler, J. A., and H. J. Lee. 1992. Exploration of Home Care Resources for Rural Families with Cancer. *Cancer Nursing* 15 (4): 299–308.

ERS (Economic Research Service). 2002. "Rural Population and Migration." U. S. Department of Agriculture, June 14, 2002. Accessed June 20, 2002 from http://www.ers.usda.gov/briefing/Population/.

Greene, J. 1999. "Prescribing a Cure for the Shortage of Rural Physicians." *American Medical News* 42 (34).

HAA (Hospice Association of America). 2002. "Hospice Fact Sheet." Accessed March 17, 2002 from http://www.hospice-america.org/facts.html.

HFA (Hospice Foundation of America). 2002. Accessed March 17, 2002 from http://www.hospicefoundation.org/what_is/.

HospiceNet. 2002. "Medicare Hospice Benefits." Accessed March 17, 2002 from http://www.hospicenet.org/html/medicare-pr.html.

Hospice Web. 2002. "More about Hospice Services." Accessed March 17, 2002 from http://www.hospiceweb.com/info.htm.

Janofsky, M. 2002. "Shortage of Nurses Spurs Bidding War in Hospital Industry." *New York Times*, May 28.

Kumar, N., L. W Stern, and J. C. Anderson. 1993. "Conducting Interorganizational Research Using Key Informants." *Academy of Management Journal* 36 (6): 1633.

Lavrakas, P. J. 1998. "Methods for Sampling and Interviewing in Telephone Surveys." Pp. 429–72 in *Handbook of Applied Social Research Methods*, eds. L. Bickman and D. Rog. Thousand Oaks, CA: Sage.

NHF (National Hospice Foundation). 2002. "What Is Hospice?" Accessed March 17, 2002 from http://www.hospiceinfo.org/public/articles/index.cfm?cat=2.

Pearlin, L. I., C. S. Aneshensel, J. T. Mullan, and C. J. Whitlatch. 1996. "Caregiving and Its Social Support." Pp. 283–302 in *Aging and the Social Sciences*, eds. R. H. Binstock and L. K. George. San Diego: Academic Press.

Pelto, P., and G. Pelto. 1979. *Anthropological Research: The Structure of Inquiry.* 2nd ed. New York: Cambridge.

Seidman, I. E. 1998. *Interviewing as Qualitative Research.* 2nd ed. New York: Teachers College Press.

Yin, R. K. 1989. "Case Study Research." In *Applied Social Research Methods*, vol. 5, eds. L. Bickman and D. J. Rog. Rev. ed. Newbury Park: Sage.

Yin, R. K. 1994. "Case Study Research: Design and Methods." In *Applied Social Research Methods*, vol. 5. eds. L. Bickman and D. J. Rog. 2nd ed. Thousand Oaks: Sage.

17

Using the Internet to Conduct Communication Research: Two Scholars' Experiences

Tara L. Crowell and Traci L. Anderson

Communication researchers Tara Crowell and Traci Anderson, who were in graduate school together when both were working on Internet-based research projects, describe their experiences in this chapter. While one was researching "safer sex" and HIV issues and the other was looking at online romantic relationships, they shared a high level of frustration with how their IRB viewed their work.

In defense of their IRB's uncertainty, in the earliest days of Internet research no one was certain what the guidelines were or ought to be. Many university boards preferred to err on the side of caution. In the age of computer identity theft and seemingly unstoppable computer viruses, it is not entirely unnatural that questions should be raised about the actual anonymity of Internet survey respondents. Nevertheless, we can also sympathize deeply with Crowell and Anderson's frustration when their dissertation research was continuously sidetracked by IRB questions they thought they had already answered.

INCREASINGLY, SCHOLARS IN COMMUNICATION, psychology, sociology, and other social sciences are conducting research online; they are also experiencing the trials and tribulations of using this medium for social research. For individuals conducting online research for the first time, common drawbacks include simply not knowing how to get started and then how to progress. Even for scholars who have prior experience conducting online research, there are potential stumbling blocks.

In this chapter, we—Tara and Traci—share our stories of conducting research online and some of the issues we faced in the process. As doctoral students in the same program, with one year separating us, our collective experiences provide a

— 239 —

useful lens for viewing many of the intricacies and much of the arbitrary nature of the online data collection process. Since one of us had no experience collecting data online before and the other had previously used the Internet for data collection, we each faced different issues and decided to structure this chapter as a dialogue of sorts, discussing our problems and successes during the process and offering some general advice for the novice online data collector.

Our respective dissertations—Tara's, which examines "safer sex" communication and heterosexually contracted HIV; and Traci's, which focuses on communication and the development of online romantic relationships—provide the backdrop for our dialogue. More specifically, we will use our experiences to examine these questions:

When is Internet data collection more appropriate than a traditional questionnaire administered to a convenience sample?[1]

What potential difficulties could arise in obtaining Institutional Review Board (IRB) approval and how might these be addressed?

How should researchers design and make the best use of online surveys?

What are the best ways to utilize participants?

This dialogue is not comprehensive, but we hope to provide the readers with a greater understanding of the online research process and some of the issues they may encounter in this kind of project—based on our own experiences.

Why Collect Data Online?

Tara: The purpose of my dissertation was to identify the characteristics of individuals who acquired HIV through heterosexual activities so that I could compare the attitudes and behaviors of individuals living with HIV with those who are not infected. Therefore, my sample needed to be HIV-positive heterosexuals, infected through sexual contact. I thought it would be difficult to enlist participants and administer a paper-and-pencil survey in a typical survey setting such as a college classroom. Due to my specific criteria for participation, and the sensitive nature of the subject matter, I believed the use of the Internet would be a more effective way to collect my data.

When a researcher is deciding whether or not to use the Internet to obtain data, he or she should consider who the target population is and what type of information he or she is attempting to ascertain. Recent studies have found that an individual is more open when responding to questions online rather than when responding to paper-and-pencil surveys, especially with personal issues (CNN 1998; Sell 1997; Read 1991). In addition, Sell (1997) contends that online surveys have the "ability to reach relatively rare, hidden, and geographically dispersed populations" (297). One study conducted by IBM (Read 1991) reveals several advantages of online surveys over traditional paper-and-pencil ones. For instance, employees may prefer them and give more open responses; and they can also be faster, more flexible and efficient, and easier to analyze. Although online surveys were still a bit suspect at the time I collected my data, they seemed to hold great promise for reaching populations with rare diseases and/or specific health behaviors and interests (Sell 1997).

I made the above arguments to justify using this method of data collection in part because I knew that my university's IRB would need to grant approval before I could continue using human subjects. This would prove to be one of my biggest problems.

Traci: As Tara points out, when deciding whether to conduct data collection online, there are obvious advantages. Other advantages include saving time and money when compared to more traditional survey methods. For example, the time spent doing data entry can be minimized by software programs that import the online data directly into a statistical program. Also, the time spent administering paper-and-pencil surveys is eliminated, a distinct advantage even when compared to the time it takes to generate an online survey. Social science scholars who have been conducting research online support these claims. Schmidt (1997), a psychologist who conducts online research, states that the Internet "presents survey researchers with an unprecedented tool for the collection of data" (274). Other scholars echo these claims (Jones 1999; Sell 1997). And online data collection is not just useful for quantitative data collection. Researchers who draw from qualitative methods find online data collection to be useful as well, using open-ended surveys or "e-interviews" (Bampton and Cowton 2002).

In my particular case, the purpose of my dissertation was to investigate online romantic relationships. Where better to collect data than online, from couples who were currently involved in online romances? As Tara indicates, there are some strong arguments for conducting research online. Carver et al. (1999) note the importance of being able to access specific populations who are interested in particular issues or who embody specific characteristics. Further, Coomber (1997) argues that target populations that are difficult to locate or those that are of a "sensitive nature," meaning that they may be less inclined to come forward and identify themselves as a member of the population for any number of social or personal reasons (e.g., abuse survivors, teen mothers, gay and lesbian persons), may be more accessible online. As there is still a rather strong social stigma associated with people who form Internet romances (although this *is* changing), I assumed I would not have an easy time soliciting respondents at a mall or in classrooms simply by asking, "Has anyone here had a romantic relationship on the Internet?"

I had conducted research online before, so I assumed this process would run as smoothly as it had in the past. However, I soon found out that as the popularity of online research had grown, so had concerns about its validity, security, legality, ethics, and generalizability. Members of my university's Institutional Review Board (IRB) expressed many of these concerns.

Tara: It seemed that the IRB questioned whether or not messages found online constitute human interactions (private correspondence) or published texts (open to public analysis). Also, the board was uncertain if obtaining consent was necessary in all online venues (e.g., chat rooms, newsgroups). These concerns resulted in it being very difficult for either of us to get approval. Following is a more in-depth discussion of the IRB problems we faced.

Institutional Review Board Approval to Collect Data Online

Tara: The first proposal I submitted to the IRB for my project, asking for "exempt status,"[2] was quickly denied approval and no further information was provided. I asked for an explanation and received the following three comments from an employee at the IRB office:

With online data collection there are ways to identify participants and to link them to their responses.
The questions on the survey dealt with sexual behavior.
If, when answering my questions about sexual activity, someone discloses to me that they had "illegal" sexual relations, I would have a legal obligation to report it to the authorities.

I was then told to submit a "full board review" proposal and did so; but that too was rejected. The second time, however, the IRB provided more comments concerning the logistics of the survey as well as the informed consent form, voluntary participation, subject anonymity, data confidentiality, and debriefing of participants. I was told that once I addressed each issue in writing and made the suggested changes, the IRB would approve my study. The whole process took me approximately fifty days from start to finish. Had I submitted my survey as a traditional paper-and-pencil questionnaire, I believe the approval process likely would have been much shorter.

Traci: Tara's problems provide the backdrop for mine. When I submitted my own proposal to the IRB, I was careful to address each of the issues Tara had been instructed to address. Since I addressed each general concern the IRB had with Tara's online data collection, I assumed I would be "home free." Instead, a mere twelve months after the IRB's members identified their focal issues regarding online data collection, they had identified a revised set of points that needed to be addressed. (In fact, a year later, another university colleague was presented with yet another set of issues.) Because of the relative newness of using the Internet for research, the IRB was particularly worried about legal and ethical issues and had yet to establish its own set of standards for researchers planning to collect data online. Following are some of the IRB's specific concerns and how we handled them.

Tara: The committee had problems because I could not acquire participants' signatures on an informed consent form, as I would with a paper-and-pencil survey. However, with online research, I could obtain participants' consent by having them click on "I Agree to Participate" or "I Do Not Agree to Participate" icons. If individuals clicked on the first icon, it took them to the survey; therefore, the only way they could access the survey was if they agreed to participate. If the participants clicked on the second icon, it sent them directly to another website, thereby disallowing them access to the survey. As Mueller (1997) states:

> By clicking the link the participant accepts the terms of the consent form and proceeds to the actual survey. Although this could be seen as problematic, in fact, this format is widely used in lieu of a signature, for example, when entering credit card information online, or when accepting the terms of a software license prior to installation. So there are ample precedents for its use.

The IRB committee also told me that participants would not have "freedom of choice" (voluntary participation) if they were filling out a survey online. One committee member stated, "If people change their minds, they will not be able to quit half-way through." I explained that, with online surveys, individuals are not pressured to begin or complete a survey. Instead, at the beginning or in the middle of a survey, they may simply close the page, open another website, or log off the computer! In traditional paper-and-pencil surveys, participants may not feel as free to withdraw due to perceived penalties, or they may refrain from expressing their desire not to participate because of face-to-face social pressures. In a "virtual encounter," however, neither of these factors influences subjects.

Traci: This "freedom of choice" issue was particularly odd to me; I wondered if these committee members had ever been online? How does one "force" anyone to visit or stay logged on to any one website, Web survey or Web page? Nonetheless, to appease the board, both Tara and I added a statement to our online Introduction/Instruction page that read, "My participation in this study is entirely voluntary, and I may terminate my participation at any time prior to the completion of this study without penalty." To this day, I am still left wondering what magical trick the committee members had up their sleeves that could coerce people into spending time on websites in which they have no interest; no doubt, marketing executives would love to get hold of such information!

Tara: The protection of participants' anonymity and autonomy were the biggest concerns of the IRB committee; and they worried that I would be able to link a name to its corresponding data set. Although on my data collection website participants were instructed not to provide their names or contact information, nor did the survey provide a "name" or "address" field, the committee pointed out there are ways that computer software can track who has visited or logged onto Web surveys. Additionally, they noted that some domains are associated with personal addresses, thereby providing information that may identify the participant.

Traci: It *is* possible for participants who complete online questionnaires to remain completely anonymous. Yes, there are several methods possible to trace the response process, including the use of CGI scripts, java applets, and log files. However, it is up to the researcher to set up such protocols. And yes, an Internet Protocol address *may* be tracked to ascertain from which computer a particular e-mail came, but this does not specifically identify the individual who filled out the survey; and again it is up to the researcher to go out of her or his way to extract this information.

Tara: I explained to the IRB that just because someone visited the site does not mean that he or she completed the survey. I also indicated I would edit the data files periodically, deleting the headers, and would not use any scripting that would allow me to track users. Even given this explanation, the IRB was not satisfied and required that more detailed directions appear on the Instruction/Introduction page. Eventually, although the slight possibility did exist that subject anonymity could potentially be breached in this online research, the committee accepted these procedures. Then it had a second concern: subject qualification. The committee members wanted to know how the researcher would ensure participants met the specific sampling requirements.[3] In other words, how could I be sure that the subjects were HIV positive? Even though the Introduction Page and Consent Form stated that participants must be HIV-positive heterosexuals who were infected through heterosexual sexual activity, some committee members expressed concern that I would have no way to monitor who was filling out the survey. (Is that not the point of anonymity?) Committee members questioned the validity of this type of online data collection because I could in no way confirm that participants were in fact HIV positive.

Traci: I had similar problems. IRB committee members wanted to know how was I to ascertain if my participants were actually involved romantically online versus *pretending* to be involved romantically online. As I could not know for certain, I had to rely on the word of the participants. I argued that, just as in many paper-and-pencil surveys, mail surveys, and telephone interviews, I would have to accept the participant's word as truth. If they said they were involved in an online romantic relationship, then I had to believe them. Could I know this any more certainly if they were standing before me?

Tara: The IRB committee suggested that I obtain verification of my participants' HIV status, which was antithetical to my rationale for using the Internet to collect data. More specifically, collecting data online allows for information to be obtained about sensitive topics and from unique populations. Also, given the prejudice and discrimination associated with AIDS, exposure of someone's HIV status could cause mental, physical, relational, professional, and/or financial harm. Why would someone continue to participate if he or she had to provide me with "proof"? If I were to require or ask for verification of an individual's status, this would certainly bias the type of person who would participate, and the resulting systematic subject bias would likely have a greater influence on the validity of the sample.

I believe that researchers should give participants the choice to maintain anonymity when at all feasible. If they choose to breach anonymity, it should be at their behest rather than the researchers'. For example, during my online study, I had over 30 percent of the participants contact me via e-mail after completing the survey. Many of them wanted to give me more information, to explain their situation in greater detail, or to thank me for doing this type of research. Others just wanted to let me know they would forward my site to someone they knew, while still others wanted to complain about the survey or to give me suggestions on how to improve my study. While I felt I could not use any of the information in these e-mails as a formal part of my study, in many ways it provided me with a better personal understanding of HIV-positive heterosexuals than I obtained from the actual data. This type of insight will be very useful in directing my future HIV/AIDS research.

Traci: Like Tara, I had many participants contact me voluntarily to provide additional information they could not include in the survey. These people did so knowing that they were providing me with a personal e-mail address, if not a name, but chose to do so anyway. Many of these people shared detailed stories of their online loves (and losses), and it seems hard to believe that these stories were passed on by people with nothing better to do with their time than "throw off" a researcher. It is possible, but not probable. It is important to keep in mind that in *any* research involving participants, there always exists the possibility of participant deception. Just because I physically see my subjects does not ensure participants' honesty. Generally, we accept this type of error as random and a natural part of the research process.

Tara: The IRB told me it believed that online studies could guarantee the same degree of confidentiality as traditional paper-and-pencil surveys.

However, with paper-and-pencil surveys, researchers establish confidentiality by locking the data and signed consent forms in two separate filing cabinets (they of course have the only key) and destroying the documentation when finished. I explained that even though online data collection produces no signed consent forms, the data is still "locked" away—just in a computer rather than in a file cabinet. Then I provided the following citation:

> For online data files, confidentiality is achieved in that the data are stored on a computer in a personal account that is accessible only to someone who knows the account user ID and password, which should again be just the researcher. In truth, a Unix account password is probably much more secure than a file cabinet that yields too often to a bent paper clip! (Mueller 1997)

Finally, to certify that participants' responses would remain confidential, I provided the IRB committee with the following statement: "To ensure participants' responses are confidential, online surveys are constructed to send data to a separate CGI bin that is accessible only by the researcher." Thus, the data is still on the Web, but at an address known only to authorized project personnel.

Given the above explanation, the IRB committee concluded that privacy would be protected with normal standards of care as for any study conducted via the Internet, even though confidentiality could not be guaranteed. It then insisted I place the following statement on the Informed Consent Form: "All information I may give during my participation will be used for research purposes only. Responses will not be shared with persons who are not directly involved with this study. As with any study conducted via the Internet, confidentiality cannot be guaranteed."

Tara: The IRB committee asked me how I could debrief participants online, because, unlike personally administered surveys, with online surveys I would not be present to debrief participants. To address this concern, a "Thank You" page was included, which let participants know they had successfully completed the survey and provided them with follow-up material (such as websites with additional information on HIV and AIDS, information on the purpose of the study, and so on), if desired.

Traci: Visit any Web survey. They are easy to find: a simple search on Yahoo or Google will yield many. Most of them have a sort of "Thank You" page that serves the purpose of debriefing (and dehoaxing, if necessary). On such a page, a researcher should include additional information about the study, when and where to find the results of the study, the researcher's contact information, and links to additional resources (such as the IRB office and information sites related to the project's topic).

Designing, Uploading, and Using an Online Survey

Traci: The most important point I would like to make is that anyone can use online surveys. Someone who does not feel "tech savvy" should not be intimidated. There are numerous tools and programs on the market to help with online survey development and data collection; some require a more "hands-on" approach than others, and some are more costly than others. Find the right tool to fit your needs. There are also many companies that will design, upload, and maintain a survey for you. These are also rather expensive services for most academicians; however, if funding can be obtained, then you might consider them.

Most people will be looking for less pricey options, so my first suggestion would be to find out if your institution has tools to help with online research. In recent years, many colleges and universities have recognized the growing trend of online research and provide support, in one form or another, for such projects. Some institutions have staff who will help faculty construct, upload, and manage online surveys. Some institutions have purchased licenses for software used to construct and manage online surveys. The survey will still need to be uploaded. There are various ways to do this (one common method uses CGI scripting, which is not as intimidating as it may sound), but again I recommend that you consult with and utilize your institution's support services.

When constructing a Web survey, many of the traditional techniques of questionnaire design are used, but keep in mind that the medium presents some unique issues regarding formatting. Witmer et al. (1990) outline online survey formatting standards that ensure ease of use. These formatting guidelines include listing response scale choices after each item to keep the response options fresh in participants' minds and to minimize continuous scrolling back and forth; aligning response boxes so that participants can use a minimal number of keystrokes; and providing explicit rules and a good deal of "white space" for ease of readability. In addition, Dillman (2000) posits that lack of navigational tools, use of pull-down menus (as opposed to radio buttons), and ambiguous or complicated instructions may intimidate those persons who have online apprehension or who are less "Web savvy." For these reasons, I try to design surveys keeping in mind my technophobic mother. If it is possible for her to complete the survey, then anyone can do it!

Be sure to include an introductory page that explains the nature of the study (criteria for participation, investigator's contact information and affiliation, and potential risks and benefits of participation) and requires participants to indicate their consent. As Tara indicated, having the participant click on an icon that indicates consent may substitute for a signature.

Tara: Based on my experiences, I have just a few side notes to add regarding online surveys. As with paper-and-pencil surveys, you need to be concerned with the length of your online surveys. Depending on the program you are using to construct your survey, your format may take up more space than it would on paper. Thus, individuals may perceive it to be more time-consuming and therefore may be less likely to participate (especially since many Internet users live in a world of high speed and quick results). In addition, once your survey is complete and uploaded but prior to recruiting participants, you should fill out your survey yourself to make sure there are no glitches, and then check your data file. I have a colleague who got the "go-ahead" from her institution's computer department that her survey was up and running. She announced it to her students and received over 300 completed surveys, but when she went to analyze the data, there was a glitch and she was unable to use any of them.

In addition to filling out your own survey, I have a few other suggestions. There should be an "error page" built into your survey, so that if people do not fill out all of the questions, they will be unable to submit the survey. Once they click the "submit" button, they will receive a message that indicates questions that have not been answered. This error page is similar to those used for purchasing products online. When you have not filled out all of the required fields, you cannot complete your order. This will eliminate receiving half-completed surveys. By the same token, you must make sure you include an "N/A" (not applicable) choice where necessary. Finally, if you are including open-ended questions, please allow enough room for the individuals to answer. Can you imagine finally getting individuals who will take the time to provide rich descriptive information, but which you never receive because they have been cut off by space limitations?

Recruitment of Participants

Traci: Recruiting participants for a study depends largely on one's population, study design, and available resources. In the case of my research on online relationships, I used a combination of volunteer and snowball sampling methods through which participants were encouraged to pass the survey link along to other people they knew who were involved in online romantic relationships. Initially, to get people to the website I solicited respondents through online romance-related websites and in online newsgroups or listservs. I chose newsgroups with subject matter that dealt with online friendships, romances, and interaction, along with a sample of newsgroups in unrelated areas. Due to the fact that much relationship research focuses exclusively on heterosexual relationships, I included newsgroups dealing with general gay, lesbian, and bisexual concerns (e.g., lesbian chat) but was careful to avoid any newsgroups that functioned as support groups (e.g., coming out, victims of abuse).

The websites were, by far, the easier of the two; I contacted the Web developers, explained the nature of my project, and asked if they would be willing to provide a link to my online survey from their websites. Most were extremely accommodating. Soliciting through newsgroups—a not uncommon strategy—proved to be significantly more frustrating. Many newsgroups have moderators whose job it is to edit and filter members' posts. Even though I was careful to read participation guidelines for each newsgroup in which I posted and made every effort to avoid being intrusive, many moderators contacted me for more information prior to posting my message. In many cases, they refused to post it altogether, stating that there was no way to verify the study was "legitimate." I countered that my full institutional affiliation was provided on both the call for participation and on the introductory page of the survey itself, and gave them the URL where the survey was hosted on the university server, but that did not change all moderators' decisions.

Perhaps the most interesting of the concerns and complaints came from a couple of moderators of lesbian-oriented newsgroups. One moderator, in particular, wrote me a quite heated e-mail stating I was "exploiting" an already marginalized group. I replied, explaining that my concern was to include, rather than exclude (as does much relationship research), persons who are gay, lesbian, and bisexual. I did not receive a response. Luckily, my final sample did ultimately include individuals who were involved in gay and lesbian relationships online.

Each researcher must decide what type and method of recruitment will work best in a given situation. Online "sampling" does not easily yield a response rate (although there are scripts and software programs to aid in this) and will likely be nonrandom. How could someone procure a list of all heterosexuals who are HIV positive or all persons involved in online relationships, in order to sample randomly or to calculate the percentage who responded? Whether a researcher can use probability sampling will depend on the population being studied; but if probability sampling is not used, the researcher must be prepared for strong criticism about the validity of results and the generalizability of findings. Remember, any sampling method has limitations, and there are arguments to support online data collection. As it continues to increase in popularity, I believe that doubts as to its utility will likely diminish.

Tara: Finally, I would like to share one other unpleasant experience I had when recruiting online participants, hoping it will help others to avoid similar mistakes. While recruiting online, I went to HIV-positive newsgroups, listservs, and chat rooms to announce my research project and provide the survey's website. However, I was unaware that some of these sites had a "Webmaster" (someone in charge of the websites and the postings) and that if you wanted to post a message, it needed to be approved. I received one very unpleasant response after posting my announcement. One person went so far as to write me a three-page letter blaming me for the demise of social science research and accusing me of being totally unethical; he complained that I was participating on a listserv strictly reserved for HIV-positive individuals. Ultimately, he wanted not only my study to be terminated, but me as well—terminated from the university, that is! So when using these types of forums, please be aware that there may be a specific protocol to follow. If you are unfamiliar with these procedures, most sites provide you with a "contact us" link. Please keep in mind that some sites may simply be "off limits," depending on your subject matter and/or target population.

Conclusion

Scholars' use of the Internet to collect data, although still a relatively new phenomenon, is growing rapidly. Over the past decade, scholars in the social sciences and other disciplines have shared with us both their online research findings and their experiences in conducting online research. These stories provide a wealth of knowledge to help others explore and understand the process. We hope that by our sharing our experiences with Internet data collection, you will have gained a better general understanding of the process. Although our dialogue is not meant to be an in-depth discussion of the whole process of online data collection, it does give an overview of some of the essential elements in the process: the appropriateness of using the Internet for data collection; potential difficulties with the IRB approval, with suggestions for addressing concerns; designing and using online surveys; and recruitment of online participants. Whether you are focusing on safer sexual communication, the development of online romantic relationships, or any number of other research areas, we hope we have illustrated why and how online research can be a viable option. Good luck!

Questions for Reflection

How exactly are online samples going to be different from the type of random sample traditionally used for survey work, whether pencil-and-paper or over the telephone? Are there any other ways to contact special populations?

Do you feel that people are going to remain eager to fill out online surveys, or will they soon become "oversurveyed" and ignore the opportunity (as has happened for phone surveys)? Why or why not?

How likely would you personally be to respond to a request to fill out a survey online regarding some aspect of your most personal behavior? What runs through your mind as you think about how to respond to this question?

To what extent do you think Crowell and Anderson's IRB concerns simply created unnecessary problems, and to what extent do you think these concerns were justified? Do you think the situation they encountered with their IRB is likely to be different today?

Notes

1. Unlike a random sample, a "convenience sample" consists of respondents who are simply readily available—convenient, as the name implies!

2. IRBs classify certain very specific types of low-risk projects as "exempt" from the most elaborate form of board review. They still require IRB approval, but the process is somewhat streamlined.

3. IRBs are not normally charged with assuring that a study's design is valid, or the research valuable, but sometimes this becomes a fine line.

References

Bampton, R., and Cowton, C. J. 2002. "The E-Interview Forum." *Qualitative Social Research* 3 (2). www.qualitative-research.net/fqs-texte/2-02/2-02bamptoncowton-e.htm/ (accessed November 14, 2003).

Carver, S., R. Kingston, and I. Turton. 1999. "A Review of Graphical Environments on the World Wide Web as a Means of Widening Public Participation in Social Science Research." www.ccg.leeds.ac.uk/agocg/report.htm (accessed August 19, 1999).

CNN Interactive. 1998. Study: "Many People with AIDS Virus Don't Tell Sex Partner." February 8. www.cnn.com/HEALTH/9802/08/sexualethics.ap/ (accessed October 7, 1998).

Coomber, R. 1997. "Using the Internet for Survey Research." *Sociological Research Online* 2. www.socresonline.org.uk/2/2/2.html. (accessed April 27, 1998).

Dillman, D. A. 2000. *Mail and Internet Surveys: The Tailored Design Method.* New York, NY: Wiley.

Jones, S. 1999. "Studying the Net: Intricacies and Issues." Pp. 1–27 in *Doing Internet Research: Critical Issues and Methods for Examining the Net,* ed. S. Jones. Thousand Oaks, CA: Sage.

Mueller, J. 1997. "Researcher Online: Human Participants Ethics Issues." www.psych.ucalgary.ca/Research/ethics/online.html (accessed August 22, 1998).
Read, W. H. 1991. "Gathering Opinion Online." *HRMagazine* (January): 51–53.
Schmidt, W. C. 1997. "World Wide Web Survey Research: Benefits, Potential Problems, and Solutions." *Behaviour Research Methods, Instruments and Computers* 29: 274–79.
Sell, R. L. 1997. "Research and the Internet: An E-mail Survey of Sexual Orientation." *American Journal of Public Health* 87: 297.
Witmer, D. F., R. W. Colman, and S. L. Katzman. 1999. "From Paper-and-pencil to Screen-and-keyboard: Toward a Methodology for Survey Research on the Internet." Pp. 145–61 in *Doing Internet Research: Critical Issues and Methods for Examining the Net*, ed. S. Jones. Thousand Oaks, CA: Sage.

18
Finding Out What's on the World Wide Web

James W. Tankard Jr. and Cindy Royal

This deceptively simple and straightforward study by James Tankard and Cindy Royal provides the perfect note on which to complete our collection. Tankard and Royal use their Web content project to illustrate many profoundly important points about research, as well as to point the way to new areas for investigation that other scholars might want to look at more closely. In so doing, they remind us that while new methods may sometimes be needed to make sense of Web content, older issues of the social significance of mediated communication remain important.

In particular, these authors talk about research design as an intensely creative process, an aspect that conventional methods texts often miss. Tankard and Royal describe their brainstorming together about innovative ways to approach an emerging, as-yet-undefined area of research—Web research. They also give us a glimpse of the evolution of their conceptual and theoretical thinking. What is the difference between "knowledge" and "information"? What does it mean to society that some subjects, time periods, and people have come to dominate the Internet landscape more than others? Is this a new form of "bias"? What are its implications? And they share some of the technical difficulties they had to resolve as their theoretical thinking emerged.

While their research does make use of some quantitative ideas we have seen before, such as correlation coefficients, this is not a methodologically complex study. Its strength is conceptual, reflecting a gradual transition from concern with the everyday, practical, concrete question of whether everything is really on the Web after all to a more abstract set of issues having to do with whether one kind of information can actually "push out" others, and under what circumstances. It is no

— 253 —

accident that some of the literature they turned to in order to make sense of their statistical results is in biology, where populations and whole ecological systems evolve according to just such principles.

Above all, this study illustrates that there are important research questions remaining to be addressed, and that finding answers to some of these questions will require conceptual innovation as much as methodological sophistication. For many researchers, this is a compelling challenge—not only because researchers tend to like challenges, but because the opportunity to think creatively about research strategies is a big part of what makes research fun.

OUR RESEARCH PROJECT WAS DESIGNED to determine what information is on the World Wide Web and what is not (Tankard and Royal 2003). The idea for the project came not from reading the research literature, but from personal observation. One of us (Tankard) had a dream about flagpole sitters—a fad of the 1920s in which someone would sit or stand for days on a platform on the top of a pole. Hoping to find more information on this curious behavior, he attempted to look up "flagpole sitters" on the Web. To his surprise, only a few sites with useful information were found. This was our first indication that while some topics are covered heavily on the Web, others are barely mentioned at all.

Some time later, Tankard was looking on the Web for the chords to "Bye Bye Blackbird." He knew the Web included the chords and guitar tabulations for thousands of songs, so he began searching. The chords for "Bye Bye Blackbird" weren't to be found. When he told a fellow amateur musician about this occurrence, he was reminded that because many Web users are young, the songs that are available online reflect youthful culture and tastes. Like the search for information on flagpole sitting, this incident also brought home the point that not all knowledge is on the Web. It was also striking that both flagpole sitting and "Bye Bye Blackbird" were popular in the 1920s. This focus on the 1920s led Tankard to think that the time dimension might be important in determining what content is on the Web. Could it be that some time periods are represented more heavily on the Web than others?

Tankard began to think about some method for testing this notion. One possibility would be to search for various years with a search engine that reports the number of sites it has found for each search. This would produce a quantitative measure of the amount of information. This kind of search could be carried out for many years over a long period of time. He realized that one difficulty might be that you would pick up all kinds of numbers that were not years (for example, a site listing a car for sale for $1,999). Something would have to be done about that problem.

At about this time, Tankard met with Royal for coffee, and they began discussing a possible research project. There are many benefits to collaborative research, including more effective generation of ideas, improved ability to catch mistakes, and a lessening of the workload through sharing. Several ideas emerged from this first session.

First, we decided to use two search engines (rather than one) as a reliability check. We found that Altavista.com and Alltheweb.com were search engines that report a "number of sites found" for every search. We also recognized the problem that the searches would pick up four-digit numbers that looked like years, but weren't. One possible remedy would be to include the word "year" in each search to force the searches to focus on years. The form of the search would become "year 1927," for example. And we brainstormed about other measures we might examine in addition to years. We thought of several time-related areas we could investigate:

Mayors of a certain city over a period of one hundred years
Academy Award–winning movies for each year up to the present
Time magazine's "Man of the Year" or "Person of the Year" for each year

Each of these "measures" would be used as an indirect measure of the time dimension. At this point, our thinking was focused mostly on the issue of time.

We also tried to think of a way to measure the comprehensiveness of knowledge on the Web—going beyond just the time dimension. This question was inspired by an earlier study by Danielson and Adams (1961) of the 1960 presidential election. Danielson and Adams came up with a probability sample of campaign events and then conducted a content analysis to determine the frequency with which a number of newspapers covered each event. We thought that we might use a similar method to sample one hundred topics from an encyclopedia and look at the extent to which each topic appeared on websites. At this point, we were using our knowledge of the scholarly research literature to expand and strengthen our study.

We speculated about possible outcomes. For the time dimension, we expected a straight line with the high end (most links found) for recent years and the low end (fewest links possible) for years in the past. At this point, we were brainstorming about ways to develop the original research idea. What are the specific questions that we really wanted to focus on? What methods would we use to answer those questions? What concepts would we look at? Were there areas of research that might have related studies that could help us shape our project in useful ways? How would our project relate to other knowledge (or claims of knowledge) in the literature? At this time, the research project was very pliable. It could have been shaped in numerous different ways. This stage of the research process is high in potential for creativity.

We strongly believe that the research process can (and should) be a creative activity. Whenever Tankard is teaching a course in basic research methods, he devotes at least one class period to the application of creativity to research. Students are assigned to read chapters from Alex Osborn's *Applied Imagination* (1953). Osborn is one of the pioneers in the now-popular field of creativity. Just one of his ideas was the technique of brainstorming, a method of using groups to generate ideas that has been applied for more than fifty years. His book is now regarded as a classic.

Methods of creativity can be utilized at many stages in the research process, from selecting a research topic to choosing variables to coming up with a name for the study. For instance, one of Osborn's techniques is to come up with a list of as many ideas as you can for solving a problem and then choose the best one. We have used that technique successfully for tasks ranging from choosing a research topic to picking a title for books and articles.

Another source Tankard has often assigned in class is a chapter by Janet Bavelas (1987) dealing with creativity in the research process. She recommends that research begin with observation of the natural world. Bavelas argues that if you only get your research ideas from the scholarly literature, you will always be just building on the research of others. It takes observation to open up new topics of inquiry. James Lovelock (2000), the discoverer of the Gaia hypothesis, also stresses the importance of observation. Lovelock says the successful researcher should be writing the literature, not reading it (104).

Bavelas also stresses that a lot of work is usually needed to develop the original idea into a feasible and meaningful research study. She tells how most of her research takes shape as a result of long, regularly scheduled discussions with graduate students or colleagues.

At some point early in our project, we wrote a brief research proposal. Writing a proposal is a useful step even if you are not submitting your research plan to a dissertation committee or a prospective funding agency. A written proposal has several advantages. It helps focus the research project. Decisions must be made about research questions or hypotheses, research methods, plans for analyzing the data, and so forth. It helps make sure that all members of the research team are thinking about the project the same way. It can also help in assigning tasks to team members. Finally, it opens the research plan up to criticism and further development—from members of the research team and others.

Deflating Hype about the Web

One of our initial purposes was to deflate some of the hype surrounding the Web. The Web is a wonderful tool, but it also has its weaknesses. The scholarly community should start looking at what the Web really can do and what it can't. While there has been some criticism of the Web, little of it has been based on evidence. In general, one of our goals was to study the Web with systematic and empirical methods. Numerous writers have argued or implied that the Web contains all knowledge, or that it will someday. We wanted to confront those kinds of claims and show that they were incorrect.

We had also noted a disturbing trend for students (and faculty members—let's face it) to rely too much on the Web. People who have a question often turn to the Web instead of going to the library. When we visit our campus library, it is common to see all the computer terminals on the first floor in use by students but hardly anyone up in the stacks searching for books.

If our research purpose was to deflate some of the exaggerated claims being made about the Web, we would need to include examples of such statements in our paper. One of the first steps was to search for statements claiming that the Web contained all or most human knowledge, or support for the notion that students have become excessively dependent on the Web (and yes, we confess it, we started our search by going to the Web!). We found the following items.

A survey reported that 93 percent of a student sample said finding information online made more sense than going to the library (Troll 2001). The same report suggested that students are "enamored of the Web. In many cases, if the information is not available on the Web, it does not exist for them." Another article on the subject of the Web as a "super-brain" stated, "We can safely assume that in the following years virtually the whole of human knowledge will be made available electronically over the networks" (Heylighen 2002). A teenage "Whiz Kid" won a prize for his efforts to design a website to contain "all human knowledge" (Miller 2002). A statement by Web programming expert John Simpson argued, "The whole body of human knowledge, experience, and understanding can be expressed in terms of plain text; if something cannot be so expressed, it might as well not exist" (Simpson 2002).

Interestingly, this last statement was strongly challenged by a reader, who said,

> I can only assume that this sentence was written specifically for shock value.... This statement is so horribly wrong. In fact little of what humanity knows, experiences, and understands can be expressed in plain text (especially at this point). (Fakerson 2002).

Such statements and events seem to reflect the unbridled enthusiasm for the World Wide Web that has been common since its invention, and the unrealistic expectations that can result. We decided to respond to the Web boosters by carrying out an empirical test of the notion that the World Wide Web contains all of human knowledge. Our initial research questions were the following:

1. Are there some obvious "gaps" in the knowledge made available on the Web?
2. Focusing on the dimension of time, are there time periods that are systematically not represented on the Web as much as others?
3. Is there a systematic bias in the coverage of time periods on the Web?

Inventing a Method

Basically, we invented our own method for answering these questions. None of the traditional methods of the social sciences—content analysis, survey research, the experiment, the case study—would provide answers to the questions we were asking. The method we came up with was a method indigenous to the Web. Our study also provides an example of a project being question-driven rather than method-driven. We didn't start with a method we liked and were good at—such as the experiment—and then try to find a problem to address.

For all of our searches, as determined in our initial brainstorming, we decided to use two search engines as a reliability check, Altavista and AlltheWeb, because they report the number of sites found for every search. We also planned to use quotation marks to focus our searches on the terms we were interested in. For instance, we would put quotation marks around "John Kennedy" so the search engines would not pick up all the Web pages that referred to a "John" and a "Kennedy." This was the same strategy we had settled on for our examination of the time dimension, when we wanted to prevent the search engines from picking up other numbers besides years and used the "year 1927" format.

Building on the Danielson and Adams study, we tried to develop a method of measuring completeness of knowledge. One idea we had was to use a standard encyclopedia (not online, but a series of physical volumes in the university library) as an operational definition of the body of human knowledge. We could take a random sample of one hundred subject entries and use search engines to find out whether they were represented on the Web, and if so, in what number. Another idea for getting at completeness of knowledge was to take a random sample of categories in the Dewey Decimal System.

The Backward L-Shaped Distribution

Very early, we tried a simple pilot study. We did searches on the term "year xxxx" with xxxx replaced by years that were ten years apart and went from

1901 to 2001. We included the word "year" to limit the websites to those actually dealing with (or at least mentioning) specific years, and to exclude numbers that were not referring to years (1900 Sycamore Avenue, for example). The results surprised us. We had been expecting a linear trend, with the number of Web pages increasing steadily from 1901 to 2001. Instead, we found that the distribution took the form of a backward L, with more recent events much more likely to be included on the Web than older events (Figure 18.1). The difference was dramatic, with 2001 producing more than five times as many links as 1901. We did not expect the sharp drop—like a precipice—as we moved back from the most recent years.

As we continued our investigation, that backward L-distribution was to become a familiar pattern. We realized we needed to get out our statistics books and read about the L-distribution. We found that the L-distribution had occurred in previous studies. The range of these studies was striking. One study dealt with plant growth and showed that the tallest plants shade the short plants from the sun, and this causes them to absorb more sunlight and grow even taller (Silvertown and Charlesworth 2001). We saw a possible analogy here to sites on the Web. People have limited attention spans and memory, and the list of bookmarks in a browser can only be so long. Perhaps the most

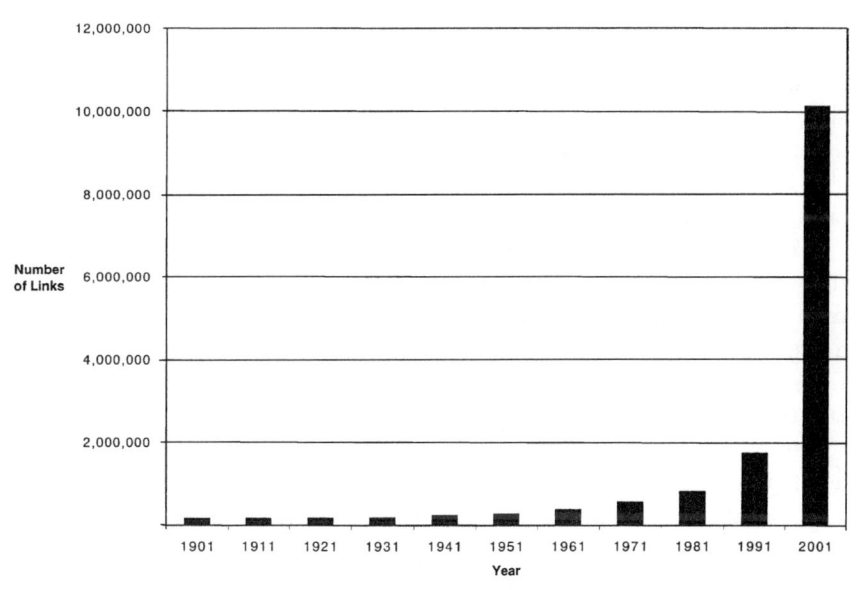

FIGURE 18.1
Results from the pilot test (searching for every decade from 1901 to 2001). The number of pages found for each year is plotted by year. The backward L-distribution is clearly visible. Search engine: Altavista.

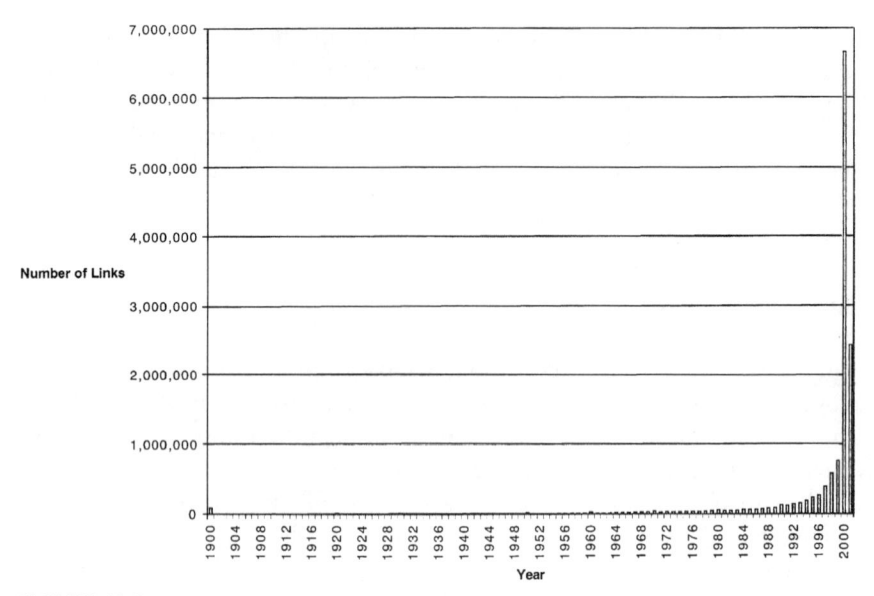

FIGURE 18.2
Results from the main study (searching for every year from 1900 to 2001). As in the pilot study, the number of pages found for each year is plotted by year. Again, the backward-L distribution is clearly visible. Search engine: AlltheWeb.

prominent sites begin to dominate and draw attention from less prominent sites. Other studies found L-distributions in the relationship between temperature and numbness in human subjects (Hoffman 1997) and in the relationship between the likelihood that recent mothers will return to work and time since the child's birth (Even 1987).

We also found that the L-distribution called for particular statistics to be used in the analysis stage. The usual parametric statistics, such as the Pearson correlation coefficient, were not appropriate because they were based on the assumption of a normal curve distribution. The preferred statistic for the L-distribution was a rank order correlation, such as the Spearman. So we carried out all our analyses using Spearman correlations.

Our next step was to carry out the investigation of the time dimension with a full sample of 101 years, from 1900 to 2001. As in the pilot test, the results fit a backward L-distribution (Figure 18.2). We tried searching for the encyclopedia sample of one hundred items. When the items were ranked according to number of links found, the results again fit the backward L-distribution.

Some of the measures we thought of worked well but others, for various reasons, did not. We had to discard the variable of number of links for mayors of a certain city over a period of one hundred years. We had intended to use the number of websites found for the names of various mayors of one city as an indirect measure of the influence of time. But it became clear that the fame or notoriety of certain mayors would play a greater role in determining Web presence than the number of years since the mayors had served.

The list of Academy Award–winning movies did not work out well because many movie names—such as "Wings," "Rebecca," and "Unforgiven"—are also common words in the language. The search for mentions of *Time* magazine's person of the year also presented problems. In some cases, the person of the year was a topic or phenomenon. Also, some names were presented by *Time* with middle names or initials, making it difficult to be sure we were finding all the mentions. For example, "John Fitzgerald Kennedy" would more likely be referred to on the Web as "John F. Kennedy" or "President Kennedy."

To produce another measure of completeness, we drew a random sample of topics from the Dewey Decimal System. This effort was not successful because this system is a classification system and many of the categories are very broad topics such as "number," "quantity," or "associations." These terms would obviously show up on many sites, distorting our results.

The unsatisfactory results for these measures illustrate another principle of research—sometimes part of your method doesn't work and you have to switch to another approach. Since several of our dimensions had not worked out, we began to try to think of other dimensions we might look at. We later came up with the ideas of looking at the Web presence of countries (using a United Nations list as a benchmark) and "Fortune 1000" companies (using a random sample of names from the list of one thousand). We also sometimes had to change a search term to make the search a reasonable one. For instance, one of the corporations on the "Fortune 1000" list was Gap. To avoid finding many kinds of irrelevant "gaps," we searched for the term "Gap, Inc."

At this point, we decided to revise our research questions to reflect the new areas of inquiry. We came up with these revised questions:

1. Are there some obvious "gaps" in the overall presentation of knowledge made available on the World Wide Web?
2. Focusing on the dimensions of time, nationality, and economic importance (power), are there systematic omissions in the information made available on the World Wide Web?

Predictors of Web Content

At some point in the research process, we began to think in terms of the predictors of the presence or absence of Web content. This addition to our study would take it beyond the level of description to the level of explanation—a more theoretically interesting level. And it would shift the research purpose from deflating the hype about the Web (although that thrust was still there) to building theory.

To find possible predictors of the frequency of Web content, we turned to previous research in the journalism area dealing with news flow and news values. This choice probably reflects our familiarity with our own field, journalism. From the classic study of news flow by Galtung and Ruge (1965), we got the idea of impact. We translated that to mean importance—the more important a topic is, the more likely it is to be found on the Web. We looked at importance as a possible predictor for the random sample of encyclopedia articles. We measured importance by the length of the article in the encyclopedia.

From other previous journalism studies, we picked up the possible predictors of magnitude and timeliness. Magnitude was tested as a possible predictor of coverage of countries (where it was operationally defined as population of the country) and "Fortune 1000" companies (where it was operationally defined as annual revenue of the company). We had already suspected that timeliness (or recency) might be an important predictor of the extent to which individual years would appear on the Web.

Sometimes we didn't know whether something we were thinking about was an independent variable or a dependent variable. We looked at this lack of certainty as a good sign. It suggested that we were breaking new ground conceptually. As the project moved along, we had to make a number of additional decisions about conceptualization. One decision we had to make was whether to use the word "bias" or not. Although it would be accurate to say that our findings indicated various biases in Web content, we decided to avoid the term because it is such a loaded word, particularly in journalism circles.

Another conceptualization issue focused on the term "knowledge." We first phrased the study in terms of what knowledge is available on the Web. But this word seemed to act like a red flag to some early readers of the manuscript, leading them to challenge our definitions of knowledge and to expect a much more philosophical discussion of knowledge than we were prepared to give. This led us to reconceptualize the study in terms of information—a more familiar term to journalists and journalism researchers and a term with fewer definitional problems.

We carried out statistical tests and found many highly significant results, but our favorite way of presenting our findings was graphs. An effective chart tells a story (Tufte 1983), and in this study the graphs told the story very effectively.

Our final paper reported that the Web was less than comprehensive in its reporting of different time periods, encyclopedia topics, countries, and "Fortune 1000" companies. The L-shaped distribution showed up with every topic. This consistent appearance of the L-shaped distribution was probably our most striking finding.

We gave some thought to how our study could be extended. We came up with additional areas in which the completeness of the Web information could be investigated, including representativeness with respect to women, ethnic groups, marginalized groups, social classes, and topics of cultural interest. In addition, we wondered whether the uneven representation of topics on the Web might be similar to the uneven representation in other media, including newspapers, books, movies, and television. Or does the Web offer a unique venue for being either representative or unrepresentative?

Finally, we thought our study should someday be extended to include the so-called Deep Web, that part of the Web that is not accessible through the standard search engines but is available through search mechanisms on individual Web pages (Bergman 2003). Will the Web be more, or less, complete and representative as increasing quantities of information are stored in these vast data warehouses?

Questions for Reflection

What things have you looked for on the Web and never found? Did you eventually find them elsewhere—by chance, in a conventional library search, from someone you knew, or in your general reading, perhaps?

Of course, we would expect that more recent material will dominate an information technology that has mushroomed in popularity in recent years. But what other forces might be at work here that have nothing directly to do with recency?

What are some of the other dimensions of Internet content (and its accessibility) that you think deserve further attention from researchers?

The Internet has been heralded as a democratizing force because it makes available a wealth of information and perspectives to ordinary citizens. If Tankard and Royal are right, what are the implications of their results for this idea?

References

Bavelas, J. B. 1987. "Permitting Creativity in Science." Pp. 307–27 in *Scientific Excellence: Origins and Assessment*, eds. D. N. Jackson and J. P. Rushton. Newbury Park, CA: Sage.

Bergman, M. K. 2003. "The Deep Web: Surfacing Hidden Value." BrightPlanet, February 5, www.brightplanet.com/technology/deepweb.asp#Introduction.

Danielson, W. A., and J. B. Adams. 1961. "Completeness of Coverage of the 1960 Campaign." *Journalism Quarterly* 38: 441–52.

Even, W. E. 1987. "Career Interruptions following Childbirth." *Journal of Labor Economics*, http://netec.wustl.edu/BibEc/data/.../ucpjlabecv:5:y:1987:I:2:p:255-77.html, (accessed August 7, 2002).

Galtung, J., and E. Ruge. 1965. "The Structure of Foreign News." *Journal of International Peace Research* 2: 64–90.

Heylighen, F. 2002. "From World Wide Web to Super-Brain." Principia Cybernetica Web1995, April 22. http://pespmc1.vub.ac.be/SUPBRAIN.html.

Hoffman, R. G. 1997. "Human Psychological Performance in Cold Environments." In *Textbook of Military Medicine: Medical Aspects of Deployment to Harsh Environments*, ed. R. Burr. Washington, DC: Borden Institute 1997.

Fakerson, F. 2002. "xml Is Insufficient." O'Reilley XML.com, May 15. www.xml.com/cs/user/view/cs_msg/516.

Lovelock, J. 2000. *Homage to Gaia: The Life of an Independent Scientist*. Oxford: Oxford University Press.

Miller, L. 2002. "The News behind the Net: Ex-Prodigy Rewards New Web Whiz Kids." *USA Today*, May 15. www.usatoday.com/life/cyber/tech/ko62200.htm.

Osborn, A. 1953. *Applied Imagination*. New York: Scribner.

Silvertown, J. W., and D. Charlesworth. 2001. *Introduction to Plant Population Biology*. Oxford: Blackwell Science Ltd.

Simpson, J. E. "Basic Training." O'Reilley XML.com, March 27. www.xml.com/pub/a/2002/03/27/qanda.html.

Tankard, J. W., and C. Royal. 2003. "What's on the Web, and What's Not." Paper presented at the Annual Meeting, International Communication Association, San Diego, CA, May 24.

Troll, D. A. 2001. "How and Why Are Libraries Changing?" Digital Library Federation, May 16. www.diglib.org/use/whitepaper.htm.

Tufte, E. R. 1983. *The Visual Display of Quantitative Information*. Cheshire, CT: Graphics Press.

Afterword: Purpose and Direction

HUMAN BEINGS ARE BOTH INDIVIDUAL organisms and members of families, organizations, cultures, and societies. Communication at all these levels is completely integral to what it means to be human; it is the way that the individual connects to the family and the group (and sometimes, the way that the group controls the individual). It is also a part of the nature of being human that we envision, design, and construct complex tools with a variety of purposes, including tools for communication itself. Communication technology is integrally intertwined with human society and raises issues of access, power, and control that reflect the more general dynamics of those societies.

Communication research concerns itself with communities and cultures, with organizations and institutions, with interpersonal and mass communication, with oral traditions and technologically mediated processes. As (arguably) the youngest major area of social science, the field has borrowed its research methods from other disciplines, primarily from psychology, sociology, and cultural anthropology. The possibilities for triangulation and fusion among methods, and opportunities for the development of appropriate new methods, are part of what make our field intellectually exciting.

And to be successful, researchers really *must* find the problems they work on interesting and challenging; otherwise the degree of commitment required would be difficult or impossible to achieve. But is this enough of a reason to do research, just because it is interesting to the researcher? Why do we do research at all—what justifies the expenditure of effort and resources? Of course, research is done in part to advance scholars' careers and to help establish that the various communication fields belong in universities and not trade schools. It is also done to help stimulate the intellectual development of students. These are all legitimate instrumental goals, but they are not the complete picture.

Research That Matters: An Ethical Foundation

This book has been concerned primarily with research about real-world problems. Communication is often an instrument of social change. Contemporary research about communication processes reflects this dynamic and is concerned with communication's role in defining and addressing social issues, from improving public understanding of health and disease to minimizing interpersonal violence, from reducing drug addiction to providing better human services (to suggest just a tiny handful of examples among so many). It seems that as societies grow more complex—culturally and politically pluralistic, based on increasingly complex science and technology, aware of complex global interdependencies—communication and communication research become correspondingly more important.

Applied research, broadly speaking, is research that has been generated by the discovery or observation of a problem or situation that needs to be understood and resolved. Most—perhaps even all—examples in this book meet this broad definition of "applied." Sometimes this term means research done to meet an objective set by someone other than the researcher (a government agency, corporation, service organization, or advocacy group seeking to produce a particular result or solve a problem it sees), rather than springing from a theoretical problem identified by the researcher. In these cases the individual researcher should be aware of his or her own ethics and their compatibility to those of client organizations. But there is no inherent reason why good research cannot be done in response to needs identified outside the "ivory tower" research community, as well as in response to needs seen from within it.

Good scholarship is often inspired by conditions in the real world and conducted in the interests of improving the human condition. Certainly no stigma should attach to the idea of applied research that contributes to social good. But each researcher must make her or his own decision as to whether her or his own scholarship contributes to a social order that is fair and just, that maximizes its members' opportunities for a high-quality life, and in which peace based on mutual understanding has the best chance to thrive. Perhaps some readers will have a slightly different list of ethical priorities, but these three seem nearly universal. These are the sorts of values that should unite communication researchers, whether they are using qualitative or quantitative methods; are concerned primarily with interpersonal, group, or mass communication; are engaged in studying new communication channels or improving our understanding of older ones. Communication research should matter in the world.

Trends in the Field

While most researchers specialize in either quantitative or qualitative research, several of the chapters in this book illustrate how the two can complement each other. Communication researchers should feel free to make their choice of methods on the basis of the research problem at hand and their goals in addressing it, rather than on the basis of an ideological commitment to one type of method or another. The particular challenge of communication research is that it often must consider many variables simultaneously. Clear identification of cause and effect, independent and dependent variables, is often difficult, especially under naturalistic rather than laboratory conditions. Right now our most promising strategy for coping with this complexity is an inclusive, rather than an exclusive, approach.

Research on new communication technologies—a type of research once seen as a sort of orphan stepchild, at times, because it did not always fit neatly with older ideas—is beginning to reflect its integration with existing scholarship. While the emergence of new technologies has challenged us on a theoretical level, restructuring mass communication theory in particular from a passive to an active audience paradigm, we are beginning to see these technologies in the context of older technologies and to understand how both old and new technologies relate to human social organization.

Finally, communication research seems to be undergoing some theoretical restructuring almost continuously. This is healthy. Researchers in this diverse field have been somewhat divided by their affiliations with academic departments that, in addition to conducting research in interpersonal, organizational, or mass communication, also teach courses in professional areas such as public speaking, journalism, broadcasting, public relations, multimedia, advertising, even visual communication and design—and sometimes in cooperation with allied areas such as information science or public health. New departmental and college configurations are being forged and reforged as some of these historical divisions make less sense in an era of "converged" communication. These trends inevitably cause us to rethink the theoretical foundations of our field.

Theory and Method

Good research also has a theoretical foundation. As our last chapter by Tankard and Royal pointed out, sometimes the ideas that generate the most interesting research are not derived directly from browsing items already published in the academic literature. Other authors in this book have used well-established theories and concepts but applied them to new problems. However interesting a finding (or however important the problem it addresses), it is through its eventual integration with a scholarly literature and a theoretical tradition that it acquires its meaning and impact. Scholarship is a collective endeavor; to be of broader value, each piece of research must be connected to this collective endeavor. It is theory—a connection to an explanatory framework—that makes these links possible.

In applied research, because it is so often driven by its subject matter rather than purely theoretical questions, theory may sometimes come into the picture later rather than sooner. Some students have the idea that applied research does not use theory or does not have theoretical implications. This is a misconception. While this particular book is primarily about the methods researchers use and the real-world advantages and disadvantages of each, a methodologically elegant study is of little value if it doesn't contribute in some small way to our theoretical understanding of how communication technologies and processes work. It is this theoretical understanding that then becomes a resource for addressing the next problem and designing the next study.

Because of the diverse intellectual and scholarly roots of communication research, sometimes the theory is a little bit less than tidy. We sometimes use "macro" social theories about the distribution of power within society, "micro" cognitive theories about how individuals process information from messages, and an enormous array of concepts and ideas that fall somewhere in between. These theories are not well integrated, and none of them quite stands alone as the one best way to understand communication. But that's a problem for another book!

Index

American Association for Public Opinion Research (AAPOR), 29–30
anonymity, 244
applied research, 266, 268
attitude questionnaires, 197
attribution theory, 79
autoethnography, 112, 143, 151–53, 159, 161–62

bias, systematic subject, 245

categorical data, 40
census data, 41
chi-square test, 40
citizen-scholar, 6, 9
civic journalism, 20
community, 6, 7; mobilization of, 37; research about, 11
confidence level, 24
confidentiality, 246
confounding variables, 116
constructivism, 73
content analysis, 70, 133–35, 137, 255
continuous scale, 40
control. *See* experimental control
convenience sample, 240

correlation coefficient, 215–18, 260
creativity, 256
cross-cultural research, 165, 167, 185–87
cultural norms, 203
cultural relativism, 171
cultural studies, 7, 171
culture, 170
culture shock, 186

deductive reasoning, 74
depth interview, 8, 62, 112, 121–22
descriptive statistics, 74
differences based on sample, 40
differential gains, 20, 22, 28
discourse analysis, 90

effects research, 115
encoding, 131
ethics, 102, 143, 151, 177–78, 180, 224, 234–35, 243, 250, 265
ethnography, 8, 74, 87, 91, 121, 144–46, 148, 150, 154, 170. *See also* autoethnography
experimental control, 35–36, 41
experimental design, 35, 38, 40, 74, 119
explanation, 74, 262

face-to-face interviews, 230–31. *See also* in-depth interviews, interviewing
factor analysis, 217–18
factorial design, 35–36
feminist research, 70, 160
field experiments, 34–35, 39, 115
field notes, taking, 94
field research. *See* field experiments
focus groups, 60–62, 87–88, 90–91, 93, 122–23, 230
formative evaluation, 44, 50, 53, 60, 62

gender, 191, 195
gender identity, 72
generalizability, 25, 35, 74, 119, 249
grounded theory, 70, 134, 160

health communication, 198
heuristic cues, 23
human subjects protections, 43, 234, 241. *See also* Institutional Review Board
hypothesis, 215, 217
hypothetico-deductive method, 74

identity, 208, 210–11, 213, 215
impact surveys, 22, 25–26, 28
in-depth interviews, 75–76. *See also* face-to-face interviews, interviewing
inductive reasoning, 74
informant, 8, 85, 170
informed consent, 243
Institutional Review Board (IRB), 12, 42–43, 87, 225, 233–36, 239, 240–46. *See also* Human subjects protections
interaction effect, 36
intercoder reliability, 135
internet data collection, 240
interpersonal discussion, 21
intersubjectivity, 160
interview guide, 200
interviewing, 58, 70, 88, 90–92, 148–50, 180, 186, 212. *See also* face-to-face interviews, in-depth interviews, telephone interviews

intracoder reliability, 235
issues of power. *See* power issues, power analysis

key informants interviews, 85, 232
knowledge gaps, 20–21

laboratory experiments, 115. *See also* experimental control, experimental design
language differences, 203
levels of measurement, 40, 216
Likert rating scales, 200

main effect, 36
media theory, 45
memory, 130–32
methodological choices, 86
minority subculture, 207

narrative, 146–47, 150, 154
naturalistic methods, 74
needs assessment, 225
nested design, 36, 39
new communication technologies, 167, 181, 223

objectivity, 162, 186
observation, 90–91
online: research, 242, 247–8; sampling, 249
operationalization, 116
opinion climates, 27
oral history, 149

participant observation, 8, 10, 85, 91, 94, 120–121
participants, recruiting, 248
participatory methods, 53
participatory rural communication appraisal (PRCA), 51–53, 54
peer influence, 114–120
population, 24, 29
positivism, 8, 160

power issues, 11, 16, 58, 62, 71, 163, 171, 195, 265, 268
power analysis, 38
pre-post design, 35, 46
prevention, 37
probability sample, 24
probes, 232
proposal, 256
protecting research participants, 42. *See also* human subjects protections, Institutional Review Board
public opinion, 24

qualitative methods, 2, 186
quantitative methods, 2
quasi-experimental designs, 38, 103
question wording, 29

rapport, 49, 58, 93, 185
reliability, 8, 35
research method, choosing, 111
response rate, 25

sample size, 29, 217, 232
sampling, 29; error, 24, 29, 40–41; frame, 24
scaling, 203
self-disclosure, 63
sense-making, 76, 79, 89
sensitizing concepts, 69, 80
snowball sample, 90, 92
social identity theory, 73
social marketing, 34–35

spiral of silence, 27
sponsor, 29
statistical significance, 41, 217
statistical tests, 30
subjectivity, 151
survey, 20, 23, 119; instruments, 200, 212; terminology, 24

tape recordings, 77
technology, 174
telemedicine, 227, 229, 232, 236
telephone interviews, 227, 231, 236. *See also* interviewing
textual analysis, 8, 12
themes, 79, 150
theory, use of, 44, 74, 268
transcription, 77–78, 95
treatment, 36, 38
triangulation, 50, 53, 265
T-test, 40

uses and gratifications, 207, 209
unit of analysis, 36, 39, 45, 129, 136–37
unobtrusive observation, 121

validity, 8, 24, 35
values, 208–11, 215, 217
videotape, using, 121
voluntary participation, 243. *See also* human subjects protections, Institutional Review Board

writing about research, 154

About the Contributors

Traci L. Anderson (Ph.D., University of Oklahoma) is assistant professor in the Department of Communication at Bryant College in Rhode Island. Her research focuses on computer-mediated communication, online interpersonal relationships, and family interaction.

Chike Anyaegbunam is assistant professor in the Integrated Strategic Communication Program, School of Journalism and Telecommunications, University of Kentucky, where he teaches communication theory and research methods. He obtained his Ph.D. from the University of Iowa and has worked as a rural development advisor with USAID, the World Bank, and various United Nations agencies, including UNICEF and the Food and Agriculture Organization.

Robert J. Balfour is Head of the Durban School of Education at the University of KwaZulu-Natal, South Africa, where he teaches courses in applied language studies and creative writing. He completed his doctorate at the University of Cambridge in the year 2000. He is a published writer and poet, and also a painter. He lives in Durban and conducts research in the province where "Interpreting Signs" is set.

Wai Hsien Cheah, Ph.D., Research Coordinator, Health Communication Research Laboratory, Saint Louis University, specializes in health and public communication campaign design and evaluation. His program of research tests the influence of personality factors and cultural orientation on the effects of fear appeal messages. Wai Hsien Cheah is from Malaysia.

Tara L. Crowell (Ph.D., University of Oklahoma) is assistant professor of communication at the Richard Stockton College of New Jersey. Her primary research emphasis is interpersonal and health communication, with a secondary emphasis in instructional communication.

Marjan de Bruin is director of the Caribbean Institute of Media and Communication (CARIMAC). She has been with CARIMAC for sixteen years, most of them as head of the print journalism department. Former editor of a Dutch weekly, she completed her doctoral degree in social psychology at the University of Amsterdam after receiving a degree from the School of Social Work. She has interests in gender, health, and environmental journalism and is a Vice President of the International Association of Media and Communication Research.

Thomas R. Donohue (Ph.D., University of Massachusetts, Amherst) is professor of mass communication at the Virginia Commonwealth University. In addition to authoring numerous scholarly publications on the impact of mass media, he was the cocreator (along with Timothy Meyer) and executive producer of a popular children's television series, "Kids Like You and Me," that aired for over six years, ending in 2001.

Lynne Edwards, Ph.D., is associate professor of media communication studies at Ursinus College, Collegeville, Pennsylvania. She is the author of chapters appearing in *Fighting the Forces: Essays on the Meaning of Buffy the Vampire Slayer* (Rhonda Wilcox and David Lavery, eds., 2002) and *Black Marks: Minority Ethnic Audiences and Media* (Karen Ross with Peter Playdon, eds., 2001). She is currently analyzing print news coverage of juvenile crime.

Elissa Foster is assistant professor at the University of Texas at San Antonio. She holds degrees in theatre (B.A. Hons. from the Queensland University of Technology) and communication (M.A. from the University of Memphis and Ph.D. from the University of South Florida). Her research interests include difficult communication in close personal relationships, health, narrative theory, and qualitative research methods.

Jennifer L. Gregg is assistant professor in the Department of Communication and research associate in the School of Public Health at the University of Louisville. She teaches courses in science and health communication, computer-mediated communication, and research methods. Her research interests include health communication and the social effects of technology. She holds a Ph.D. from Michigan State University in media and telecommunications, as well as an M.S. from Iowa State University, and a B.A. from Drake University (both in journalism and mass communication).

Joy L. Hart (Ph.D., University of Kentucky) is professor in the Department of Communication, University of Louisville. Her research and teaching center on organizational and interpersonal communication. For the last two years, she has been part of an interdisciplinary team providing health education and health care to rural Gales Point, Belize, in Central America. This project, sponsored by the University of Louisville, is part of an international service learning initiative.

Aaron Karnell holds a B.A. from Cornell University, an M.A. from Syracuse University, and a Ph.D. from the University of Kentucky. He works for the U.S. government and maintains an interest in international communication research, with an emphasis on policy and human rights.

Robert L. Krizek (Ph.D., Arizona State University) is associate professor and director of graduate studies in the Department of Communication at Saint Louis University. He teaches and conducts research in organizational culture, sport communication, communication in "third places," and ethnographic methods. In addition to studying socialization and storytelling in organizational contexts, he looks at the significance of nonroutine public events through the examination of the personal narratives of those in attendance.

Timothy P. Meyer (Ph.D., Ohio University) is Ben J. and Joyce Rosenberg Professor of Communication and Chair of Information and Computing Sciences/Communication at the University of Wisconsin, Green Bay. He has published nearly one hundred books, book chapters, and scholarly journal articles on the impact of varying types of media content on different audiences, using an array of methodological and theoretical approaches.

Loreen N. Olson (Ph.D., University of Nebraska, Lincoln) is assistant professor of communication at the University of Missouri, Columbia. Her research focuses on social issues facing today's couples, such as intimate and family aggression, family secrets, effects of adult dementia on relational functioning, and communication issues in various family forms. She was recently awarded the Steve Duck New Scholar Award from the International Association for Relationship Research.

Susanna Hornig Priest is associate professor and director of research at the College of Mass Communications and Information Studies at the University of South Carolina, Columbia. She has published over forty research articles and two books, *A Grain of Truth: The Media, the Public and Biotechnology* (2001) and *Doing Media Research: An Introduction* (1995). In recent years she has focused on public responses to controversial technologies. In addition to her Ph.D. in communications from the University of Washington, she has degrees in anthropology and sociology.

Lana F. Rakow, Ph.D., is professor of communication and women's studies at the University of North Dakota, where she is director of the new Center for Community Engagement. She recently completed her second term as president of the North Dakota Professional Communicators. She is author or editor of four books and numerous articles on gender and communication, curriculum reform, new technologies, and communication and communities, and she is principal investigator on a project to assess the needs of rural communities and nonprofit organizations in North Dakota.

Karen Ross, Ph.D., is reader in mass communication at Coventry University and visiting professor at the School of Politics, Queens University, Belfast. She has written extensively on issues of equality/inequality in communication and culture, and her most recent books include *Gender and Newsroom Practice* (with Marjan de Bruin, 2004); *Women and Media: International Perspectives* (with Carolyn Byerly, 2004); *Media and Audiences* (with Virginia Nightingale, 2003); *Mapping the Margins: Identity, Politics and Media* (2003); and *Women, Politics, Media* (2002).

Cindy Royal is a doctoral candidate in the School of Journalism at The University of Texas at Austin. Her research interests include the effects of the Internet on communication and culture. She has an MBA from the University of Richmond in Virginia and a B.S. in business administration from the University of North Carolina at Chapel Hill.

Dietram A. Scheufele, Ph.D., is professor in the School of Journalism and Mass Communication, University of Wisconsin, Madison. He teaches courses in public opinion, media and politics, and research methods. His current research examines the roles that the Internet, traditional mass media, and interpersonal communication play in promoting social capital.

Michael D. Slater (Ph.D., Stanford University) is professor of journalism and technical communication at Colorado State University, with a joint appointment in the Department of Psychology. His recent research is on community-based substance abuse prevention, alcohol-related risk perceptions, and responses to alcohol-related messages. He has published approximately eighty-five articles, book chapters, and reports. He is chair of the Coalition for Health Communication and former chair of the International Communication Association's Health Communication Division.

Brian G. Southwell (Ph.D., University of Pennsylvania) is assistant professor in the School of Journalism and Mass Communication at the University of Minnesota, where he also holds an adjunct appointment in the School of Public Health. His research focuses on human information processing, particularly for health and science information. His dissertation was selected as the International Communication Association/National Communication Association Health Communication Dissertation of the Year.

David I. Tafler, Ph.D., is head of the Communication Department of Muhlenberg College in Allentown, Pennsylvania. He has written extensively on interactive media and new technologies and coedited (with Peter d'Agostino) *Transmission: Toward a Post-Television Culture*. Since 1997, Tafler has been doing research involving Pitjantjatjara Yankunytjatjara Media (PY Media) in central Australia. He is currently working on a book about new media technology and cultural transformation.

James W. Tankard Jr. is professor emeritus at the School of Journalism at The University of Texas in Austin. His interests include literary journalism and computer-assisted reporting. He holds a Ph.D. in communication from Stanford University, as well as a B.S. from Virginia Tech University and an M.A. in journalism from the University of North Carolina at Chapel Hill.

Paaige K. Turner (Ph.D., Purdue University) is associate professor in the Department of Communication at Saint Louis University. She teaches and conducts research in the areas of organizational communication, feminist theory, health communication, and research methods. Her research has looked at the creation and negotiation of contradiction within such topics as organizational socialization, midwifery and birth, and the body in the workplace.

Kandi L. Walker (Ph.D., University of Denver) is associate professor in the Department of Communication at the University of Louisville. Her teaching and research focus on interpersonal and health communication. For three years, she has been part of an interdisciplinary health care team providing services to the village of Gales Point, Belize, in Central America. As participants in the University of Louisville's International Service Learning Program, faculty and students collaborate in this effort.

Pamela Whitten is associate professor in the Department of Telecommunications at Michigan State University and senior research fellow for Michigan State's Institute of Healthcare Studies. She conducts technology and health-related research and teaches graduate and undergraduate telecommunications courses. She holds a Ph.D. in organizational communication from the University of Kansas, an M.A. in communication from the University of Kentucky, and a B.S. in management from Tulane University.

John D. Youngblood, born and raised in Texas, graduated in 1998 with a B.A. degree in speech communication and English from Sam Houston State University and obtained his M.A. degree from the Department of Communication, Auburn University in 2001. In 2004, he received his Ph.D. from the Department of Communication, University of Kentucky. John's research focuses on community membership of individuals with multiple marginalized identities.